Japanese Management

Japanese Management
Tradition and Transition

Arthur M. Whitehill

London and New York

First published 1991
by Routledge
11 New Fetter Lane, London EC4P 4EE

Simultaneously published in the USA and Canada
by Routledge
a division of Routledge, Chapman and Hall, Inc.
29 West 35th Street, New York, NY 10001

Typeset by J&L Composition Ltd, Filey, North Yorkshire
Printed in Great Britain by Mackays of Chatham PLC, Kent

British Library Cataloguing in Publication Data
Whitehill, Arthur M. (Arthur Murray)
  Japanese management.
  1. Japan. Business firms. Management
  I. Title
  658.00952

ISBN 0–415–02253–3

Library of Congress Cataloging in Publication Data
Whitehill, Arthur M. (Arthur Murray)
  Japanese management: tradition and transition / Arthur M.
  Whitehill
     P.   cm.
  Includes bibliographical references.
  ISBN 0–415–02253–3
  1. Industrial management—Japan.   I. Title.
HD70.J3W49 1990
658'.00952—dc2   90–8357
                                                                          CIP

Contents

Contents

Figures

Tables

Preface

During the past twenty years, there has been a veritable deluge of publications dealing with bits and pieces of Japanese management. Hundreds of articles and more than a dozen books have discussed such so-called 'sacred treasures' as lifetime employment, seniority wage and promotion, consensus decision-making, and enterprise unionism. Others deal with macro-level problems such as Japan's aging population, plans for 'restructuring' the economy, and the need to combat worldwide trends toward protectionism.

With this outpouring of words, it is difficult to believe that there is no up-to-date book covering all aspects of the Japanese management system. Popular volumes such as *Theory Z* (Ouchi 1981) and *The Art of Japanese Management* (Pascale and Athos 1981) have tempted business readers in their search for a comprehensive analysis. Both were excellent and highly regarded books which focused upon comparative case studies of American and Japanese firms. But neither made any pretence of dealing with the basic principles of management as practised today in Japanese corporations. The outstanding book, *Kaisha: The Japanese Corporation*, by Abegglen and Stalk (1985), most closely achieves this goal. But it, too, is at a rather general level.

This book represents an effort to fill this gap. Its purpose is to integrate and update our knowledge of the Japanese management system. So many changes have taken place in management philosophy and practice during recent years that earlier books – including several by this writer – are no longer entirely current. Some 'sacred treasures' have become heavy burdens for the leaders of Japanese industry. Important trends in economic and social conditions have deeply eroded the unique approach to management which served Japan so well between the end of the Second World War and the historic oil shocks of the early 1970s.

Nevertheless, management in Japan remains a very special blend of tradition and innovation. No attempt will be made in this book to perpetuate the futile distinction between what is traditional and modern. But it would be a disservice to ignore the historic and cultural roots from which have grown Japan's present management practices.

Part I, therefore, describes the distinct imprint of history upon the present system. Since this is not an historical treatise, it was felt sufficient to go back only several hundred years – a very short span in Japan's long history as a nation. The first chapter deals with the Tokugawa feudal period, which lasted from the early seventeenth century until 1868, the year the Emperor Meiji was restored to the throne. Chapter 2 covers the period from 1868 to the present time. In these two brief chapters an attempt is made to create a meaningful perspective for viewing modern Japanese management in the context of history and tradition.

Part II provides an overview of the contemporary setting within which Japanese managers live and work. Chapter 3 stresses the impact of culture, and identifies the most critical values which influence management structure, process, and behaviour. Chapter 4 presents a chronology of recent social, political, and economic trends relevant to the subject of this book. In Chapter 5, the 'big picture' of Japanese industry is drawn – the units, the links, and the adhesive which together form what will be described as Japan's integrated national system.

In Part III the policies and practices in each of the major functions of management – Japanese style – are analyzed. Chapters 6–12 deal with such basic activities as organization and planning, staffing, leadership style, compensation and benefits, motivation and evaluation, communication, and improving organizational effectiveness. When appropriate, a comparison with Western management systems will be made.

Finally, in Part IV, some attempt is made to enter the risky business of forecasting. What are the current challenges to Japanese management, and what will they be in the future? Will the next hundred years truly be the 'Century of the Pacific', and what role may Japan be expected to play? There are no firm answers to such questions, but some meaningful clues have emerged in recent years.

Writing any book is, at best, a long and lonely task. The finished product depends heavily upon the input, support,and generosity of many people. This volume surely is no exception. I am grateful to the many Japanese executives who interrupted their busy schedules to share their understanding with me. Their candid discussions of the problems they now face as their companies enter the new Heisei era were invaluable during my numerous trips to Japan for consultation and research. Mr Masu-ichi Honda, former personnel director of Kokusai Denki Company and lifelong friend, was especially generous in sharing his wisdom and insight concerning the practice of management.

Thanks also are due to Dean David Bess and my colleagues in the College of Business Administration, University of Hawaii, for their enthusiastic support. Opportunities over a period of many years to develop and teach courses on Japanese management, both at the university and at the Japan–America Institute of Management Science, have provided the constant exposure and depth necessary to deal with this fascinating subject.

It is not possible to express adequately my gratitude to my wife, Lynn, an experienced practitioner in the difficult world of international business. Her balanced and creative ideas contributed much to this book, and her patience and understanding made it possible.

I hope that this volume will make some small contribution to a better understanding of Japanese management. Only through such understanding will international business executives be successful in achieving their goals, and avoiding costly blunders, when dealing with their Japanese counterparts.

Arthur M. Whitehill
Honolulu, Hawaii, USA

References

Abegglen, J. C. and Stalk Jr, G. (1985) *Kaisha: The Japanese Corporation*, Tokyo: Charles E. Tuttle Company.
Ouchi, W. G. (1981) *Theory Z*, Reading, Mass: Addison-Wesley Publishing Company.
Pascale, R. T. and Athos, A. G. (1981) *The Art of Japanese Management*, New York: Simon & Schuster.

Part one

The imprint of history

Chapter one

Shoguns and merchants

Imagine, if you can, an isolated island nation of about 25 million people enjoying an unprecedented 250 years of peace and prosperity. This is a highly sophisticated, vital country with a well-developed government bureaucracy, relatively advanced educational facilities, and many cultural refinements. Such was Japan in the feudal Tokugawa era from 1603 to 1868.

Perhaps even more difficult to visualize is the fact that this thriving, peaceful nation had no industry – no steel mills, no high-tech factories, and only the most primitive weapons of defence. Virtually sealed off from the rest of the world, Japan had developed a vibrant, yet increasingly vulnerable society. Under the leadership of Tokugawa Ieyasu, founder of the Tokugawa Shogunate, the country was a tightly organized and managed hereditary dictatorship.

Guarding the status quo

Many clever devices were used to consolidate and perpetuate political power during the feudal period. For example, the Shogun divided the nation into more than 250 domains ruled by his vassal lords, or daimyo. To make sure all the daimyo remained totally dependent upon the Shogun, each was required to establish his family in Tokyo, known then as Edo, but he himself had to live during alternate years in his domain. In a sense, therefore, the families were hostages, whose well-being depended upon the daimyo's proper behaviour and loyalty to his lord.

In addition, tight class distinctions were used to keep each person in his place (Yoshino 1968:3). Below the Shogun and his imperial household was the samurai, or warrior class. To them went the most generous benefits in education, status, and political power. A long step below the samurai were the peasant farmers, who enjoyed their considerable status largely because they were the only true producers of wealth from whom substantial taxes could be extracted.

Artists and artisans followed in the status hierarchy. Many of the treasured woodblock prints enjoyed today were created during the feudal period in a style known as *ukiyo-e*. Lovely courtesans, scenes from various stages on the Tokaido Road linking Tokyo and Osaka, and, of course, Mount Fuji from every conceivable angle, were favourite subjects for this art form. Such artists as Hokusai and Hiroshige provided an almost endless stream of more than 10,000 prints, which probably depicted the society of the times better than any other medium.

In the theatre, Kabuki drama shared popularity with the famous life-size puppets. Kabuki, more lively and understandable than the medieval Noh plays, offered the forerunner of the modern revolving stage to provide quick changes of scenery. And in the world of poetry, the seventeen-syllable *haiku*, which must be the most compact literature in the world, was much admired.

Finally, at the bottom of the social totem pole, were the lowly merchants, viewed as creating nothing and engaged only in the moving of goods from here to there. But the merchants' time was soon to come. These experts in commerce developed a cohesive society of their own, a subculture that formed the embryo for Japan's industrial explosion that was to follow the feudal era. Codes of conduct and supporting financial institutions were established which became increasingly important in the nineteenth century. As the power of the merchant class increased, their social status also gradually improved.

To meet this incursion of their traditional superior position, the Shoguns and samurai decided to follow that famous slogan of pragmatism – if you can't beat them, join them. And in joining them they managed to control them, creating a close liaison between government and business that persists, in spirit if not in form, even today.

In many ways the Tokugawa period was one of growth – growth in education, in the arts, and in commerce. It was a time for consolidation and, perhaps most important, a time of peace.

Though almost completely sealed off from the rest of the world, there were a few 'approved' leaks, notably with the Dutch and Chinese through the southern port of Nagasaki. Ultimately, it was through these communication channels that the seeds of doubt were spread concerning the long-term viability of Japan's isolation policy.

The roots of modern management

In examining the origins of modern Japanese management it is important to keep one basic fact in mind. Although links surely can be established with the past, almost every business policy and practice for which the Japanese are justly famous today is of distinctly post-Second World War vintage. True, tap roots may extend deep into the feudal and even earlier periods. But present-day management is 'modern' in every respect, and mirrors the remarkable environment and events which have moved Japan from humility in defeat to intense national pride in the 'economic miracle' which is the envy of the world.

Yet the imprint of history is impressive and provides a perspective from which to view the Japanese management system which is unavailable from other sources. Therefore, it may be useful to look briefly at several aspects of the feudal period from which modern management is derived.

National identity

There were many reasons for the Japanese to develop a strong sense of national identity during the Tokugawa years. After a long history of civil wars, and the inevitable rise and fall of competing warlords, Japan welcomed the more than two centuries of peace under the Tokugawa clan. There was a sense of order and stability in society which, in spite of the dictatorial control, was reassuring and tended to promote a comfortable feeling of belonging.

Japan, for most Japanese, was the world – a world of one race, one language, and a firm but beneficent leader. Each person knew and accepted his proper place in this orderly society. A high level of literacy for the times, plus a knowledge of printing, made communication within the country extensive and effective in promoting a national identity.

Any communication outside the country, however, was discouraged in every possible way. For example, European Catholic missionaries were viewed as potential competing thought leaders from abroad. Therefore, Japanese citizens were prohibited from having any contact with them. Even the size of ships was limited so that ocean travel would be impossible. An extreme restriction forbade overseas Japanese, considered to be contaminated by Western culture, to return to their homeland.

With such an inner-directed society, homogenized and standardized as it was, a widespread feeling of national identity emerged quite naturally. As former US Ambassador to Japan Edwin Reischauer points out, 'Peace and stability also permitted the Japanese to work over and perfect their own rich culture' (Reischauer 1977: 70).

For all of these reasons, identity with and loyalty to the nation was extremely strong. And this national identity may be seen today as an important element in the well-oiled mechanism of Japanese management. When the good of the nation is at stake, Japanese business leaders will quickly rally to the cause. Statements of business ideology promoted by such management organizations as Keidanren, Keizai Doyukai, and Nikkeiren often have a strong nationalistic flavour. And, in fact, the recent drive to 'restructure' Japanese society owes much of its widespread acceptance to the willingness of all sectors of the populace to join in a common cause for the good of the nation.

Confucian doctrines

Although scholars continue to debate the validity of simply extrapolating Confucian doctrines to present-day Japan, there is little doubt that Confucianism underlies the thinking and behaviour of managers in subtle, yet important, ways. Three of the teachings of this most influential of Chinese philosophers are particularly relevant: unquestioned obedience to family; total loyalty to one's superior; a reverence for education.

Constant obedience and fidelity to family, often referred to as filial piety, was at the core of Confucianism. Responsibility and respect between father and son, husband and wife, and among older and younger siblings, were considered essential. The family itself was at the very heart of society. Strict familistic norms were quite consistent with the vertical society of Japan's feudal period.

And they continue today to influence relations not only in the natural family but in the 'corporate family' as well.

The second Confucian doctrine of significance to management is total, unswerving loyalty to one's superior. This precept was given strong support by the traditional samurai military code known as Bushido . Under this code, the samurai were encouraged – in fact ordered – to demonstrate full and constant loyalty to their lord. Those who ruled, and those who followed, were frozen in their respective roles. Authoritarianism and paternalism were constant companions at that time, and are by no means strangers today. Modern Japanese managers are, as we shall see throughout this book, benevolent yet firm – paternalistic yet demanding – in their relations with employees. Subordinates are expected to show their gratitude for such treatment in their total commitment and dedication to their superior and to the company.

Finally, the tremendous impact of the Confucian reverence for education and self-development cannot be overstated. The extremely high prestige accorded teachers and scholars in China transferred rather easily to the peaceful environment of Tokugawa Japan. Extensive reading, creative writing, and the pursuit of culture and art were highly regarded among a rather leisurely peacetime 'warrior' class. Today, Japan's educational system has been criticized for its centralized, inflexible administration. But the proof of its effectiveness is in the almost totally literate population and in the impressive Japanese abilities in mathematics and science. To assure a quality education for their children is the number one goal of most Japanese parents. The extreme sacrifices that all family members make to achieve this goal truly are awe-inspiring.

Furthermore, the urge for self-development as an end in itself, rather than merely a means to an end, is a quality unmatched in any other nation of the world. The thousands of bookstores throughout Japan, open to the streets and always packed with readers, attest to the innate curiosity of people of all ages. Everybody can read, and it seems that they do read – on trains, at bus stops, in waiting rooms – whenever an opportunity arises.

Similarly, company-sponsored courses are extremely popular and are available for almost every interest from English to flower arranging, from engineering to poetry readings. For most Japanese, there is no need to see some material pay-off in the short-term future. This inner drive for satisfaction through self-development is rooted in Confucian values and affects many aspects of the modern Japanese management system.

Councils and group decisions

The tight organization and lengthy existence of the Tokugawa era continued and reinforced a traditional reliance upon collective organization and group identification. Even before the feudal period, reliance upon rice culture in Japan demanded collective action. In the small farming communities, family groups worked closely together and cooperated in the various stages of rice cultivation from planting to harvest.

The welfare of each individual depended upon the integrity of the family. And the prosperity of each family was possible only through close cooperation with other family units. Groupism, therefore, has been a fact of life existing from the earliest periods of Japanese history. This is in sharp contrast to the legacy of American frontier psychology, which puts so much stress upon rugged individualism.

Furthermore, the central Tokugawa administration was a huge bureaucracy in which authority was shared through many offices and at many levels. The Shogun delegated much of his authority to councils of daimyo who, in turn, delegated to councils of lesser officials. In the various domains throughout the country, the same general pattern of rule through delegation to numerous levels of bureaucratic offices was followed.

Groupism, as opposed to individualism, is one of the most significant differences between the value systems of Japan and the United States. The roots of Japanese collectivism, as described previously, reach deep into tradition and history. Again, we see a basic characteristic of Tokugawa Japan which is mirrored in the way organizations are structured and managed today.

Regional competition

Perhaps one of the great strengths of Japan has been the spur of competition among different industrial centres – notably between Tokyo in the Kanto region and Osaka in the Kansai area. This intense rivalry goes back to the early 1600s, when the Tokugawa samurai crossed swords with those loyal to Toyotomi in the famous Battle of Sekigahara. The victorious Tokugawa lost no time in establishing his capital in Edo (Tokyo) and the country's political centre shifted from Kansai to Kanto. This was a change of major importance, since the capital for ten centuries had been Kyoto, just a short distance from Osaka.

In pre-Tokugawa days, Osaka was the commercial centre of Japan. With an excellent harbour, the city was the hub of merchant activity and the centre of Japan's growing textile industry. Also, it was here that the big rice warehouses of the feudal lords were located. But as political power shifted to the new capital in Tokyo, so, gradually, did the focus of business activity move to the east. By the end of the Tokugawa period, Osaka's monopolistic position had weakened, and Tokyo's economy started a long period of steady growth.

With both government and business developing in Tokyo, a close relationship grew up between these two sectors of society. In a sense, the close government–business links which characterize the Japanese economy today had their beginnings in the feudal era.

In contrast, Osaka businessmen tended to reject any ties with government and to be more entrepreneurial in their activities. As Masaki Nakajima, chairman of Mitsubishi Research Institute has observed, 'Unlike the Tokyo businessman, the Osaka merchants believed in liberalism and scorned government intervention. The Osaka businessman believes diligence is the most valuable ethic.'[1]

Even today, Kansai business leaders are considered more aggressive, more independent than those in the Kanto district. Yet Tokyo has become the undisputed leader, with its tremendous concentration of corporate headquarters, influential management associations, and powerful governmental ministries. Not all Osaka entrepreneurs would agree with this contention. But its widespread acceptance seems to be demonstrated by the popular expression 'going up to Tokyo'. Whether coming from Kansai, Kyushu, or the northernmost tip of Hokkaido, one always goes 'up' to that incredible centre of economic, political, and social activity – Tokyo.

The Tokaido Road

Though the Tokyo–Osaka rivalry is still very much alive today, Japan's two largest cities are closely linked together by the world's busiest transportation artery – the Tokaido Road. Originally a single road in the most primitive sense of the word, the Tokaido is now a route embracing every conceivable mode of transportation. Because Japan is a country with only a narrow belt of reasonably level land between mountains and sea, the resulting corridor now contains a modern expressway, the original Tokaido rail line, and the bullet train system. Two-fifths of the population and 70 per cent of the industrial plant are packed into this eastern sea route which has been called 'the spine of Japan'.

Travelling the Tokaido Road was a common pastime even before the Tokugawa era. When Kyoto was the nation's capital, warriors went up the road to fight back invaders from the northeast. When the capital moved to Tokyo, however, traffic up and down this vital artery became the lifeblood of commerce as well as the favourite subject of artists and poets.

There were fifty-three stations, or resting places, on this route, each a day's journey apart. Noted author, William Forbis, gives us the following description of the lively scene on this busiest of highways:

> Surfaced with sand and stone, lined by rows of firs, this wide avenue carried a ceaseless two-way trample of runners, pilgrims, merchants, samurai, sumo wrestlers – all afoot on horse; no wheels allowed. The finest sight was the passage of a lord traveling to or from his fief, borne on a stately palanquin by eight half-naked men, and accompanied by noblemen, porters, footmen, and soldiers.
>
> (Forbis 1975: 230)

Today, the size and shape of Japan's industrial conglomerate still reflect the constraints of this corridor bordering the sea. Government efforts to disperse industry more widely have not met with great success. The dictates of geography and history seem to have cast in concrete this super concentration of industry and people along the ancient Tokaido route.

Recent programmes to restructure Japan's economy and to increase domestic consumption include an ambitious plan to construct a tunnel under Tokyo Bay linking the industrial sprawl of Kawasaki with Chiba Prefecture. Though entirely consistent with government strategy, this new link may contribute to even further industrial concentration in the Kanto area. Thus the configuration of industry started many centuries ago is perpetuated today, with well-established geographic parameters for Japanese industry and management.

Burdens of obligation

In searching for the roots of the present Japanese management system, we cannot ignore the web of shared obligations which exert a strong influence on managerial behaviour and practices. Isolation and loneliness for the Japanese are two of the most dreaded states of being. This can be physical isolation, as was the case in ancient times when exiled to a distant island. Or it may be psychological, as would be the case when an individual's act brings shame and ridicule upon himself and his family. Three reciprocal, or shared, obligations deserve brief mention here: *on*, *giri*, and *ninjo*. Each was highly developed in traditional Japanese ethics, and each remains an ever-present force in modern business relationships.

The concept of *on* originally referred to the benevolence bestowed by a feudal lord, parent, or other authority figure. Today, it seems the emphasis has shifted to the feeling of gratitude and heavy obligation felt by the recipient of such benevolence. In any event, there is a tightly binding relationship established between a superior and an inferior when the former does an important favour for the latter.

It is said that one can never repay an *onjin*, a person to whom you owe such a heavy debt. Yet each person will struggle with a number of these non-repayable obligations during his or her lifetime. An individual who 'does not know *on*' is hardly worthy of being Japanese.

A present-day example of *on* would be when a graduating senior from a top university has shaped his entire educational career in the hope of being hired by one of Japan's most prestigious companies. The student's father mentions to a close friend, who is a director of the company, that his son wants very much to join the corporate family. If the director is influential in securing the

11

coveted position for his friend's son, both father and son would assume an *on* toward the bestower of this very significant favour. Any request from the director would be fulfilled if at all possible, and many efforts would be made to repay, at least in part, this tremendous favour. Benedict refers to *on* as 'one's constant shadow like a small New York farmer's worry about his mortgage or a Wall Street financier's as he watches the market climb when he has sold short' (Benedict 1946: 115).

At a lower level on the scale of obligatory relations is the concept of *giri*. Again quoting Benedict, 'These debts are regarded as having to be repaid with mathematical equivalence to the favor received and there are time limits' (Benedict 1946: 116). Without attempting to unravel the enormous complexities of such obligations, let us just say *giri* is a something-for-something obligation that sooner or later occurs in almost every person-to-person relationship. Transferred to the business setting, favours done must be repaid, whether the relationship is superior–subordinate, salesman–customer, buyer–supplier, or any other mutually beneficial connection.[2]

Finally, a somewhat different concept, *ninjo*, is included in this discussion, even though it is not strictly an obligation in the same sense as *on* and *giri*. Meaning 'human feelings', *ninjo* is obligatory only in the sense that all true Japanese are expected to demonstrate this quality. Though perhaps closest to the Western concepts of sympathy and empathy, it goes beyond such feelings. In the Western context, one expresses sympathy ('I am so sorry'), or empathy ('I know how you feel'), *after* being told of another person's problems. To show *ninjo*, however, is to understand another's personal anguish, anxiety or grief *without* being told. Yoshino describes this subtle ability as 'an understanding response to another's *hidden* feelings of deprivation and despair' (Yoshino 1968: 8).

In the rigidly structured society of feudal Japan, the need for the human kindness inherent in *ninjo* was acute. Because duty always came first, and obligations always had to be met, some emotional escape valve was a necessity. The sensitive understanding of one's innermost feelings by another human being provided welcome relief from inevitable tensions and frustrations in such an environment.

This kind of helpful understanding and sympathy is at least

equally crucial in Japan's fast-paced, stressful business world today. Not all Japanese salarymen are workaholics, but there is little doubt that most work long hours for their companies. No matter how much loyalty, diligence, and productivity they lavish on the company, it never seems to be enough. Each day, as one observer notes, is another 'samurai duel'.

High levels of expectation at work are compounded by the constant pressure arising from too many people in too little space. While the Tokugawa samurai girded their loins for battle, in much the same way the Tokyo salarymen prepare for their daily commute and the long hours of work to follow. In their stressful life-style, an unsolicited smile of understanding, or unexpected offer of help, from one who demonstrates *ninjo* must be extremely welcome. Thus, a human quality which was well-developed in the feudal era is perhaps even more highly treasured in Japan's modern, post-industrial society.

The rise of the merchant class

William Forbis, in his book *Japan Today*, recalls an incident in the 1840s that reveals the low esteem in which the lofty shoguns and samurai held the merchant class (Forbis 1975: 190). The father of Yukichi Fukuzawa, who was to become one of Japan's greatest statesmen and educators, reproached his son's teacher for burdening him with the study of arithmetic. 'It is abominable,' said the class-conscious father, 'that innocent children should be taught to use numbers – the tool of merchants.' It is ironic that with these tools the despised merchants were to take the leading role in Japan's own 'Great Leap Forward' following the Meiji Restoration.

In a traditional society, agriculture is the backbone and major source of wealth. Tokugawa Japan was traditional in this sense, with about 80 per cent of the population engaged in agriculture. Artisans and merchants made up another 14 per cent, while the ruling class of Shogun, lesser feudal lords, and samurai accounted for the remaining 6 per cent. Among the commoners – that is the farmers, artisans, and merchants – the latter were assigned the lowest rung on the ladder of prestige.

It is particularly interesting, therefore, that during the last half century of the Tokugawa period it was the lowly merchants who prospered while the upper classes increasingly faced serious financial difficulties. Taxes no longer provided sufficient revenue to support the large and demanding bureaucracy needed to run the country. Foreign trade was almost non-existent and thus offered no income. Increasingly the government had to turn to commercialization to survive. Some of the more progressive fiefs established small, rather primitive industries. Most of these were related to national defence: iron smelting and casting, ship building, and armaments. And in the cities and towns a vigorously expanding merchant class was building a business economy far beyond anything expected in a feudal society. There were banks, letters of credit, and even the buying and selling of futures in such commodities as rice.

It was not long before the ruling class fell heavily in debt to these rich city merchants. Many of the lower-level samurai left their warrior–administrator status to engage in the scorned, but more profitable, commercial activities. Others took the easier route of marrying the daughters of wealthy merchants in order to improve their deteriorating economic status.

A few of the merchants amassed very large fortunes. The Mitsui family, destined to become one of the four major *zaibatsu* conglomerates in later years, already was a powerful force by the early 1800s. The importance of this shift in control in terms of developing an elite corps of experienced businessmen cannot be emphasized too much. These were the men who would lead Japan's rapid industrialization after the doors of commerce were opened to the rest of the world.

It was the affluent merchants, as mentioned earlier in this chapter, who also established a unique cultural milieu in the larger cities. In the entertainment quarters of Osaka and Tokyo, businessmen (and no doubt some samurai in disguise) relaxed in the company of lovely *geisha*. These were the professional singers and dancers who also acted as a kind of mother-confessor for the harried businessmen. In addition, the art, drama, and literature which is so highly appreciated today can be traced to the emerging business class. Fine pottery, gorgeous brocades, and exquisite lacquer products were created to meet the growing market for such one-of-a-kind items.

Thus, two cultures existed side-by-side in the fading days of the Tokugawa era: that of the still-proud but economically hard-pressed ruling class of warrior–bureaucrats; and the increasingly feisty city merchants. The die was cast and the foundations laid for a modernized Japanese economy. By the mid-nineteenth century, a carefully conceived strategy was emerging that would end, once and for all, feudalism in Japan and propel the isolated country into an interactive role with nations throughout the world.

The beginning of the end

The Tokugawa system began to crumble in the latter half of the nineteenth century because of internal problems as well as ominous military developments in the big outside world over which the Shoguns had no control. The ruling class faced escalating financial problems and was unable to adjust to the persistent spread of commercialization. There was little it could do to halt the rising wealth and power of the merchant class. Nor was it any longer able to stem the worrisome news from abroad that Japan could be ripe for picking by a number of well-armed, ambitious, 'barbarian' nations.

Much has been said about Japan's 'survival mentality', in an effort to explain certain actions which appear brazen – even hostile – to Western observers. Recent instances triggering such discussions include negotiation of bilateral oil purchase agreements well above world prices, dumping semiconductor chips at prices below cost of production, and the maintenance of various strategies to protect the inefficient but politically powerful small farmers of Japan. None of these tactics have done much to warm relations between Japan and the Western nations. But one must remember that Japan, despite her tremendous success as an export-driven economy, still is a fragile, island nation.

Throughout her long history, the country has experienced almost every known natural and man-made disaster, including earthquakes, fires, typhoons, and the holocaust of war. After each such catastrophe, Japan not only has survived but has seemed to gain strength from her adversity. Furthermore, she has done this in the face of severely limited natural resources and a life-threatening dependence on foreign trade. Under the circumstances, who can fault Japan for doing what she must do to survive? But it is a response that one must consider when interpreting Japanese actions – past, present, and future.

This survival mentality has been close to the core of the

Japanese value systems for a very long time. It was this same basic instinct that encouraged the younger samurai to join with the leading merchants in the later Tokugawa years. Together they were able to mastermind a plan which would open the country and restore the Emperor as its full and legitimate leader.

The grand plan for the Meiji Restoration did not culminate until 1868. But in 1852, as a prophetic meteor streaked across the sky, four black ships steamed into Tokyo harbour and set the seal of doom on feudalism in Japan. Under the command of US Commodore Perry, these vessels symbolized to the Japanese the beginning of the end of their nation's isolation from the world. No shots were fired, but the implication was clear: the ships could cut off coastal shipping upon which the capital depended for its vital food supplies.

Such a radical upheaval did not come easily, and public support for opening the country was by no means unanimous. This lack of consensus was used by the daimyo of two powerful domains, Satsuma in southern Kyushu and Choshu in Western Honshu, to mount a campaign to replace the Tokugawas with a strong imperial regime. Combining traditionalism with modernism was seen as the only way to contain the West and still profit from its advanced military and industrial technology.

Finally, in 1868, a coalition of the more powerful daimyo from the rebellious domains seized the government and restored the Emperor Meiji to the throne. In actual fact, direction of the government fell largely to a group of ambitious, well-educated young samurai who were realistic enough to accept the Western treaties. It was they who launched Japan on the high road to industrialization. The young Emperor and his entourage were quickly moved to a new capital in Edo, which then was appropriately renamed Tokyo, or 'Eastern Capital'.

General discontent with the rigidity of Tokugawa society during its final years sparked an important surge of nationalism and a renewed interest in Shintoism. Though the Tokugawas attempted to force upon society unquestioning acceptance of Confucian doctrines – which tended nicely to reinforce the totality of their paternalistic rule – intellectuals continued to preach the importance of preserving traditional Japanese values. Pride in the past, veneration of ancestors, and belief that Japan was a 'divine' nation gradually developed into an intense nationalism. This rebirth of Shintoism and worship of the past was destined to become a central force in the years of the Meiji era and beyond. Furthermore, it is an historical cornerstone of what will be described in a later chapter as modern Japan's integrated national system.

Such a sketchy overview of Japan during the 250 years preceding the Meiji Restoration would not satisfy historians. But the purpose here has been merely to set the stage for a discussion of the century of modernization which followed. Though brief, this chapter also has highlighted some of the more significant values and events which provide important clues to understanding the present-day Japanese management system. We now turn to the period of incredible economic miracles – marred only by the debacle of the Second World War – which have made Japan an undisputed leader among the industrialized nations of the world.

Notes

1 This quote can be found in 'New look at the economy – the roots of Japan's industrial development' in the *Tokyo Newsletter* of the Corporate Communications Office, Mitsubishi Corporation.
2 A brief, lucid discussion of these shared obligations may be found in Yoshino and Lifson (1983).

References

Benedict, R. (1946) *The Chrysanthemum and the Sword*, Boston: Houghton Mifflin Company.
Forbis, W. H. (1975) *Japan Today*, New York: Harper & Row.
Reischauer, E. O. (1977) *The Japanese*, Cambridge, Mass.: Harvard University Press.
Yoshino, M. Y. (1968) *Japan's Managerial System*, Cambridge, Mass.: MIT Press.
Yoshino, M. Y. and Lifson, T. B. (1983) *The Invisible Link: Japan's Sogo Shosha and the Organisation of Trade*, Cambridge, Mass.: MIT Press.

Chapter two

Emperors and entrepreneurs

The road from the obscurity of Tokugawa feudalism to the glitz and glamour of modernity has been neither an easy nor a straight- and-narrow path for Japan to follow. With the coming of Perry's black ships, and the restoration of the Emperor Meiji to the throne, Japan joined the world community of nations. But there were tremendous obstacles to be overcome, and many detours to be followed, before the country would arrive at its present pinnacle of industrial leadership.

During the 120 years from 1868 to 1988, Japan experienced incredible changes and made remarkable progress. In this chapter we shall trace the outstanding events which not only have a bearing on the nature of the present Japanese management system but, in a real sense, helped shape the destiny of an amazing nation and its people. Not everyone feels comfortable with the present dominance of Japan in the world of industry and commerce. But few would deny that her outstanding accomplishments deserve the study and understanding of all business people who are sensitive to the realities of an emerging global marketplace.

The following discussion is structured around four major periods: the Meiji era, from 1868 to 1912; the brief period of Taisho democracy, from 1912 to 1926; the long era of Showa, extending from 1926 to 1989, and the newly entered Heisei period. Each time interval coincides with the coronation of an Emperor. Some of the key events covered in the sections which follow are the opening of Japan, the resulting 'first economic miracle', the tragic waste of the Second World War, and the now-familiar story of Japan's 'second economic miracle'.

The Meiji era (1868–1912)

In the preceding chapter, the orderly transition from Tokugawa feudalism to the guided capitalism of the Meiji era was described. Evolutionary rather than revolutionary, the emergence of Japan into the real world of industry and commerce was accomplished smoothly and efficiently – one might say in 'true Japanese style'.

It is important to know that immediately after the Restoration in 1868, study missions were dispatched to Europe and America to determine just how far Japan was behind the rest of the world in industrial (particularly military) technology and know-how. They found a disturbing gap, and steps were quickly taken to remedy it.

Some of the more radical young samurai advocated a new form of nationalism. This was summed up by the slogan *sonno joi*, meaning 'honour the Emperor and expel the barbarians'. Honour the Emperor they did, but few really wanted to repel the advanced technical knowledge and skills of Westerners. As Professor Edwin O. Reischauer, one of America's most popular and successful ambassadors to Japan, points out, 'Some Japanese had realized from the start that the only defense against the West was to adopt its superior military and economic technology and thus to "expel the barbarians" in the modified sense of achieving security from the West and political equality with it' (Reischauer 1977: 80).

Top priority was given to industries considered strategic to the national defence. Such basic industries as railroads, mining, shipbuilding, and military arsenals were essential not only to Japan's defence but also to keep the peace in a nation undergoing rapid and traumatic change. The government itself financed, developed, and administered these strategic industries for the first quarter-century following the Restoration. There were, after all, no experienced corporate leaders – no 'captains of industry' comparable to the Mellons, Carnegies, or Fords who led America's industrial revolution.

Such a restructuring of society was not accomplished without risks, experimentation, frustrations, and occasional failures. But the underlying administrative skills carried over from the Tokugawa period sustained the government during these difficult times. Furthermore, the strong self-identity and homogeneity of the Japanese people provided a cohesiveness that contributed greatly in this early surge of development. Perhaps it is not stretching things too far to suggest that the Japanese thirst for learning, a trait often mentioned today as a prime mover in the nation's economic successes, provided the basis for assimilating the 'best of all worlds'.

Similarly, the early Meiji leaders were notably eclectic in their acceptance of Western methods and ideas. They were determined to preserve the special values and practices that were essentially Japanese while, at the same time, adopting Western developments on a highly selective basis. This discriminating approach to the nation's industrial growth was expressed in the popular slogan, *wakon yosai* – Japanese spirit and Western technology. To achieve these twin goals posed a dilemma which continues to haunt the leadership of Japan today.

It is not surprising that the political leaders at the time were strict, autocratic, and paternalistic in dealing with their constituents. Reflecting their samurai origins, they shrewdly substituted the Emperor for the Shogun and made much of the 'divine' leadership vested in the imperial household. The concept of *ie*, or extended family, was fostered at the expense of individualism. And loyalty to the Emperor was considered the most important obligation for all those worthy of their Japanese heritage. Shintoism, restored as the state religion with the Emperor its God, encouraged an almost universal commitment to national goals and policies.

In such an environment, the strong central government made the rather surprising decision in the 1880s to divest itself of most of Japan's basic industries. The foundations had been established, and it was now time to spin off the industrial–commercial ventures to the private sector. The significance of this move hardly can be overstated. Not only was its immediate impact important, but at least two of the fundamental relationships it engendered are reflected today in the modern Japanese management system.

First, the shift from public to private ownership of the means of production rewarded an elite of rich and influential families for their support during the early years of the Restoration. The modern plant and equipment were sold to the chosen few at bargain prices. An added bonus was the fact that start-up problems had been eliminated and employees already had several decades of training and experience. This resulted in a tremendous concentration of wealth and power in the hands of a small elite. And it fostered close personal ties between the government power-brokers and these favoured big-business leaders. The nurture of such relationships between government and business persists today as an essential element of Japanese management.

Second, it established a high degree of tolerance – even active support – for huge financial combines which clearly would have been frowned upon under early American anti-trust laws. The Japanese did not, and still do not, have an innate fear of monopoly or oligopoly. In fact, the conventional wisdom always has been that in size there is strength. Big business, then, always has been interpreted as good business in the Japanese context.

Such warm support from the government did not, however, come without its price. Big-business interests were expected to show their appreciation by accepting the guidelines laid down by the political and military bureaucracy. With the Emperor firmly entrenched as a divine father-figure, each sector of society was viewed as a 'branch' of the extended family which was Japan. Divine guidance, therefore, was furnished from the Emperor, through his political and military chiefs, to the leaders of the young industries. All worked together for the collective good of the nation family.

The important families which were the recipients of this great power and trust became the core of the vast industrial combines known as *zaibatsu*. Names such as Mitsui, Sumitomo, Mitsubishi, and Yasuda soon became familiar words to all Japanese, as each family group extended its empire. Though presumably purged by the Occupation forces after the Second World War, these remarkably resilient cartels continue to play a key role in Japan's modern industrial development.

Japanese capitalism leans heavily upon the close ties between business and the government bureaucracy on the one hand, and between business and the ruling Liberal Democratic Party (LDP) on the other. As one observer puts it, 'In Japan, the government bureaucracy, the political system and the private sector are tied together in an incestuous relationship' (Sethi *et al.* 1984: 16). Though not as monolithic as the simplistic phrase 'Japan, Inc.' would indicate, the close and supportive relationship between government and business clearly has contributed to Japan's remarkable accomplishments throughout its industrial history.

The Meiji era, then, was a period of innovations, consolidation and, most important, of growth. A useful perspective is provided by one writer in these terms:

> The old feudalistic order proved to be a wonderful nursery for the Meiji bureaucracy to grow. 'Selfless devotion to the group', which had been the moral code of the feudal society – the esprit de corps of the Japanese – became the impetus for the efficient growth of bureaucracy and the diligent efforts of workers in the modernized Meiji organizations. Efficiency and diligence in turn accelerated the industrialization process.
>
> (Masatsugu 1982: 39)

Large industries flourished, backed up by a growing number of small subsidiaries, sub-contractors, and service companies. This was the beginning of what is known today as the 'dual structure' of Japanese industry. That is, a limited number of extremely large and prestigious companies at the top; and a plethora of struggling small firms at the bottom. Most of the glowing accounts of the Japanese management system written by Westerners during the past several decades have focused almost exclusively in the upper half of this dual structure – the top echelons of Japanese industrial society. Perhaps this is because so little can be said about the 'troops' at the bottom. It is a dog-eat-dog world down there, with survival the name of the game. More will be said about this less fortunate scenario – in which long hours, hard work, and fear of tomorrow prevail – in later chapters of this book.

It may not be amiss to add a few words about the Emperor Meiji himself – unquestionably a rather colourful person. An excellent description is offered by William H. Forbis as follows:

> Sir Harry Parks, the British ambassador, perceived that if the emperor were about to regain importance, it would be useful to have an audience with His Imperial Highness. Ushered into the Kyoto court, he was shocked to find a boy of fifteen, dressed in white brocade and trailing crimson trousers, face whitened and cheeks rouged, one lip painted gold and the other red, teeth blackened, eyebrows shaved and replaced with arches – a kind of stylized and archaic toy-man. This was the Emperor Meiji, in whose name and under whose authority Japan was to be transformed yet again.
>
> (Forbis 1975: 199)

Forbis hastens to add, however, that the rapid changes in the Emperor which were to follow were no less dramatic than the changes in the country he was to lead. Within a few years, he had adopted Western military dress (complete with medals and white gloves), grown a moustache, and matured into an impressive and useful symbol of authority. With the Emperor as its rallying point, a small oligarchy of former samurai had created the strong Japan it wanted.

Yet, inevitable winds of change were stirring, and it is to these new and divergent trends that attention now is directed.

The Taisho period (1912–26)

Though given sparse treatment in the literature, the brief reign of Taisho, the Emperor Meiji's son, deserves serious attention. This was a period of transition from concentrated leadership by an oligarchy of ex-samurai to a far more diffused power base. The new and aggressive leaders included not only military officers and bureaucrats but businessmen and intellectuals as well. Some characterize the latter years of Taisho and the remaining 1920s as the era of 'Taisho democracy' and, indeed, it was a period of a growing popular voice in government.

There were two earlier events that provided the legal and moral bases for at least an experimental fling with democracy: the drafting of Japan's first Const tution in 1889, and the establishment in 1890 of an elected bicameral legislature known as the Diet. A politically conscious public, with a plurality of factions, had replaced a docile citizenry led by a recognized elite.

Symbolic of these changes, and perhaps in part a cause of them, was the death of Emperor Meiji in 1912, and the new reign of Taisho (meaning Great Righteousness) until 1926. Though at first considered an apt successor to the throne, Emperor Taisho suffered a brain thrombosis in 1919 which left him extremely eccentric. A widely circulated story tells of one occasion when, while addressing the Diet, the Emperor rolled up the script for his speech and, holding it like a telescope, peered long and hard at the assembled dignitaries. Other similar stories did little to bolster the image of the ill-fated Taisho, and in 1921 he was forced to yield even ceremonial functions to his son, who became the Prince Regent. Five years later, when the Emperor Taisho died, the era of Showa (meaning Bright Peace) began with the coronation of Emperor Hirohito.

Happily living with an ambiguity which would be intolerable to Westerners, the Japanese embraced both a reverence for centralized authority and a yearning for democracy. The former was symbolized by the centrality of the Emperor; the latter was given life, as mentioned earlier, by the reality of a Constitution and an elected two-house legislature. Furthermore, a new generation was coming into power with strong representation from reformers in the fast-growing Socialist Party and from rural landowners. Even small businessmen were demanding that their views be heard in the Diet, which had become the proving ground for all groups competing for a place in the sun. As author Frank Gibney reminds us, 'The fight between democracy and authoritarianism in Japan was a long one; and the democrats got in some good blows' (Gibney 1975: 267).

The First World War gave a powerful boost to the conservative big-business class, since the entire industrial sector was fully mobilized for Japan's role as the primary power in East Asia. It is safe to say that by the end of the 1920s, Japan had achieved a full transition from an agrarian to an industrial society. At the time, it was widely assumed that she also had fully moved from a feudalistic oligarchy to a parliamentary democracy. But the rising forces of militarism and ultranationalism proved this to be a mistaken assumption. The fact is, as Reischauer emphasizes, 'the roots of liberalism were still shallow' (Reischauer 1946: 166).

There were many additional forces at work toward the end of the Taisho regime which tended to put a damper on democracy. While the urban middle classes honestly sought a new social order based on democratic ideals, the far more numerous peasantry remained unimpressed. It valued its comfortable familiarity with a conservative government anchored in the omnipotent and omniscient Emperor. Needless to say, the peasants distrusted the newly popular Western movies and jazz, and they deplored the appearance of 'modern' girls, or *moga*, in the large cities. Perhaps there is a parallel here between the *moga* and so-called 'new human beings' (*shinjinrui*) causing so much heated debate in Japan today. To conservative groups, the spread of liberalism was nothing more than an unfortunate illness which had to be cured.

The end of the Taisho era witnessed two antithetical events

which seem to mirror the indecision concerning the best course for Japan to follow. In 1925, a major achievement of the liberal movement was the granting of universal male suffrage. Ironically, this was the same year in which the notorious Peace Preservation Laws were passed to gag dissent and stamp out 'dangerous thoughts'. A dangerous thought was identified as anything critical of entrenched political leaders or in any way questioning the sublime authority of the Emperor. It was on this sort of ideological seesaw that Japan was poised at the beginning of the new era of Bright Peace.

The era of Showa (1926–89)

The year 1926 was a momentous one for Japan. Isolation was far behind her, and the 'First Economic Miracle' of industrialization was an accomplished fact. Furthermore, the untidy tug-of-war between democracy and centralization in government was beginning to show a winner. To the eventual deep regret of the new Emperor Hirohito, his divine star was to rise, and the feisty beginnings of democracy were to be eclipsed by a growing militarism.

The truth is, a firm ideological foundation for democracy simply was not there. Most Japanese were uneasy with the confrontations, endless harangues, and political settlements of the nation's differences inherent in the parliamentary process. Deep in their hearts they believed that the ultimate goal was *wa*, or harmony. And this happy state was best achieved by compromise and consensus. Decisions thus reached could be carried out most effectively by dedicated, loyal servants of the state, guided by the unquestioned wisdom of its divine leader.

The forces of democracy, therefore, lacked broad emotional and intellectual support. It was too 'Western' a concept to be digested by Japan, and it came to be associated with all other corrupt and barbaric foreign institutions. In its place was the reassuring strength of a growing industrial–military coalition. This new oligarchy was to lead a generally willing populace, step by step, toward the cataclysm of the Second World War. This sad story has been told in its entirety elsewhere. For our purposes, a brief recounting of the Showa era before and after Pearl Harbor will be sufficient to fill out the historical background in which modern Japanese management has its roots.

Pre-war Showa (1926–41)

Militarism and imperialism were not newcomers on the scene when the Showa period began. As early as 1905, the mighty Russian Bear had been tamed by tiny Japan in the most amazing naval victory of all times. The victor's spoils included the ice-free Port Arthur in Manchuria as well as Korea – which the Japanese formally annexed in 1910.

Therefore, it was no shock when, on 18 September 1931, a small group of army officers blew up a stretch of the Manchurian railway. Blaming the incident on the Chinese, the Japanese Army proceeded to overrun the whole of Manchuria and established the puppet state of Manchukuo. Though not officially sanctioned by the Emperor or the civil bureaucracy, neither was willing to publicly condemn this military coup.

The seeming capitulation of the government to the military must be viewed in a larger context – spreading acceptance of the Japanese version of Nazi Germany's *Lebensraum*. More living space was needed for a mushrooming population. The United States had slammed the door on Japanese immigration in its Exclusion Act of 1924. In addition, the whole British Empire and Australia had excluded Orientals on purely racial grounds in a manner particularly humiliating to the proud Japanese. It did not take much urging from the military to get broad popular support for the Great East Asia Co-Prosperity Sphere – a clever euphemism to make Japanese expansionism more palatable to her Asian neighbours.

Carrying on in this tradition, a new incident was created in July 1937 near Beijing in North China, sparking off the ruthless war to conquer all of China. Beijing, Tianjin, Hankow, and Nanjing fell in rapid succession to Japanese forces. In little more than a year, a good part of northeastern China was occupied by Japan. Such startling military victories led the Japanese people to support further aggression with a fervent sense of duty and righteousness. The military gradually penetrated key government positions and, at the same time, extended its control over industry. Leaders of the *zaibatsu*, who formerly opposed imperialism, now entered into a marriage of convenience with military leaders. The mutual benefits were obvious, and those who were not 'in' the ruling clique realized that they would be 'out' for ever.

Parliamentary power almost vanished, and in 1940 all political parties were ordered to disband. Instead, rival factions were 'encouraged' to join together in the new Imperial Rule Assistance Association, a monolithic, nationwide organization which bore rather sinister resemblance to the German Nazi Party.

Revolutionary shifts in power had taken place but, as Reischauer reminds us, 'There was no revolution, no successful *coup d'etat*, no formal change of the political system.' (Reischauer 1977: 101). Everything had taken place within the rather ambiguous framework of the 1889 Constitution. As we shall see, this was an early example of the fact that written documents, whether a Constitution or a business contract, are not taken literally, and will be interpreted by the Japanese as shifting circumstances dictate – an attitude that causes some concern among Western diplomats and business people.

One might ask what the US reaction was to Japan's aggressive moves in East Asia. A few perceptive observers were, of course, deeply concerned. But until complacence was jarred by the fall of France to the Germans in 1940, no strong measures had been taken. Finally, when pacts signed between Japan, Germany, and Italy revealed an alliance that could not be ignored, the United States imposed strong economic sanctions and banned all oil shipments to Japan.

The die was cast. Without adequate oil supplies Japan would be unable to expand the war in China or, indeed, to fight off feared attack by the United States. Taking a bold initiative, win or lose all, seemed the only alternative. The stunning attack on Pearl Harbor on 7 December 1941 was Japan's answer to her dilemma. With General Tojo at the helm as both Prime Minister and Commander-in-Chief, bolstered by the divine guidance of Emperor Hirohito, military victory seemed assured.

A key to what actually was to happen is found in a simple, one-sentence observation by Forbis: 'One might say that the Japanese thoroughly understand only the Japanese' (Forbis 1975: 210). Never expert at predicting the reactions of other peoples in crisis situations, Japan badly miscalculated the unity and determination of 200 million outraged American citizens. US mobilization was swift and total; the crippled navy was rebuilt, and a vast armada of ships and planes fought its painful way across the Pacific.

Because of the final victory, many younger Americans today do not fully realize that this was a war which their country seemed close to losing a number of times. The Japanese inflicted heavy losses on US forces and proved themselves particularly adept at the island-hopping, cave-dwelling, primitive warfare the situation required. But unbelievable communication difficulties, conflicting strategies favoured by the Emperor, the armed forces, and the government, compounded by impossible demands for logistic support, were their undoing. When fire-bomb raids on Japan herself incinerated cities and eliminated crucial production sites, the end was in sight. The atomic *coup de grâce* was delivered at Hiroshima and Nagasaki in 1945, and soon thereafter Japan admitted total defeat and accepted 'unconditional surrender.' Coming before his subjects, the Emperor renounced his divinity as a whole nation mourned. The old Japan was finished; a new Japan was born.

Post-war Showa (1941–1989)

From the ashes and rubble of defeat, Japan started the seemingly impossible task of rebirth and growth. Progress was painful and slow for the remaining 1940s, and Japan's 'Second Economic Miracle' was not to burst forth until the next decade. Yet, due to an unbeatable mix of hard work, determination, national pride, and the most benevolent Occupation in the world's history – plus a little bit of luck – Japan re-emerged as an independent nation in 1952 with a solid basis for her rapid climb to prosperity and industrial leadership. Let us look briefly at just a few incidents in this remarkable story which shed some light on Japanese management today.

An ironic bit of the luck mentioned previously was the outbreak of the Korean War in 1950. Japan benefited tremendously as United Nations' forces poured billions of dollars into the country for war materiel. These funds, enriched by additional billions in US aid, provided much of the capital for building and equipping some of the most modern, efficient factories in the world.

It was also fortunate that the Allied Occupation was almost solely an American effort under the leadership of General MacArthur. This unitary command simplified strategic plans for recovery, and under MacArthur's ever-present charisma the Japanese people offered almost complete loyalty and cooperation.

With nowhere to go but up, the entire nation pulled together in reforming and rebuilding the economy.

Since demilitarization was a primary goal of the Occupation, the armed forces were completely disbanded and all remaining ships and weapons confiscated or destroyed. Furthermore, because the concentration of industrial power was considered equally guilty in waging the war, former *zaibatsu* leaders were purged and banned from future public life.

A more difficult problem was MacArthur's strong desire to bring true democracy to the defeated nation. To that end, Diet members, high-level civil servants, and leading intellectual leaders who had overtly supported the war effort, were replaced by new, usually younger, persons.

By far the most significant step toward democracy was drafting an American-style Constitution backed up by a number of supporting laws. Though at first this task was to be shared with the Japanese, it soon became clear that the Americans would have to do it themselves. The fact is that it took MacArthur's staff less than two weeks in early 1946 to draft a Constitution that ironically started with 'We, the Japanese people...'. Among its many provisions, perhaps most important were those redefining the role of the Emperor, restoring civil rights, and renouncing war and the maintenance of armed forces except for defence. The ultimate demonstration to the Japanese of American democracy came in 1951 when MacArthur himself was fired by his boss, President Harry S. Truman.

It was about this same time that US attention shifted from reforming Japan to using her as a crucial staging area, and as a source of more than $4 billion worth of war materiel, in the Korean War. To activate this shift, some of the strictest curbs on industry and its leaders were relaxed. The National Police Reserve, created by MacArthur, was allowed to be called the Self-Defence Forces which, greatly enlarged, exist today. And less support was given to the leftist labour unions which, in earlier Occupation years, had been created as a check against the powerful *zaibatsu*. Thus, as Japan became America's major ally in the Pacific, democratic reforms yielded to a push for economic recovery.

By the late 1950s, Japan had completed her economic recovery and was poised at the starting line for a period of phenomenal growth. A quick look at the changes in real GNP growth rate provides the best overall measure of the nation's remarkable progress in the 1960s and early 1970s. Table 1 shows these trends to the mid-1980s. Today, Japan's total GNP is about half that of the United States. But on a per capita basis, and depending upon the currency exchange rates used, Japan's is equal to or exceeds that of the United States.

In a very real sense, the sudden rise in oil prices in 1973 signalled the end of miraculous, double-digit growth in Japan. Real growth in 1974 plummeted to an astonishing -1.2 per cent, recovering to slightly more than 5 per cent from 1977–9. Since that time, the rate has been in the 3–5 per cent range and seems likely to remain there for the foreseeable future.

A glance at Table 1 shows an international comparison of several measures of economic performance for Japan, the United States, and the Federal Republic of Germany during roughly the past decade. As the data indicate, Japan's era of spectacular growth is over, and is now not much higher than that of the United States or Germany. Though Japanese unemployment rates are shown as being comparatively low, we shall see in a later chapter that differences in reporting methods explain much of the difference.

Table 1 Comparison of economic performance of the USA, Japan and the FRG

		Average '78-'82	'83-'87	1987	1988*	1989*
United States	Growth	1.6	3.8	2.9	2.9	2.7
	Unemployment	7.3	7.5	6.2	6.0	5.9
	Inflation	8.2	3.3	3.0	3.2	3.5
Japan	Growth	4.5	4.0	4.2	4.1	3.8
	Unemployment	2.2	2.7	2.8	2.8	3.0
	Inflation	2.9	1.0	(0.1)	1.2	1.5
Federal Republic of Germany	Growth	1.6	2.3	1.7	1.7	1.7
	Unemployment	4.4	8.0	7.9	8.1	8.2
	Inflation	4.3	2.5	2.1	2.0	2.0
Average of industrially advanced nations	Growth	2.1	3.3	3.1	2.8	2.6
	Unemployment	6.2	8.0	7.6	7.4	7.4
	Inflation	8.1	3.9	2.9	3.0	3.1

Source: Economic Planning Agency, 1988 White Paper on the Japanese Economy
Note: *IMF Estimates

The Heisei era (1989–)

The opening days of 1989 were momentous ones for the people of Japan. The beloved, yet controversial, Emperor Hirohito died at age 87 after an incredible record of sixty-two years as symbolic leader of his nation. At that moment, the era of Showa (Bright Peace) ended and the Heisei era (Achieving Peace) began.

No Japanese monarch has lived or ruled so long. Hirohito's reign began in 1926 upon the death of his father, the Emperor Taisho. Debate continues even today as to Hirohito's actual role in the events leading up to and during the Second World War. But few doubted the true statesmanship of the man when, as unconditional surrender became inevitable, he proclaimed with the circuitousness worthy of a Japanese linguist that 'the war situation has developed not necessarily to our advantage', and called upon his people to 'endure the unendurable'.

Now, more than forty-three years after that fateful statement of surrender, his son, 55-year-old Akihito, has ascended to the throne. The new Emperor is a worldly and highly educated man who has continued his father's scholarly interest in marine biology. On the other hand, he has shown himself to be different from his father in many ways. Akihito captured the imagination of all Japanese when, at age 25, he married Michiko Shoda, a commoner and daughter of a flour mill executive. They met on the tennis court, and the popularity of tennis remains today an almost national obsession. There is a widespread feeling that the well-liked couple will go far toward humanizing the traditionally mystical perception of the Emperor and the imperial family.

As a new era begins, the 'age of miracles' seems to be over. Yet, Japan continues to demonstrate a post-industrial level of strength that remains the wonder of the world. While growth rates since 1975 have not been spectacular, they have exceeded those in the United States and in every nation of Europe. This modest but steady growth resulted in a cumulative advantage for Japan that brought her to an impressive rating among the very top industrialized countries of the world.

Japan as number one?

This raises the much-debated question as to whether Japan truly qualifies for Ezra Vogel's rating in his book, *Japan As Number*

31

One. The truth is that the Japanese did not appreciate Vogel's accolade and have become increasingly weary and uneasy with it. Reflecting this uneasiness, Naohiro Amaya, a former vice minister in Japan's powerful Ministry of International Trade and Industry, admits that 'The Japan I know is Number Two' (Amaya 1984: 3). Amaya argues that a country must satisfy several conditions in order to qualify for world leadership.

First, it must have power – particularly military and economic power – overshadowing that of any other nation in the world. Japan, however, has specifically rejected all aspirations to becoming a first-rate military power. While Japan allocates only about 1 per cent of her GNP to defence, the United States devotes more than 7 per cent of GNP to military expenditures.

Second, Mr Amaya points out that for a country to be Number One it must have a viable, exportable economic system. Japan's economic system and management practices certainly have served her well for the past several decades. On the other hand, the United States continues to lead the world in GNP, gold reserves, and in both exports and imports. America also leads in a vast range of industrial exports, including nuclear reactors, aeroplanes, radar, telecommunications equipment, digital computers, and central processors to mention just a few.

Furthermore, other countries that have tried to adopt Japanese practices have found the task exceedingly difficult. Japanese management is indeed a system, with highly interdependent parts. To transplant a desired policy or practice seems to require acceptance of the whole system. Few developed or developing nations are willing to go that far.

Finally, a third prerequisite for world leadership is what Amaya calls 'a distinct, viable, and transferable culture'. Most experts would agree that Japan's potential for transmitting her culture is severely limited. Japanese traditions, values, and aesthetics are all anchored in the country's rich past and are peculiarly inaccessible to people of other cultures.

Such an evaluation in no way detracts from the remarkable progress and achievements of Japan during the past several decades. While Japan may not offer a viable model which is easily transferred to other nations, she does none the less provide a source of inspiration and challenge to the rest of the world.

Political stability

A final historical note should be added before moving on to Part II and its focus on the modern setting for business in Japan. Because business and government work so closely together, a brief look at the political system may be of interest. For more than thirty years, Japan enjoyed unprecedented political stability which contributed significantly to her rapid climb to a position of world leadership. It was not until the influence-peddling and pay-offs surrounding the so-called Recruit Company scandal of 1989 that serious cracks began to appear in the tough skin of the Liberal Democratic Party (LDP).

As the Japanese are fond of saying, they have lived under a 'one-and-a-half-party-system'. The one part is the Liberal Democratic Party (LDP) which has been in power since 1955; the additional half is made up of all the opposition parties taken together. The 1987 selection of Noburo Takeshita as the president of the LDP, and hence the country's Prime Minister, continued the long history of strong, party leadership. Initial public opinion polls indicated an even higher level of support for Takeshita than for his popular predecessor, Yasuhiro Nakasone. However, the Recruit scandal was his downfall, and he announced on 25 April 1989 that he would resign because of his role in the affair.

Finding an untainted successor within the party leadership turned out to be an increasingly difficult problem as the sordid details unfolded. After many weeks of painful searching, Mr Sosuke Uno, former Minister for Foreign Affairs, was selected to succeed Takeshita; unfortunately, Uno was to remain in office only seven weeks. Reports quickly surfaced concerning his alleged paid relationships with professional *geisha*. This new scandal, together with rising opposition to a newly-imposed 3 per cent consumption tax, led to a humiliating defeat for the LDP in the 23 July Upper House election. The next day, Uno submitted his resignation accepting 'full responsibility' for the election loss.

Again, a scramble began to find a new 'Mr Clean' who, as prime minister, would be able to overcome the scandals and quell the revolt against the unpopular consumption tax. After an agonizing two weeks, Mr Toshiki Kaifu, a two-time former education minister, was overwhelmingly elected president of the troubled governing party and thus became yet another Japanese prime minister.

Various reasons have been advanced for the long reign of the Liberal Democrats. First, the party is the conservative body, and a strong representation of conservative votes from rural areas, government bureaucrats, and big business form a formidable alliance. Even though faction-ridden and, in the eyes of many Americans, more corrupt than their own government during the infamous Watergate capers, the LDP kept a reasonably firm grip on its long-standing control of Japanese politics.

A rather obvious second reason is the awesome record of economic growth. At least until very recent years, Japan certainly has been a super-success story. As Koichi Kato, a representative in the Diet, recently said, 'Japan is almost on a par with America in terms of the quality of consumer life'. The Japanese are well aware of their remarkable achievements and have thus far shown little desire to oust the political party that led them through these rewarding years.

The past hundred years reviewed very superficially in this chapter have been called the 'Century of Modernization' in Japan. In the next three chapters comprising Part II, we turn to major aspects of the present-day environment of management. These include the influence of today's culture and values upon management, some recent trends that have made a significant impact on the management system, and the macro-level structure of the Japanese industrial system.

References

Amaya, N. (1984) 'Japan is number two', *Japan–American Journal*, July–August.

Daikichi, I. (1988) *The Culture of the Meiji Period*, Princeton, New Jersey: Princeton University Press.

Forbis, W. H. (1975) *Japan Today*, New York: Harper & Row.

Gibney, F. (1975) *Japan, the Fragile Superpower*, New York: W. W. Norton & Company Inc.

Masatsugu, M. (1982) *The Modern Samurai Society*, New York: AMACOM.

Reischauer, E. O. (1946) *Japan: Past and Present*, third edition, New York: Alfred A. Knopf.

Reischauer, E. O. (1977) *The Japanese*, Cambridge, Mass.: Harvard Universtity Press.

Sethi, Namiki, and Swanson (1984) *The False Promise of the Japanese Miracle*, Marshfield, Mass.: Pitman Publishing Inc.

Part two

The modern setting

Chapter three

Culture and values

All of us are creatures of our culture. It is important, therefore, to be aware of just what the concept of culture means and to understand its critical role in international business. As we shall see, many costly blunders occur primarily because expatriate managers are not sufficiently knowledgeable concerning the different cultures within which they must conduct operations.

In this chapter, attention will be directed to the meaning of culture as it is relevant to cross-cultural management. How does culture relate to such qualifications for the expatriate as technical competence, cross-cultural communication, personality traits, and language abilities? What can be done to alleviate behavioural problems, such as culture shock, which often contribute to executive failure in foreign assignments? In the discussion, we shall also compare some of the basic values held by Japanese managers with those of their American counterparts. It will be necessary in this chapter to rely very heavily upon the behavioural scientists – anthropologists, psychologists, and sociologists. For it is from these disciplines that the most useful theories and research have developed.

What is culture?

There are so many definitions of culture that it is difficult to know where to begin. Perhaps it is fitting to turn first to Professor G. Hofstede, who devoted his career to the study of culture and its impact upon organizations. Hofstede defines culture as 'the collective programing of the human mind, obtained in the course of life, which is common to the members of one group as opposed to another' (Hofstede 1978).

There are a number of key points embedded in this brief definition. First, culture is transmitted within a collectivity – the family, school, peer group, corporate organization, region, or nation. Basically it is learned behaviour rather than the outcome of biology. Culture comes mainly from our brains rather than from our genes.

Second, acculturation is a continuous process. It starts on the proverbial 'mother's knee', and continues to build during the formative school years and throughout our exposure to organizational and social collectivities in the course of life.

Finally, culture is shared, and thus communicated and reflected in groups. These groups may be quite small or extensive, as in the case of international comparisons. In this book, emphasis is upon the cultural similarities and differences between Japanese managers and their American counterparts. Within each nation, regional groupings also produce cultural differences: in America, New Englanders versus Southerners; in Japan, Tokyoites versus natives of Kyushu or Hokkaido. The most obvious symbol of culture – language – varies considerably even among such sectional sub-cultures. At the corporate level, too, certain forms of behaviour are common to the members of one organization as opposed to another. This is true for companies within one country (General Motors versus Citicorp), and even more dramatically when corporations are located in different countries (Fujitsu versus IBM).

More a description than a definition, the following concept seems especially relevant to the world of international business: We are immersed in a sea. It is warm, comfortable, supporting and protecting. Most of us float comfortably in the water; some bob about catching glimpses of different lands from time to time; a few emerge from the water entirely. The sea is our culture.

Most business people live and work within the reassuring stability of their own culture. These are the ones who float comfortably in the water. Understanding is shared, there are common symbols, and co-ordinated action between human beings is possible. Behaviour is relatively predictable, and in most cases stimulus 'A' will produce reaction 'B'.

Those who catch glimpses of foreign lands from time to time are the short-term sojourners – the tourists, consultants, and many business people whose trips abroad seldom exceed a few weeks.

Then there are the few – the true expatriate managers – who leave the water entirely and accept the many rigours of business operations in a culture quite different from their own.

Cultural awareness

There are many reasons why a careful study of the various cultures within which multinational organizations do business is so important. First, the concept is so widely misunderstood. It is a complex and mutually interactive phenomenon in the sense that culture influences an organization and the organization, in turn, exerts an influence upon the culture.

Furthermore, culture has a visible, practical effect upon organizational performance and individual satisfaction. Understanding and working within cultural constraints is essential for organizational effectiveness. In addition, it is a changing phenomenon and hence requires constant study of, and adjustment to, its impact upon organizational structure, process, and behaviour.

Cultural imperatives affect every aspect of an expatriate manager's overseas experience. One way to appreciate this simple fact is to examine the personal qualities that contribute to success in a foreign assignment. According to top executives in more than a dozen large international corporations, four categories of qualifications are considered essential for success: (1) technical competence; (2) cross-cultural knowledge; (3) a unique 'mix' of physical and personality characteristics; and (4) language ability (Whitehill 1987). Let us look at each of these requirements and the cultural elements involved.

Technical competence

The vagaries of cultural differences, and the considerable effort and time required to understand and cope with them, give top priority to unquestionable ability to do one's job. A candidate in accounting or finance, must be the greatest financial wizard around. An engineer must be the best engineer encountered by the foreign hosts. Expatriate managers are viewed as outsiders, strangers, who are guilty until proven innocent. Their technical expertise, therefore, must be totally convincing.

Cultural differences create enormous difficulties and many

surprises in any foreign assignment. Overseas managers, therefore, simply do not have the time or energy to sharpen their basic job skills when each day brings some new, unexpected crisis. Their credibility with foreign managers must at all times be impeccable. An impressive past record of achievement will go far towards impressing their hosts that they are, indeed, dealing with an expert.

To illustrate the element of surprise so common in foreign cultures, a few examples may be helpful. Take the matter of engineering standards, which are by no means universal in nature. Standards in Asian countries may be European or American, depending largely upon historical association. Even with respect to contracts, which Westerners believe to be binding in every respect, Asian companies may ignore a key clause simply because 'circumstances have changed' since signing the agreement.

On a less serious scale, there are many 'little surprises' encountered every day in a foreign assignment. For example, the concept of time may vary widely among different cultures. In many Asian countries, a meeting called for ten will convene at twelve – with no apology for the delay. And there always are the surprises arising from semantics – that is, differences in the meaning of words. An answer assumed to be 'yes' may turn out to be 'no', or at best 'we will give the matter further thought'.

Cross-cultural knowledge

Most obvious is the need for overseas managers to have a deep and sensitive understanding of the host country. But for the majority of busy executives, the pressure of their jobs has prevented them from doing their homework, and their familiarity with foreign cultures is superficial at best. This is true even with respect to Japan – perhaps the most researched and documented nation in the industrialized world. Unfortunately, as mentioned earlier in this book, much of the information on Japan's management system tends to be superficial or, in some cases, misleading. To achieve up-to-date cross cultural understanding is not an easy task. For global salesmen moving from one country and culture to another every few days, it is an impossible goal. But for those expatriate managers who are assigned to a single country for an extended period of time it is an achievement which can mean the difference between success and failure.

A few illustrations from a variety of Asian countries will illustrate the need for careful, cross-cultural preparation:

1. Business cards are always used in Japan when one business executive meets another. They should be a standard pattern and size to fit Japanese filing systems and must have square corners, since round corners are used only by women. They should be bilingual and presented Japanese side up, with the printing facing the receiver.
2. A key requirement in Korean business is *kibun*, meaning inner feelings or mood. A Korean will not do business with a person who has offended his inner feelings.
3. In the Philippines, the common saying, *bahala na*, or God wills it, indicates that success is considered more a matter of fate than of individual merit.
4. In Indonesia, there is an ancient and 'honorable' custom of using 'speed money' to grease financial deals.
5. Malays view life as a passing thing, and to avoid personal chitchat or show too much concern for profits can lead to total rejection.

(Whitehill 1987: 53–8)

The pervasiveness of cultural constraints requires study before, as well as during a foreign assignment. The Business Council for International Understanding estimates that international personnel going abroad without cross-cultural preparation have a failure rate ranging from 33–66 per cent. This is in contrast to less than 2 per cent for those who had the benefit of such training.

Physical and personality traits

A special 'mix' of traits which are congruent with cultural norms is a further requirement for expatriate success. Little need be said about the tremendous importance of good physical and mental health. A foreign assignment naturally means changes in climate, diet, and exercise habits. The difficult adjustment to a new environment leaves little time for medical treatment or therapy. Furthermore, medical practices differ sharply among countries. Japanese physicians, for example, typically double as pharmacists.

And in Japanese hospitals, a family member is expected to stay with the patient and help with his care. Many Westerners are particularly surprised to learn that it is by no means unusual for patients to tip a doctor upon completion of treatment.

Beyond basic good health, there are a number of personality traits which contribute to success in a specific cultural environment. Patience and humility are particularly prized in many Oriental cultures. These are not traits for which Western managers are well known. Closely related is the need for a high tolerance for silence. Europeans and Americans tend to be articulate and outspoken, and find long periods of silence almost unbearable. Many Asians, on the other hand, will consider the prolonged silences during negotiations to be the most productive time. A Japanese friend once commented, 'You Westerners like the expression "Don't just sit there . . . do something". We Japanese would reverse it and say "Don't just do something . . . sit there".' Silence, while considering the full range of alternatives in a difficult situation, will earn high marks for the expatriate dealing with Asian counterparts.

A healthy respect for age is another cultural norm widely observed in many cultures. In most Oriental societies the age/wisdom equation still prevails. Older executives are wiser, and thus should be recognized first and listened to with an awe approaching reverence. It is difficult for managers from American and other youth-centred cultures of the West to accept this deference to age.

A final comment has to do with cultural differences regarding proper dress codes for business. For example, the Japanese salaryman's 'uniform' is a dark suit, white shirt, dark tie, and highly polished black shoes. While total conformity to this norm is not expected of foreign businessmen, very loud clothing does create the feeling that the visitors are not taking the negotiations seriously. It is good advice for the expatriate in Japan to leave the wild sports coats, aloha shirts, and splashy ties at home.

Language ability

The last, and sometimes most painful, cultural barrier is that of language. Perhaps the most misleading and overworked expression in international business is, 'Don't worry . . . they all speak English'. It is true that the language of international business is English. But it is also true that colleagues with whom an expatriate must work, day in and day out, will not all be able or willing to 'work in English'. Being confined to those foreign executives who can handle the special vocabulary of managerial English means being limited to a small, and usually atypical, group of associates abroad.

It is clear, therefore, that each one of the qualities most needed for success in a foreign assignment will be significantly affected by the cultural constraints of the country involved. The ability to understand, and work within, the accepted value system and codes of behaviour is essential for effective managerial performance. This is nowhere more true than in Japan, since the management system is, in many important respects, unique to that country. The next section deals with some of the critical variables encountered in the cultural milieu of Japan.

Critical variables

A useful conceptual framework for comparing the industrial societies of different nations focuses attention on three critical variables: (1) values; (2) relations; and (3) structure. A conceptual framework is no more than a systematic way of thinking about something. In this case, the framework of values, relations, and structure in one culture as opposed to another provides a useful model for comparative management studies (Davis 1971: 10–23).

Values

Every culture reflects a system of values. Basically, values are deep-rooted sets of convictions to which individuals, groups, and societies attach strong sentiments of approval. These shared convictions serve as useful guides to behaviour. In addition, they are the foundation for what is believed to be 'good' or 'right'. They underlie beliefs, shape attitudes, and stimulate the expression of opinions. In a very real sense, values are the primary determinants of human behaviour.

It is useful to distinguish between values and ideology, since the two often are confused. Values tend to be broad, general orientations towards experience. In the next section, we shall compare some Japanese and American values that affect the management system of each country. An ideology, on the other hand, concerns a particular phenomenon as perceived by a special sector of society, such as, for example, the business community. Furthermore, an ideology usually results in a publicly stated position on an important and controversial issue.

Most relevant to this discussion is business ideology – that is, the stated position of business leaders regarding a current issue. Ideologies often are expressed in 'white papers', or 'position papers'. In most industrialized nations, one organization has emerged as the principal ideological spokesman for the business community. In the United States it is the Committee for Economic Development (CED); in Japan it is Keizai Doyukai . There are, of course, in both countries other management organizations which also spread the prevailing convictions of their members. With respect to the sorts of subjects treated, some recent examples would include protectionism, inflation, interest rates, national debt, and the role of government. Labour unions, consumer groups, and other sectors of pluralistic societies have similar channels to spread their own ideologies.

Both values and ideologies do change over time. But values tend to be more sticky and resistant to change. The more fundamental the value, the slower any change will be. For example, individualism is a basic American value influencing a wide range of attitudes, preferences, and behaviour. In a study which tracked Japanese and American management–worker relations over a turbulent fifteen-year period, the individualistic orientation of American employees showed little change (Takezawa and Whitehill 1986: 92–6). It continued to exert a strong influence on the responses to a variety of questions raised in the study. This particular American value seems to persist no matter what changes take place in society. Some values, in contrast, may gradually weaken while others emerge under serious pressure of change.

Relations

Values create norms and roles which, in turn, specify desirable terms of relationships. The expected behaviour depends largely on the relative positions of the parties involved. A student behaves in a certain way when dealing with his or her teacher. This behaviour will be quite different from that he or she displays when with other students. A father and son, boss and subordinate, husband and wife, are all expected to conduct their relationships in certain acceptable ways.

Professor Stanley M. Davis suggests that 'five broad patterns of social relationship exist in every society and historical period' (Davis 1971: 17). These are: kinship; fealty; status-based; contractual; and bureaucratic. A comparison of Japan and the United States, indicating differing forms and relative importance of these relationships, will indicate how deeply they are embedded in each culture.

Kinship, in modern terms, refers to the role of the family in its broadest sense. In feudal Japan, the concept of *ie*, or house, meant an extended family which often reached far beyond blood lines. Though substantially modified, this notion still affects many aspects of Japanese management. For example, we often hear that Japanese recruits join the 'corporate family' directly from high school or university. The intention is that the new recruit will stay with the company for his entire working lifetime. Human resource management tends to be familistic (paternalistic) in such a firm. The company itself may be an integral part of a larger 'family' or grouping of related firms.

In the broader context of Japanese society, the nuclear family – father, mother, and children – is replacing the extended family as the basic social unit. Yet the crucial role of close, family-type, personal relationships in all aspects of life reflects the persistence of the broader concept of kinship.

In contrast, the notion of an extended family is virtually unknown in the United States. Children 'move out' of their homes at a rather early age and establish their own nuclear family units as soon as possible. Furthermore, the companies for which they work are not considered 'home', and paternalism in any form is normally rejected. Therefore, it seems safe to conclude that kinship relations exert far more influence upon Japanese than upon American management.

Turning next to fealty relations – that is, the commitment to fidelity, or the obligation for loyalty – we again find substantial differences between the United States and Japan. As mentioned earlier, extensive personal contacts are the hallmark of successful managers in Japan. Working through such contacts naturally creates for each manager a complex web of obligations. The important concepts of *on*, *giri*, and *ninjo* have been discussed already in the opening chapter of this book and will not be repeated here. But there is little doubt that the burden of such interpersonal obligations weighs heavily on Japanese managers and influences almost every aspect of their business operations.

American managers seem to be much less concerned with 'psychological contracts' of any sort. Of course they, too, develop personal relationships which are helpful to them in business. But the clear separation of work life from personal life tends to make these relations more superficial and less binding. It is contracts, written policies, and standard operating procedures far more than implied reciprocal obligations which tend to guide the behaviour of US executives.

Status-based relations also appear in every industrial society, but they are manifested in quite different ways. Simply defined, status means who outranks whom. It is, therefore, a concept which creates a vertical hierarchy based upon some measure of relative importance. An individual's status, or rank, is important because it carries with it certain privileges and powers. There is considerable truth in the popular saying that 'Rank Hath its Privileges', and one's relative status is something to be prized and protected.

In both Japanese and US corporate society, status is a key determinant in organizational structure and functioning. It would be difficult to say in which country it is more important. But a distinction must be made between status *per se* and symbols of status. The latter include such familiar 'perks' as reserved parking spaces, corner offices on a lofty floor, private dining rooms, carpets on the floor and, today, the inevitable array of high-tech information systems on the executive's desk.

US managers seem much more concerned with these indicators of status than do their Japanese counterparts. In fact, the Japanese deliberately seem to play down the importance of superficial status symbols. Private offices are rare and are reserved usually for only a few top-level executives. The president often wears the same cotton work jacket as that worn by the lowliest employee. And in most companies, employees at all levels eat in the same dining room or canteens.

This in no way lessens the importance of the status hierarchy in Japanese companies. Everyone has his or her proper place, and everyone typically knows that place and accepts the rationale for the rigid vertical structure. To a considerable extent, this is equally true in American companies. It is only with respect to the outward evidences of status that Americans seem far more concerned.

Contractual relations offer a rather easy topic for comparison of Japan and America. While Americans are perhaps the most legalistic, contractual people in the world, the Japanese have a healthy disdain for lawyers, legal action, and written agreements of all sorts. At the last count, there were more than twenty times as many lawyers per capita in the United States as in Japan. Large US corporations employ as many as 400 full-time lawyers, most of whom occupy plush private offices and operate in a hushed atmosphere of awe and respect. In a very real sense, these lawyers represent an entire law firm – but in this case there is only one client.

The number and complexity of US laws restricting business operations may make more than half a million attorneys essential. However, there are those who feel an appropriate US export to Japan to help the trade imbalance would be several thousand American lawyers. But it seems unlikely that the Japanese would take kindly to this suggestion. Their need for attorneys is limited, since they are not a contentious or legalistic people. Personal bonds are considered far more binding than legal contracts. To the dismay of Western negotiators, Japanese companies often ignore a key clause in a contract simply because 'circumstances have changed' since signing the agreement. There is little doubt that the United States 'wins' when considering the importance placed upon contractual relations.

Now we turn to bureaucracy and the special pattern of social relations it tends to create. A bureaucracy encourages rather impersonal, formalized, and specialized links among its members. In return, it is said to offer a high level of efficiency and a permanence that goes beyond the lifespans of those associated with it.

Though large government agencies are the classic examples of bureaucracy, large corporations run a close second. This is as true of IBM as it is of Fujitsu; or as true of Matsushita as it is of General Electric. In most cases, it seems a natural law that the larger an organization grows, the more bureaucratic it becomes. Ownership is divorced from management, and the bureaucracy takes on a life and 'personality' of its own. The structure itself demands certain roles and relationships among its members. Bureaucracy appears to be equally endemic in large organizations no matter where they are located.

From this brief overview of five types of relationships found in all industrial societies we see again the heavy hand of cultural constraints. In each case, the importance assigned to such relationships, and the way in which they evolve and influence systems of management, must be viewed within the relevant cultural environment.

Structure

The third critical variable when comparing industrial societies is structure. This may be studied at both the societal and corporate levels. Chapters 5 and 6 deal specifically with structure at the macro and micro levels respectively, so discussion here will be limited.

At the macro level, we must be concerned with the number, size, and nature of the organizations which together make up the fabric of industrial society. Some organizations are unique to a given culture – for example, the Japanese *sogo shosha*, or general trading company. Others, such as transportation, utility, or retailing companies, are common to all societies, but their operations may be shaped by cultural forces. We would also want to include in a cross-cultural comparison the role of such groups as government agencies, management associations, and labour unions.

At the micro level, corporate structure clearly is influenced by cultural factors. Centralized versus decentralized organization, span of control, debt/equity ratios, channels for communication, size and power of the board of directors, and many other structural characteristics all reflect cultural norms. Structure, therefore, as well as values and relations, must be considered a critical variable in cross-cultural management studies.

Modern Japanese values

Because value orientations have such a profound impact upon the Japanese management system, it is essential to give some specific illustrations of such values. Their origins often are found in earlier periods of history. Some examples were discussed, with special reference to the Tokugawa era, in Chapter 1. Here we shall look at several current value orientations as they affect the practice of management.

'We Japanese'

The majority of the Japanese firmly believes that there are only two groups of people in the world – 'We Japanese' (*Ware Ware Nippon-jin*) and everyone else. The term *gaijin*, frequently interpreted as foreigner, but perhaps more accurately as outsider, tells us much about this value orientation.

The Japanese are an unusually homogeneous ethnic group, a nation-family. Everybody speaks Japanese; everyone looks Japanese; everyone thinks Japanese. This striking likeness becomes obvious when one compares a stroll along Tokyo's Ginza with a walk down New York's Fifth Avenue. In Tokyo, the vast majority of passers-by clearly are Japanese. Most of those whose looks differ from the bulk of the crowd either are tourists or expatriate business people. There is a feeling of solidarity in this sameness; a sense of security in being an insider.

In New York the scene is totally different. Individuals in the passing crowd come in all shades of the rainbow, all heights and weights, and babble a variety of languages. No one is assumed to be 'in' until, as individuals, they earn the right to be there. In this sort of environment there is little stability or security, and a constant need to mix and communicate with a variety of people.

The expression, 'We Japanese', is heard frequently and not only reflects the insider–outsider syndrome but also implies a uniqueness of which the Japanese are very proud. And, it is true, there are characteristics of the nation, her people, and her management system which are unique. On the other hand, there are many similarities. Both the similarities and differences between the Japanese and US ways of managing provide the core of the discussion in the chapters which follow. A prominent Japanese executive once observed: 'The Japanese and American management systems are 95 per cent the same, and differ in almost all important respects.' The wisdom of this remark will become clear as our analysis develops.

Group identity

To be lonely, to be a stranger, to be isolated from one's group – these are constant dreads among Japanese people. Therefore groupism, in the sense of total commitment and identification to the group, is a treasured cultural value. This groupism starts at an early age with very close family ties. Japanese familism (*kazokushugi*) is a basic value which is reflected in many aspects of management such as the so-called lifetime employment system, emphasis upon length of service, and a generally paternalistic approach to human resources management which is sometimes referred to as 'welfare corporatism'.

In contrast to Western individualism, Japanese groupism requires subordination of self to the goals and norms of a collectivity. This may be one's family, class in school, university, corporate department or section, or Japan itself. It is considered right and good to be dedicated and loyal to such groups, and to be satisfied with basking in the glories and accomplishments gained through collective efforts.

There have been many attempts to explain the reasons for the sharp contrast between the dominant values of groupism in Japan and individualism in America. One such explanation which seems quite plausible views groupism as emerging from the collective orientation and interdependence required by Japan's traditional rice culture. In contrast, American individualism is traced to a frontier psychology. The early pioneers, pushing west through an uncharted and hostile environment, had only themselves to rely upon. It was 'every man for himself', and individuals survived by their own wits and ambition. In any event, there is hardly any facet of management in either country which is not in some way touched by this striking contrast between groupism and individualism.

Strong work ethic

That the Japanese are hard workers is hardly front-page news. In what other country has the central government mounted an all-out campaign to encourage its citizens to work *less*? Yet, that is just what the Prime Minister's office is promoting among Japanese employees. Shorter hours, longer vacations, and full enjoyment of leisure-time activities are all being advocated. To Americans it is incredible that the indefatigable Japanese take only about 60 per cent of their paid vacations.

Furthermore, many Japanese employees continue their work long after normal business hours. They arrive home late at night with too few hours of rest to prepare themselves fully for another 'samurai duel' the next day. A recent survey shows that more than half of all middle-aged white-collar workers return home well after 8 p.m., and seldom eat dinner with their families more than twice a week. A related fact is that little entertaining is done in the Japanese home. As one writer observes, 'Americans entertained even their most distant companions more frequently at home than the Japanese did their most intimate friends' (Barnlund 1989:135).

This high value placed on work, and a corresponding suspicion of leisure, is said to reflect a Confucian work ethic even more powerful than America's Protestant work ethic. Neither is a good description today. There is no more recognition of Confucianism in Japan's modern will to work than there is a conscious reflection of Protestantism among hard-working Americans. Yet the terms indicate the early origins in each country of a strong, healthy work ethic which persists today.

Frugality

According to the Bank of Japan, household savings in Japan in 1987 were about 18 per cent of disposable income. This compared with about 12 per cent in West Germany, 5 per cent in Great Britain, and about 6 per cent in the United States. Although the Japanese have been spending somewhat more of their income in the past several years, they continue to save at least three times as much as Americans.

Why this high value placed upon personal savings? There seem to be several good reasons. First, Japan is a country with a long history of natural disasters. Earthquakes, devastating fires, and typhoons have plagued the country with alarming regularity. Therefore, putting aside sufficient funds to meet these 'rainy days' is an understandable reaction. Furthermore, the high priority given to education means a substantial investment for families, second only to home ownership. Savings for this purpose, often from semi-annual bonus payments, are very common. And, finally, there are many convenient and rewarding outlets for savings. For example, the postal savings system, established in 1875, now does business through 22,000 postal offices throughout the country. Postal savings account for about 20 per cent of total individual savings. In addition, stock and bond ownership has expanded rapidly in recent years. And, of course, investment overseas has become increasingly attractive – almost irresistible – with appreciation of the yen.

There is reason to believe that Japan's rate of household savings will show a moderate decline in the years ahead. Less rapid salary increases in an era of low growth, increasing longevity and the financial demands of old age, and a weakening of the long-standing expression, 'sacrifice now, enjoy later', will all tend to lower the propensity to save. But most experts agree that the savings rate will remain substantially higher in Japan than in other advanced countries (The Economic Planning Agency 1983: 63–8).

Sense of duty

There is a strong compulsion among Japanese people to fulfill their obligations. This may mean the sorts of reciprocal commitments described in Chapter 1, such as *on* and *giri*. One must repay a favour or service in kind as promptly as possible. But this sense of duty also extends to all social and business matters. For example, it is one's duty to abide by the behavioural norms required to avoid collision or confrontation in a small country with too many people. It is equally one's duty to be a dedicated employee and to be loyal to the company which provides the privilege of employment. A further obligation, deeply felt by most Japanese, is to avoid bringing shame on oneself, on one's family, or on any group with which one is associated.

In a sense, one of the several reasons why Japan is such a tense society is this heavy burden of obligation. To many Westerners, the steady escalation of attention, favours, and gifts as the Japanese strive to repay their obligations can easily get out of hand. Yet this is a practice which is deeply embedded in their strong sense of duty.

Conformity

Who has not seen the cadres of Japanese tourists all following their leader, doing the same things, buying the same gifts to take home, and eating in the same restaurants as did thousands of their predecessors? And who has not marvelled at the sameness of the dress and demeanour of the Japanese salaryman? Conformity comes easily to the Japanese; to be different is most uncomfortable.

There is a popular expression in Japan that 'the nail that sticks up will be hammered down'. This is a fate that most businessmen wish to avoid at all costs. How does a salaryman dress when he goes to work? As mentioned earlier, in order to appear inconspicuous and to blend with the crowd, he wears drab suits of dark blue or grey, white shirt, conservative tie, and black shoes. A tailor who specializes in men's suits said, '60 per cent of our salaryman customers choose dark blue.'

It is not entirely clear why the Japanese prefer dark dress. But it is probably because they retain traces of their ancestors' sense of value which regarded self-effacing modesty as a virtue. Even today, they dislike showy or loud clothing. This was a painful lesson learned by one Hawaiian exporter who sent a large shipment of brilliantly hued aloha shirts to Japan. Almost the entire shipment was returned unsold. Conservatism generally is admired, and Japanese people tend to conform to this norm.

Networkers par excellence

It is not an overstatement to say that the engine of Japanese business is built largely of personal contacts. Who you know assumes great importance in spelling success or failure. Long before even entering a business career, a perceptive person will start the never-ending process of networking. In Japanese, the term *jinmyaku* means a web of human beings, and this network is relied upon in almost all management actions.

For example, to work effectively through the complex Japanese distribution system requires close and long-standing relationships with individuals at all levels. It takes many years to build such a network. This creates obvious limitations for foreign business executives, who simply cannot create the necessary web of intimate contacts during relatively brief overseas assignments.

In more general terms, it is absolutely essential to build a network of personal friends. They stand ready to help you now and in the years ahead. And, it hardly need be added, you will stand ready to return the courtesy extended to you. Many practical applications of this value orientation will be discussed in later chapters.

Avoidance of shame

The Japanese value system includes an absolute obsession to avoid bringing shame to themselves, to their families, to their company and immediate work group, or to Japan herself. Nothing must ever be done which will cause disgrace and tarnish the reputation of oneself or of others.

The delightful outcome of this deeply held value is one of the safest, relatively crime-free societies in the world. A simple comparison with the United States will prove this point. The United States has ten times the number of murders, and more than two hundred times the number of robberies per hundred thousand population as does Japan. And it is true that women can walk the back streets of Tokyo at night without fear.

The level of day-to-day honesty among the Japanese comes as a pleasant surprise to most foreign visitors. An umbrella left in front of a restaurant is most likely to be there a week later when the owner returns. Vending machines, of which there are more than 5 million in Japan, are located prominently with no fear of vandalism. Merchants display their wares on the sidewalks in front of their shops knowing they will be safe. And the absence of graffiti on fences, walls and subway trains also indicates a widespread respect for, and reluctance to deface, public property.

Many other values could be discussed which help to explain the behaviour of Japanese people. Most have an observable influence upon the organization and conduct of Japanese businesses. This cultural component of management will be referred to many times throughout this book.

Cultural adjustment

For the Westerner, whose values are so different from those of the Japanese, the need to adjust to this new cultural 'sea' is often very difficult. When such adjustment becomes too painful the expatriate will find some excuse for ending his foreign assignment and returning home. Experience indicates that as many as 50 per cent of personnel sent abroad may be expected to return prematurely. Exact figures on the cost of aborted overseas assignments are difficult to obtain. But a 1985 study indicated, 'American companies are losing $2 billion a year in direct costs, and there is no figure for costs of lost business and damaged company reputation' (Mendenhall *et al.* 1987). Estimates place the average cost per failure from $55,000 to $150,000, but in some instances it may be as high as $500,000.

At least three major barriers to success warrant our careful consideration: (1) culture shock; (2) self-reference tendencies; and (3) reliance on questionable stereotypes.

Culture shock

The term 'culture shock' has become almost a cliché in the literature of international business. Yet, it is a very real and upsetting condition experienced by any individual who, especially for the first time, are 'on their own' in a foreign culture. Culture-shocked people suddenly find that all the familiar and predictable cues for acceptable behaviour are missing. Their cultural support system has been pulled from beneath them. They become anxious, nervous, irritable, and confused.

In this upset state of mind, an expatriate manager may respond by progressive withdrawal from contacts with the foreign hosts. Americans will spend more time at Tokyo's American Club than at Japanese gathering places. In a similar manner, Japanese executives in New York will retreat to the smart Japan Club in order to enjoy the warmth and support of their fellow countrymen. Not all, however, follow this pattern. Some become defensive, some become excessively critical and blame their disorientation on their foreign hosts. In time, fortunately, most individuals learn to comprehend, survive in, and grow through immersion in a new and different culture.

There is, however, a time frame within which acceptance of, and adjustment to, a foreign environment takes place. One way to think of this transition is in terms of a 'W-curve', which illustrates the typical stages a foreigner goes through when assigned overseas. An American sent to Tokyo, for example, will first experience a 'high' upon arrival which typically lasts two to three weeks. He is an honoured guest – a VIP – and the Japanese roll out the red carpet for him. The polite and generous treatment the new arrival receives is almost overwhelming.

But soon the expatriate must get down to work, and the honeymoon is over. Now he is an outsider – that is, he is outside the 99 per cent who are insiders and refer to themselves as 'We Japanese'. His language ability, if any, is primitive, his fantasies linger on American hamburgers, he resents the insiders, to whom he now refers as the 'Japanese mafia'. It is this stage, lasting perhaps twelve to eighteen months, that is reflected by the initial sharp fall in the W-curve.

All is not lost, however, and if this difficult period can be lived through, the curve will rise again. Our transplanted American begins to enjoy Japanese food, has attended Japanese language classes each morning before work, is familiar with Tokyo's marvellous transportation system, and thoroughly enjoys living in a clean, safe environment with honest people. He has weathered his attack of culture shock and survived.

When this now well-adjusted expatriate completes his assignment and returns home, another period of trauma, known as reverse culture shock, or re-entry crisis, may be experienced. This condition is best illustrated by thinking of the individual who has spent a long time abroad. Returning to the United States may mean return to long-forgotten unpleasant experiences, such as dealing with rude taxi drivers, tolerating careless service in 'greasy-spoon' restaurants, and rediscovering that not all sales people believe that the customer is always right.

The Japanese, too, often experience reverse culture shock when returning to their country. The case history of a Japanese woman returning from graduate work in California illustrates a rather typical re-entry crisis. She was surprised by the narrow streets, dark rooftops, and sombre clothing which she had almost forgotten. Now she preferred a shower to Japanese-style bathing, drank cola with her meals, and seemed brusque, almost 'masculine', to her old friends. As the case writer states, 'She was no longer *kateiteki* (homelike), and some relations feared that she might have trouble finding a husband. Japan had not changed, but she had' (JETRO 1979).

Most cases of reverse culture shock do not last more than a few months. Then the curve turns upward again as the comfortable, warm, and supporting 'sea' begins to provide predictability and stability. It might be added, however, that the adjustment curve never rises to its original level. The individual who has lived and worked abroad never will be quite the same person he was before the experience. He will be more questioning, more aware of alternatives and, it is hoped, a more humble individual. He will have taken a difficult, but necessary, first step toward becoming a true *kokusaijin*, or international person.

Self-reference tendencies

A second common behavioural trap is for the expatriate to assume that others will think and act as he does. This tendency to use oneself as the sole reference point in assessing behaviour rests on a particularly slippery assumption: that 'my way' is the best way, and that any deviation from this ideal should be corrected as soon as possible.

In a way, this tendency was at the heart of Henry Higgins's wistful question, 'Why can't a woman be more like a man?' in the famous musical *My Fair Lady*. He goes on to point out that men are such 'reasonable chaps'. Many Americans overseas wish that their Japanese counterparts would be 'more like us'. But the fact is that they are not, and are not likely to be in the foreseeable future.

A typical situation evoking this self-reference tendency is promptness in keeping appointments. The Japanese are ambivalent regarding punctuality: their trains must run on split-second timing, but it is quite all right to be an half-hour late for a business appointment. Perhaps the thing most upsetting to Americans is not the half-hour wait in a reception room, but the typical lack of apology for being late. From the Japanese viewpoint, the delay was unavoidable – therefore, why discuss it?

Many other situations in Japan trigger the temptation of Americans to use themselves as points of reference. For example, the long periods of silence encountered in business meetings; the 'tiresome' delay in getting down to business; the Japanese aversion to asking for information; or the casual treatment accorded written documents. Irritation with such cultural differences can lead to frustration and failure in establishing a close and understanding relationship with those who do not think and act as we do.

Reliance on stereotypes

All Americans are abrasive, boisterous, and impulsive. All Japanese are overly polite, evasive, and circuitous. The word 'all' in these short-hand descriptions is the clue to the fact that a highly questionable stereotype is being used. A stereotype is a quick-and-easy way to identify and think about a group of people. While it usually is true that some small germ of truth underlies these sweeping generalizations, the vast scope of individual differences is ignored. And the serious danger is that expatriate executives will rely upon their stereotypes in shaping their own behaviour vis-a-vis their foreign hosts.

It is not unfair to say that it is ignorance concerning a group of people that encourages the use of stereotypes and makes them dangerously dysfunctional. American misconceptions concerning more than a billion Chinese were openly expressed and widely believed before relations with the Peoples' Republic were normalized. Furthermore, an isolated instance, if widely publicized, can foster an unrealistic stereotype. One need only recall the negative image created in Japan when a handful of US Congressmen took part in the smashing of a Japanese television set on Capitol Hill.

With respect to all three of these behavioural traps which may catch the expatriate manager, the most effective preventatives are awareness and understanding. Awareness of the fact that one is not alone in facing such stumbling blocks is very important. In addition, an understanding of the prevalence and nature of all such behavioural difficulties will improve one's resistance. Pre-assignment training, selective screening of applicants, and exposure to support groups of others who have served overseas can go far in minimizing failure due to these problems.

The observations in this chapter concerning variations in cultures and values are by no means confined to Japan. Nor are the problems of cross-cultural adjustment relevant only to the American manager sent to Tokyo. But the fact that Japanese culture, and its system of management, are so complex and in many ways unique makes expatriate selection and training particularly crucial. Yet, too few American companies offer comprehensive cross-cultural skills training to managers and their families prior to moving overseas. Given the many problems of adjustment every expatriate must confront, it is not surprising that many fail to complete the full term of their foreign assignment.

References

Barnlund, D. C. (1989) *Communicative Styles of Japanese and Americans*, Belmont, California: Wadsworth Publishing Company.
Davis, S. M. (1971) *Comparative Management*, Englewood Cliffs, N. J.: Prentice-Hall Inc.
The Economic Planning Agency (1983) *Japan in the Year 2000*, Tokyo: The Japan Times Ltd.
Hofstede, G. (1978) 'Culture and organization – a literature review study'. *Journal of Enterprise Management* 1: 127.
JETRO (1979) 'Reverse culture shock', *Focus Japan*, August: 16.
Mendenhall, Dunbar, and Oddon (1987) 'Expatriate selection, training, and career pathing', *Human Resource Management* 26, 3: 331.
Nihon Keizai Shimbun Inc. (1981) *Salary Man*, Tokyo: Nihon Keizai Shimbun Inc.
Takezawa, S. and Whitehill, A. M. (1986) *Work Ways: Japan and America*, Tokyo: The Japan Institute of Labour.
Whitehill, A. M. (1987) 'How to pick your "man in Asia",' *Southern Business Review*, 13, 2: 53–8.

Chapter four

Economic and social forces

So much for our brief look backward at the history, tradition, and culture of Japan. Now it is necessary to sketch the current environment within which that nation's highly successful management system operates. We already have discussed the outstanding events during the earlier decades of the post-war Showa period from 1945 to the mid-1980s. But many dramatic changes have taken place during even more recent years, particularly since the sudden appreciation of the yen (*endaka*) which began in 1985.

But first just a few words about the nature of change in Japanese society. An important part of the country's highly integrated national system is a clear, compelling, and easily communicated sense of mission. Basic changes considered vital to Japan's prestige and, in some cases her survival, are accepted and acted upon with impressive speed. The advantages of being a small country with a homogeneous people are nowhere more evident than in such situations.

Important national goals which demonstrate this phenomenon include harmonious labour–management relations, control of all forms of pollution, development of a modern social security programme, and many others. Now the crucial need for economic reform has moved into the leading position among national goals. There is every reason to believe that the broad base of support, and the determination to take quick action, will once again result in successful achievement of this latest facet in Japan's overall national mission.

This chapter will describe several broad sectors of the dynamic, present-day environment which are of particular relevance to management. Specifically, we shall consider economic reform, the social environment, and the educational system.

Economic reform

No system of management can be divorced from the external environment within which it must operate. For Japanese managers, this fact never has been clearer than in recent years. Fundamental changes have taken place in the Japanese economy, all part of a national consensus on the urgent need for extensive economic reform.

To sort out the most significant from among the many programmes for economic reform is not an easy task. None the less, two major changes in the Japanese economy during the past few years can be identified. These are: substantial appreciation of the yen; and broad-scale restructuring of the economy.

The rising yen

The sudden and extreme appreciation of the yen, following the five-nation Plaza Accord of September 1985, triggered a national determination to embark upon economic reform. The yen has since appreciated as much as 100 per cent against the dollar, surging from a ¥240 level to a high of about ¥120. Led by the United States, the exchange rate adjustment was aimed at correcting the trade imbalances among major countries. While some improvement has resulted, this ambitious objective has yet to be fully realized.

The US initiative was based upon what seemed to be perfectly sound reasoning. A higher yen against the dollar would raise prices of Japanese goods exported to America and hence decrease sales. Conversely, prices of US exports to Japan would decrease and thus stimulate demand. Unfortunately, the effect was much more modest than anticipated. In fact, the US trade deficit with Japan alone rose to a record $59.8 billion in 1987. However, the rate of increase levelled off, and by 1988 the corner was turned and the deficit declined to almost $50 billion.

Unfortunately, the deficit began rising again in 1989 and the imbalance remains disturbingly high. As a result, much to Japan's chagrin, the country was targeted in mid-1989, under the US Omnibus Trade and Competitiveness Act passed the year before, as a nation engaging in unfair trade practices. Increased tension between the two countries was, of course, the natural result of this harsh action.

The limited success of currency revaluation merely reconfirms the malignancy of other economic problems. Much has been written about the inferiority of US autos, electronic goods, and other items in terms of quality, design, and packaging. Competitive pricing – the specific target of currency revaluation – never has been an overwhelming concern.

Basically, the still-unresolved problem is how to create consumer demand for US products, which are perceived as being less attractive and less reliable than comparable items from alternative sources. I have asked this question of a broad sample of Japanese executives: 'If you could buy a new Ford or Chevrolet in Tokyo at the same price as a Nissan or Toyota, would you be likely to do so?' The disquieting response in every case has been an abrupt 'No!' or, at best, an amused smile. This is the fundamental issue which must be addressed before any market-induced correction to the US trade imbalance can be achieved.

Clearly, there are limits to how much can be accomplished solely by upward adjustment of the yen rate. Further appreciation to levels of ¥110–100 are, of course, possible but could have some very painful effects. At some point in the adjustment process the Japanese economy must suffer from rising unemployment in the regions and industries hardest hit by a sharp drop in overseas demand. The 'hollowing out' of regional economies is being experienced already in certain sections of Japan, with the jobless rate peaking at 2.8 per cent in 1986 and 1987, the highest since records started being kept in 1953.

Restructuring the economy

Most experts agree that the benefits of exchange rate adjustments cannot continue indefinitely and that further yen appreciation could start having disastrous results. Attention, therefore, has shifted to exploring a number of basic changes in Japan's economic structure. The 1987 Maekawa Commission Report, published by the influential Economic Council, set the stage for restructuring by making three key recommendations. First, Japan should take a number of specific steps to reduce the current account surplus. By 1987, the export-driven economy was still creating more than an $80 billion surplus in trade with the rest of the world. Second, the Commission urged an immediate and substantial increase in domestic demand. And third, a broad range of programmes should be implemented to improve the quality of life enjoyed by the Japanese people.

The Council, which serves as the chief advisory body to the Prime Minister, reiterated its position on these three points in its new five-year economic plan for Japan which began in 1988. This report carries tremendous political force and no doubt will contribute substantially to the shaping of Japan's development in the years ahead. By adopting its proposals, the Council rather immodestly suggested that Japan could 'take over the current US role in the world economy'. Accomplishment of this ambitious goal can be proved only in the future. But the seriousness and importance of these proposals should not be underestimated.

An important step toward the Council's first objective, to reduce the current account surplus, has been taken by enacting substantial market liberalization. Import restrictions on industrial products have been eliminated, and Japan's average industrial tariff is now the lowest in the world. An important point often missed is that, all 'rules of the game' apply equally to Japanese and foreign firms. In spite of this fact, foreign firms still consider the Japanese market difficult to penetrate. In this case, the perception may be more important than the reality, and the problem of market access therefore remains.

It may be useful to comment briefly on Japan's distribution system, with its layers of secondary and tertiary wholesalers. Some foreigners claim that this is a conspiracy to restrict imports and hence works against the goal of improving the current account surplus. Actually, the primary reason for the large number of wholesalers in Japan is the prevalence of so many small family-run retail outlets. There are almost twenty retailers per thousand persons in Japan, a figure twice that of the United States or Great Britain. These small retailers are not sophisticated in marketing techniques, have limited capital, and work in very small quarters. Therefore, the so-called 'hand-holding wholesalers' are needed to provide such essential services as generous credit terms, assistance with displays and advertising, and acceptance of returns of slow-moving merchandise. As in almost all of Japanese business, the long-standing personal contacts between wholesalers and retailers are of the utmost importance.

Furthermore, most wholesale firms also are very small. About three-quarters have fewer than ten employees. As one advocate of rationalizing the distribution system points out, 'When we consider the fact that many of the wholesalers are in the same boat as the retailers in terms of their financial resources and the size of business, we must also take into account the wholesalers' wholesaler, and so on down the line into the complex distribution web' (Okamoto 1980: 57–63).

Recognizing that increasing imports through easier market access will help reduce Japan's current account surplus, the government is making a strong effort to simplify the distribution system. Although small retailers, like small farmers, are considered political dynamite in Japan, there is evidence that some progress toward simplification will be accomplished in the future. Foreign companies, along with Japanese manufacturers, can expect to benefit from these developments.

Even in the still-protected area of agricultural products, American exports are not as severely restricted as often claimed. Actually, Japan has long been the world's largest and most reliable market for US farm products. According to US Department of Agriculture figures, as early as 1981 Japan was importing 62 per cent of US beef exports, and 44 per cent of US citrus exports. And in 1988, a firm agreement was negotiated to remove all quotas on these two important products by 1991. Though Japanese farmers no doubt will demand and continue to get some government protection, Japanese markets can hardly be considered closed to foreign competition.

The second recommendation of the Economic Council to increase domestic demand is another important phase in the overall restructuring of the Japanese economy. While the lion's share of publicity has focused upon Japan's booming exports and the persistent imbalance in foreign trade, a significant fact often overlooked is that her dependence upon exports is less than in any other industrialized nation except the United States. Japan's export dependence – that is, the percentage of GNP accounted for by exports – was approximately 10 per cent in fiscal 1987. This modest ratio, of course, does not reveal the tremendous importance of these exports in financing crucial imports, such as oil, which are essential for the nation's survival. But it does show that Japan already is oriented toward internal demand and positioned for further growth in this area.

A set of emergency economic measures, announced by the government in 1987, called for a ¥6 trillion package (about $40 billion). This is an ambitious programme to stimulate domestic demand, and calls for ¥5 trillion in public investment, of which more than ¥1 trillion will go into housing alone. An additional ¥1 trillion of demand will be generated by tax reform, which already has resulted in substantial cuts in personal income and other taxes.

The need for equally bold action by the private sector is emphasized by a leading Japanese economist in these terms: 'It is hoped that the private sector will step in to take the lead in fiscal 1988 and beyond, with the government performing a supportive role. This is an essential condition for substantial expansion in domestic demand' (Okumura: 1987).

Under former Prime Minister Noboru Takeshita, a major portion of the projected public expenditures were scheduled to take place in rural areas. Raised in a small town, his intention was to shape his domestic policy around a concept of *furusato*, or 'hometown environment'. Though it is too early to be certain, it seems likely that Prime Minister Kaifu will continue this emphasis. Consequently investment, both public and private, will be encouraged to improve rural roads, bridges, water and sewage systems, and schools.

Not all improvement projects, however, will be placed in rural areas. One mind-boggling project along the coastal area of Tokyo Bay is underway that combines both public and private resources. This is an ambitious re-urbanization plan called Minato Mirai 21, or the New Port City Plan for the Twenty-First Century. The plan aims to transform Yokohama, Japan's second largest city, into a model showcase for future international information centres. The project includes a 5,000-seat international convention centre, an international exhibition hall, 'smart' office buildings, shopping centres, hotels, museums, and parks. The overall goal is to remake Yokohama totally, turning it into an international culture and high-tech information city, with completion scheduled for the year 2000.

In addition to the Yokohama project, a similar scheme is taking shape for Chiba Prefecture across the Bay. Here a large-scale Makuhari Messe, or trade fair city, is being created. This new centre will include international exhibition halls, conference rooms, hotels, and parking facilities. Makuhari Messe is expected to revitalize the local economy by adding an integrated and balanced industrial sector to what is now largely an agriculture-based area.

Numerous other projects adjacent to the crowded Tokyo Bay area include expansion of Haneda International Airport, construction of a coastal highway, and the dramatic plan to build a bridge–tunnel link across Tokyo Bay to join the Kawasaki industrial complex with fast-growing Chiba Prefecture.

Perhaps of at least equal importance in stimulating domestic demand is the constant introduction of 'hit products' – that is, totally new consumer goods which will provide, as one advertising agency explains, 'a new and pleasant lifestyle for the people of Japan'. Highly successful hit products in recent years included an automatic bread baker in which ingredients are placed the night before to provide freshly baked bread for the next morning's breakfast. More than a million units were sold in one year at a price of about ¥30,000 ($250).

Another success story is the fully automatic washing machine, designed for silent operation and called Shizuka Gozen, literally 'Lady Quiet'. A uniquely Japanese item is the 'Tick Punch' vacuum cleaner which sucks up ticks, along with the dirt, from tatami mats and kills them with heat. The diffusion rate for durable consumer goods in Japan has reached the 100% level, and the trend is toward purchasing top quality machines and high technology products.

Such creative ventures are exciting and receive constant exposure in the Japanese press. In addition, underlying the whole concept of expanded domestic demand are many opportunities arising from a new wave of innovations in microelectronics, telecommunications, and information processing. Each techno-logical breakthrough creates new user and service demands in the domestic economy. Add to this the investment commitments already made for social infrastructure, especially housing, and there is every reason to believe that the Economic Council's call for a revitalized domestic economy will be answered long before the turn of the century.

The social environment

Turning now from economic reform to a reappraisal of the social climate within which Japanese companies operate, the broad issue of *ikigai*, or quality of life, will be addressed. Improving the quality of life is a subject of continuing concern at all levels of both the government and private sectors. It is also, as mentioned earlier, the third major issue addressed in the Economic Council's five-year economic plan launched in 1988.

The Japanese people

Fundamental to an understanding of a society is an appreciation of the composition and dynamics of its population. In Japan, this may be especially true because of the many unique characteristics of her people. There is little doubt that these demographic features exert a profound influence upon the nature and conduct of the Japanese management system.

An immediate reaction of foreigners is amazement at the incredible sameness of the passersby on any of Japan's busy thoroughfares. The Japanese population is indeed singularly homogeneous in race, religion, values, and language. In striking contrast, America is a heterogeneous, multi-racial, multi-religious, and multi-lingual society. Japan's homogeneity leads to a high degree of conformity in thought patterns, and a general absence of the conflict and confrontation so typical of American society.

Throughout her history, Japan has pursued a strict exclusionary immigration policy. Though skilled foreign workers and professionals, in limited numbers and when critically needed, have long been accepted, unskilled foreigners have been almost totally excluded. Legally registered aliens in Japan make up less than 1 per cent of the population, and the vast majority of these foreign residents are Koreans. Chinese and American resident aliens follow, but in much smaller numbers. It is true that the lure of high wages and salaries, and the many opportunities for profitable business ventures, have attracted a steady increase of foreigners. As one young American who gave up graduate studies to work for an investment counselling firm confided, 'Japan is no longer a place for lovers of the "Tales of Genji". It's for lovers of money.'

For those foreigners who speak Japanese, starting salaries are generous, club memberships and company cars are available, and luxury apartments often provided. One indication of the recent influx of US business persons is the rising number of members in the American Chamber of Commerce in Japan – 1600 members, of whom about 500 have joined during the past five years.

The other side of the immigration coin is the illegal alien problem, which has escalated in recent years. Illegal foreign employees are those who are working but hold only tourist or student visas, or those whose passports or visas have expired. When discovered, they usually face prompt deportation. In 1986, a total of 8,131 illegal foreign workers were apprehended, three-quarters of whom were from the Philippines. Other major sources included Thailand, China, Pakistan, and Korea. Men continue to be a minority, only accounting for about one-quarter of the violators in 1986, but their numbers are increasing more rapidly than those for women.

The strong yen has, of course, greatly increased the attractiveness of working in Japan. Wages, for example, are likely to be five to ten times the pay for comparable work in these other countries. A year's pay in Japan could pay in full the cost of a modest home in the Philippines. Fewer Japanese are willing to perform menial, physically demanding jobs in today's atmosphere of affluence. To fill this gap, illegal aliens will continue to run the risk of apprehension and filter into Japan. Though clearly increasing, the total number of foreigners living and working in Japan remains a small proportion of the population as a whole. The vast majority are, and will continue to be, 'insiders' – that is, 'We Japanese'.

A further characteristic of the Japanese people is their middle-class identity – that is, a self-perception as living a middle-class life-style. This is in spite of recent evidence of polarization between increasing numbers of the very rich and all others. In an annual survey on national life, the Prime Minister's Office asked a representative sample of 7,857 citizens what standard of life they were enjoying. A middle-class consciousness was apparent among an impressive 87.6 per cent of those who responded. Of these, 6.4 per cent saw themselves as upper-middle class, 51.8 per cent as middle-middle class, and 29.4 per cent as lower-middle class. In the light of widespread prosperity in Japan, it is particularly interesting that only 0.2 per cent felt that they belonged to the upper class. Here is further evidence of the tight homogeneity of

Figure 1: Type of life-style

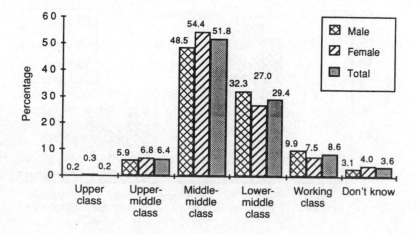

Source: Focus Japan, January 1987

Japan's citizens. Figure 1 presents these perceived types of life-style in greater detail.

The same survey asked people if they were satisfied with life at present. Reflecting at least the material affluence of today's society, 68.2 per cent indicated that they were satisfied. Of special interest, considering the oft-quoted expression that Japan still is 'a man's world', was the fact shown in Figure 2 that more women (71.7 per cent) than men (63.7 per cent) expressed satisfaction with their lives.

The housing problem

Perhaps the most worrisome gap in Japanese society is that between the dreams and reality concerning housing. It is the dream of almost every Japanese salaryman to own a single-family, detached house on a small lot, no more than an hour from work. The reality is that fewer each year can afford to buy even a tiny

Figure 2: Degree of satisfaction with life

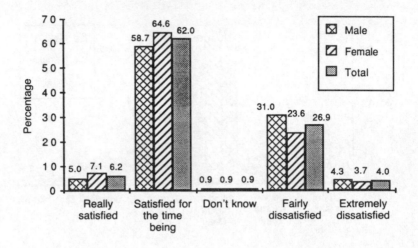

Source: Focus Japan, January 1987

condominium, let alone a private home. Even the most basic housing in Tokyo costs ¥100 million ($750,000) and up. A luxury home recently built in Denenchofu, one of the city's best residential areas, cost ¥3 billion, or more than $20 million. The average price for land zoned for residential use in the Tokyo metropolitan area rose a record 73.5 per cent in 1987 alone. Little wonder that the wide-open spaces and comfortable homes of American suburbanites are irresistible bargains for Japanese investors.

Such numbers may be difficult to comprehend fully. A simple way is to visualize standing on one square foot of land in the crowded Ginza area of Tokyo. It requires some careful shifting around for an average-size American to plant both feet within such a small square. Yet such a tiny scrap of land sold recently for more than $15,000. Move your feet just a bit apart, and the price of the land you are standing on doubles to $30,000.

The construction industry continues to boom in Japan, but little affordable housing for the ordinary citizen has resulted thus far. Large public works, and luxury hotels and office complexes in central Tokyo, currently attract major attention from investors. Modest, individual homes are not profitable for the tightly controlled construction firms. There is little real competition or bidding in the industry, with most contracts awarded under the so-called *dango* system. This is a web of bribes in the form of cash and gifts, usually arranged in secluded restaurant meetings, to prime contractors from general contractors, and to general contractors from subcontractors, to 'buy into' a project. Many construction firms are under the control of gangster syndicates, and the ordinary citizen longing for a home of his own is the innocent victim.

According to the *Housing Industry Handbook*, only 58 per cent of Japanese homes throughout the country had flush toilets in 1985. At the same time, an astounding 66 per cent were still without sewage systems – including some communities within the greater Tokyo area. For a nation with the second largest GNP in the world, the lag in providing world-class housing for her citizens is a persistent and highly political problem.

Many reasons could be cited for the exorbitant price of real estate in Japan. Antiquated building codes, many small construction firms, and preferential tax treatment for so-called 'urban farms' are just a few. Thus far, any meaningful land reform to lower prices has not been a major part of the general economic restructuring effort.

Japanese tourists returning to their country are sobered by the endless cluster of drab, cramped houses seen on the long drive from Narita Airport to central Tokyo. Not quite the 'rabbit hutches' claimed by some foreign critics, such dreary structures do not compare well with the average European or American home. For the Japanese government, they represent a festering sore on an otherwise healthy body politic.

Discrimination, Japanese-style

America, in her zealous crusade for equality at any cost, has attacked discrimination with the determination and force of a reformed sinner. Former downtrodden minorities have become noisy, favoured majorities. Those who were in the former majorities now are rebelling and crying 'reverse discrimination'. To be discriminating, in the sense of being properly selective within a given context, is no longer an acceptable American trait, and any form of discrimination is seen as reprehensible – and probably illegal.

Sometimes the United States seems to assume that she shares the burden of discrimination solely with such prime offenders as South Africa. But this is a mistaken conclusion. Every country in the world is guilty to some extent – and Japan is surely no exception. Because of their strong cultural identity and striking homogeneity, Japanese do discriminate against persons different from themselves. It is the familiar insider–outsider syndrome. And because many outsiders are of a different race, the discrimination becomes racist in nature. As Professor Edwin O. Reischauer points out, 'In essence it is a deeply racist concept, almost as though Japanese were a different species of animal from the rest of humanity' (Reischauer 1977: 411).

Though more frequent contact with Westerners has weakened any present-day marked bias against Caucasians, the history of such prejudice goes back to the opening of Japan to the world at the time of the Meiji Restoration. Again quoting Reischauer's perceptive observations:

> When the Japanese first came into frequent contact with
> Caucasians in the nineteenth century, they found them strange
> and revolting. Their big noses and curious coloring – blue eyes
> and red hair – made them seem more like mythical goblins than
> human beings, and they were distressingly smelly because of
> their richer diet of animal fats and their heavy woolen clothing.
> Batakusai, meaning 'stinking of butter', once was a common
> pejorative for Western.
>
> (Reischauer 1977: 411–12)

Fortunately, times have changed, and today almost anything Western is considered very 'now', or 'in'. Yet beneath their wish to become truly *kokusaijin*, or international people, the Japanese cling to their conviction that they are, if not always better, at least very different from other people. If a Westerner also happens to be black, the prejudice is even deeper. Basically, the Japanese tend to align themselves with the whites in America – an alliance which many consider to be the lesser of two evils.

Westerners are not the only targets of racial bias in Japan. Koreans, though constituting the largest group of registered aliens in Japan, are treated as second-class citizens. At the time of writing, Koreans – even second- or third-generation families in Japan – still are subjected to annual registration and fingerprinting. Even other Japanese are not totally exempt. Those living in Okinawa, and the so-called 'hairy Ainu' in the northern island of Hokkaido, are considered somewhat inferior to the superior, sophisticated Tokyoites.

Aside from racial discrimination, Japan continues to assign women a role in society much lower than that of men. This wording is chosen with care, since from the viewpoint of many Japanese – both male and female – this is not discrimination in the Western sense. However, the notion of male superiority starts almost before conception of the Japanese child. Most families desperately want, and show continuing preference to, a son. The eldest son always seems to be first in line for distribution of everything from candy to college educations. The net result is that the self-perception of Japanese males is one of distinct superiority over mere females.

This distinction extends to all walks of life. A simple, yet dramatic, example took place on a crowded train as it arrived in Tokyo station. On one side of the car was a distinguished-looking, middle-aged Japanese couple; on the other side were their American counterparts. As the train slowed down, the Japanese wife shook off her shoes, climbed on the seat to retrieve her husband's coat, helped him put it on, and only then got down her own coat. Her husband showed his gratitude by leaving her far behind as he rushed to the station platform. On the other side of the car, a reverse sequence was unfolding. The American husband reached for his wife's coat, helped her put it on, and then retrieved his own from the overhead rack. His wife showed *her* gratitude by rushing out of the car leaving her husband behind to fend for himself.

This little scenario tells a big story. The Japanese wife did not feel that she was an object of sex discrimination. She was merely fulfilling her role as a Japanese woman and wife. Nor did the husband feel particularly favoured – he simply was receiving the deference due all males. The American husband, in turn, did not feel chivalrous and considered his actions merely good manners.

His wife expected and received the priority to which she had long been accustomed.

During recent years, sexual equality in the workplace has been 'suggested' under Japan's relatively new Equal Employment Opportunity law of 1986. More will be said about this law and its effects in later chapters. Here we shall just point out that, though there are more women working in Japan these days, mere numbers do not tell the whole story. Most are still in low-paying jobs, and more than a third are self-employed or working in family businesses. Almost all women returning to work after raising their families work as part-timers with none of the security and few of the benefits of full-time employment. Those few who do enter the professions still gravitate toward teaching and nursing. One of the handful of Japanese females who have made it to the top in business says the best advice she can give ambitious women is to 'Think like a man, act like a lady, and work like a dog'. A later discussion of the staffing function in management will show this to be excellent advice.

Paradoxically in a country which shows extreme deference and respect for the elderly, Japan does in one sense discriminate against them. For many years, the mandatory retirement age of 55 pushed still-active persons into a long and often difficult retirement. Now with forced retirement creeping up to age 60, the problem is somewhat alleviated. But even at 60, Japan's record-setting life expectancy means many years during which some marginal means of support will be necessary. In contrast, America, so often accused of flagrant discrimination of all kinds, has almost abandoned the whole concept of mandatory retirement in both government and industry.

Discrimination is not new to Japan. For many centuries an outcast class, known as *eta* (full of filth) or *burakumin* (village people), worked at jobs involving slaughter and use of animals – tanners, butchers, furriers, and so on. Living together in *buraku*, or villages, these people even today are isolated from the mainstream of Japanese society. Many actually are farmers. But if they were born into the outcast class there is no way to escape. Though legally freed by the Meiji Restoration in 1868, their lot has not greatly improved. Fear of contamination and loss of purity perpetuates the deep prejudice against the more than 2 million outcasts now living in Japan.

Male–female relations

A final aspect of the Japanese social environment which affects the practice of management is the nature of relationships between the sexes. Subtly, yet visibly, sexual roles and behaviour do influence many business policies and practices, particularly in the general area of human resource management.

The alleged problem of sexual harassment so much talked about in US companies today is not likely to be a big issue in Japan in the foreseeable future. Many Japanese office women feel themselves fortunate if they are even noticed by their male co-workers. Nevertheless, such important management concerns as supervisor–subordinate relations, patterns of leadership, promotion decisions, and development programmes clearly are influenced by the accepted, conventional male–female relationships.

Separation of the sexes in Japan tends to be more extensive, and to last longer, than in the United States. Many private schools still cater exclusively to one sex, with the girls specializing in such fields as music or art, and the boys focusing upon such subjects as engineering and science. Even at university levels, many social activities tend to segregate men from women, and casual dating is still less common than in the typically integrated, coeducational US colleges.

In the workplace, too, most women are on a different track to men and frequently are considered little more than *shokuba no hana*, or office flowers. Many top Japanese companies continue to select all of their female recruits from high schools or junior colleges. In too many cases, the major selection criteria are that the graduate must be younger than 24, attractive, well-mannered, obedient, and totally lacking in ambition. In general, the relationship between male and female employees tends to reflect distance rather than intimacy while at work.

On the subject of pre-marital sex, studies indicated that a rather small portion of young people in Japan are sexually very active, but that the vast majority are sexually repressed. A government survey throughout the country in 1983 indicated that only 12.7 per cent of females between the ages of 15 and 23, and 18 per cent of males in the same age group, had experienced sex. A young woman from Tokyo, in a recent seminar conducted by the author, responded to these figures by exclaiming, 'That doesn't sound like my friends!' Young, wealthy city dwellers no doubt are far more active. In any case, the figures are considerably below those of many Western countries.

Paradoxically, Japan has no tradition of sexual immorality. Sex is a bodily function which, like good food and fine wine, is to be enjoyed. Yet permissiveness is tempered by the ever-present fear of shame. Though prostitution has been illegal since 1958, sex is openly available at the famous *toruko*, or turkish baths, and at hot-springs resorts throughout the country. Furthermore, the pattern of male-only entertaining at the thousands of hostess bars and cabarets opens the door to many opportunities for sexual encounters.

Of course marriage is the ideal goal of most young people in Japan. Economic limitations, however, make it necessary to postpone marriage until perhaps 27–30 for men and 24–28 for women. According to a recent survey, the average Japanese couple will spend about $30,000 on getting married and enjoy their honeymoon in Hawaii or Guam. Although the bride's family covers most of these costs, the groom's family is expected to contribute a substantial monetary gift. Guests to the wedding also offer cash gifts, averaging perhaps $50 each. Wedding receptions tend to be large, elaborate, and rather lengthy affairs with many shouts of *banzai*!

Though coercive, strictly arranged marriages are a thing of the past, 'semi-arranged' matches are still the path followed by most couples. In these cases, a relative, good friend, or supervisor at work will encourage prospective partners to exchange photos. If either party wishes to halt the proceedings at this point no one loses face. Sometimes a particularly choosy man or woman may reject as many as a dozen possible mates on the basis of pictures alone. However, if both parties like what they see the next step is an informal meeting, or *omiai*, usually at a popular restaurant or coffee shop. Again, either side may retreat without shame.

But if the couple then decides to continue meeting, the ties become more binding and marriage is the most likely result. The initial sponsor of the match becomes a master of ceremonies on the festive occasion. There is little doubt that impromptu, so-called 'love marriages' are becoming more popular these days, but the semi-arranged matches have a better success score and tend to be favoured by the majority of Japanese youth.

The education system

One of the most impressive characteristics of the Japanese people which sets them apart from others is their constant, insatiable thirst for personal development. Furthermore, much of this pursuit of learning is not to get a promotion or salary increase this year or next, or to meet any immediate need. Rather, it is simply a deep-rooted conviction that education must be a life-long endeavour. Most Japanese want to better themselves, and learning new things is seen as the best way to achieve their goal.

This extraordinary taste for learning has solid foundations in Japanese history. According to Confucius, the sixth-century Chinese philosopher whose teachings have profoundly influenced Japan's value system, the ideal social order is achieved not by law, but by an educated populace. He stressed the moral obligation to improve oneself and to serve as an example for others. This is an obligation which most Japanese accept from an early age and continue to feel well into retirement age. Ambitious parents constantly remind their children that only through a high level of education will people achieve success, the nation prosper, and Japan enjoy the international prestige which she deserves. This appeal is irresistible when posed within the broader mix of Japanese culture and values.

Because there is such a clear gap between the extreme rigours of pre-university schooling and the relative ease of the university experience, each phase will be discussed separately in the sections which follow.

Pre-university education

The dream of most Japanese mothers is for their children – and especially their sons – to graduate from a top-flight university and thus have a better-than-average chance to enjoy a lifetime career in one of Japan's large, prestigious corporations. From pre-kindergarten through to high school, this is the main priority in most Japanese families.

The pressure starts early in a child's life. Pre-kindergarten cram schools flourish in the larger cities, with toddlers studying the fundamentals which will help them meet the entrance requirements for elite kindergartens, often owned and operated by one of the leading universities. The private, pre-kindergarten cram schools start the long series of financial sacrifices every family will make for their children's education. Tuition for a six-week summer programme for 3 to 4 year olds can cost as much as $10,000. But the head start thus gained is considered to be worth it in one of the world's most competitive educational systems.

Kindergartens in Japan are a far cry from the 'play schools' of other countries. Discipline is stressed, and the fundamentals of reading, writing, and arithmetic are introduced. By the time they enter first grade, students will be able to construct sentences and will have mastered simple number relationships. In a sense, they are poised at the starting line to begin the fierce struggle for ultimate admission to the university of their choice.

Japan's education system underwent a series of reforms during the Occupation period following the Second World War. For example, the US 6–3–3–4 model was adopted with six years of elementary school, three years of junior high, three years of high school, and four years at the university level. In addition, compulsory education was increased from six to nine years – no longer very relevant, with 95 per cent of the eligible age group attending high school. Not all American-imposed reforms, however, have survived. The Occupation's purge of moral education (*shushin*), stressing such values as filial piety, loyalty, and nationalism, was soon discarded. By 1957, moral education, with some modifications, had been restored and today is considered one of the essentials of Japanese schooling.

The curriculum for all public schools is standardized by Japan's prestigious Ministry of Education (Monbusho). Textbooks are prescribed and course content established. These standards, in turn, become the guidelines for private schools to follow. While often criticized as being narrow and bureaucratic in nature, such national standards set a rigorous pace to which all students must conform. The impressive result is a national level of competence that is the envy of other countries throughout the world. A maths test given recently to 125,000 students from twenty countries resulted in Japanese junior and senior high school students both coming out on top. In more general terms, Japan can boast of a uniformly well-educated citizenry, solid character training for the young, and a highly qualified workforce.

Japanese children currently attend school 240 days a year,

including half day on Saturdays, compared with 180 days in US public schools. This gap, however, will gradually ease in the years ahead. The Ministry of Education has decreed that beginning in 1992, children will attend school only five days a week, although at first on a biweekly basis. But until then, the extra days, plus shorter vacations and fewer holidays, add up to almost two additional years of schooling. By the time they reach high school, students are ready to tackle such courses as electronics, physics, statistics, and calculus – subjects usually reserved for college level in the United States.

The shift to even a partial five-day school week may, in fact, merely increase attendance at an already booming Japanese institution – after-school cram schools, or *jukus*. The Ministry of Education recently reported that one out of every six primary school students and one out of every two junior high students attend a *juku* after regular school hours. In 1986, it was estimated that fees paid by anxious parents totalled ¥870 billion (about $6.5 billion). Younger children are exposed to the arts, the abacus, and calligraphy, while older students study more academic subjects to help them prepare for the inevitable university entrance exams.

With their long hours in the classroom, sports and other extra-curricular activities, attendance at *juku*, and four to five hours of homework each night, Japanese children have little time for relaxation or even for sleep. There is a popular Japanese saying that is all too true: 'Sleep four hours, pass. Sleep five hours, fail'.

Even with such intensive preparation, not all high-school students pass the crucial university entrance exams given in February of their senior year. Experience indicates that only about 40 per cent taking the exams pass on their first try. The rest will have to attend another year of intensive *juku* and try again – or simply settle for a terminal high school degree.

As with most Japanese institutions these days, there are cross currents of opinion and pressures for change in the education system. Some defend the enviable level of scholarship the system has achieved. Others criticize the rigidity of the system and the tremendous stress under which it places students. Furthermore, there is a spreading worry that rapid change and international-ization may require a different end product – that is, graduates who are more creative, more daring, and more open to change. But the present system is so successful and well entrenched that changes are likely to be modest and slow in coming (see Table 2).

Table 2 Education in Japan and the USA

Category	Japan	United States
1 Expenditure on education: percentage of GNP	6%	7%
2 Percentage of students graduating from senior high school	90%	77%
3 Average time spent on homework per day (senior high school students)	2 hours	30 minutes
4 Percentage of students absent per day	very low	9%
5 Years required studying mathematics	3 years	1 year average
6 Years required studying foreign languages (junior and senior high school)	6 years	0 to 2 years
7 Percentage of university students majoring in technological fields	20%	5%

Source: Nippon Steel News, March/April, 1988, p. 7

The university experience

Once the stress and strain of years spent preparing for university entrance exams are over, both parents and students are ready for a break. The Japanese university provides just that – a four-year interim, described by many as a 'paradise', before entering the tough, real world of business. Since academic grades are not considered to be very important by recruiters seeking college graduates to join their corporate family, the most sacred GPA (grade-point average) watched so carefully by US students is of little concern to their Japanese counterparts. As one experienced American professor states after twelve years of teaching in Japan, 'One clear tendency among 90 per cent of the Japanese college students I've taught is their strong determination *not* to study' (Gold 1988).

The four years of college life are spent primarily developing social skills for which they had little time during the gruelling years of public schooling. Their emphasis is upon meeting new friends, developing social maturity, making general plans for their future careers, and enjoying themselves. Classes are often held just once a week, and attendance is sporadic.

Tremendous loyalty and school spirit are developed during

university years. Close friends and classmates who join the same company upon graduation will form the important *gaku batsu*, or school clique, within the organization. These cliques cement lifelong, intimate ties. University caps and T-shirts are worn with pride, and alumni clubs prosper throughout the world. These precious years, after all, are the reward for many years of hard work and sacrifice.

Professors in Japanese universities tend to be well-trained, and now well-paid, professionals. Yet many are more interested in research than in quality classroom performance. An exception should be noted – the students' 'senior seminar'. This is a relatively small class during the senior year which brings professor and student close together. Professors are on the lookout for exceptional students for whom they can give the highest recommendation. Companies rely upon professors with whom they have had a successful relationship to do this essential pre-selection screening for them. Students, in turn, will try very hard to please their senior-seminar professor because his evaluation and recommendation to company recruiters can mean success or failure in securing a coveted position upon graduation. Students frequently devote the entire last summer vacation of their university career to helping their professor with his research, asking for no pay and being grateful if the professor takes them on an overnight excursion to the mountains or the sea at the end of the summer. There is a degree of mutual dependence here that is almost never found in American universities.

Though the university provides a pleasant interim for most students, there are exceptions. Those in the demanding fields of science and engineering do have to master a respectable body of knowledge in their chosen fields. Lab work must be completed and experiments tended. But even these students would be dismayed at the pressure and intensity of similar courses in American universities. However, in Japanese universities as in all educational settings, the opportunities for learning and self-development are there if students care to take advantage of them.

A discussion of the remarkable opportunities and facilities available within Japanese corporations for continuous training will be reserved for a later chapter. Because of the expectation of lifetime employment with a single company, the very extensive in-house educational programmes are both necessary and cost effective.

In this chapter, the discussion has dealt with the present-day external environment to which Japanese managers must be responsive. We have examined the ambitious programmes for economic reform which are receiving top priority among the nation's goals. Such programmes include accommodation to the rising yen, and extensive restructuring of the economy. Analysis of the current social environment included a careful look at the Japanese people themselves, the sensitive issue of adequate housing, the extent of discrimination in Japanese society, and relations between the sexes. Finally, the education system, from pre-kindergarten cram schools through to university graduation, was described. In the next chapter we move on to an examination of the macro-level components, and connecting links among components, of the industrial structure of Japan.

References

Gold, S. (1988) 'Inside a Japanese university', *Japan Update*, Winter: 3.
Okamoto, M. (1980) 'Rationalizing the distribution system', in P. Norbury and G. Bownas (eds) *Business in Japan*, London: The Macmillan Press.
Okumura, A. (1987) 'Japan's changing economic structure', *Journal of Japanese Trade and Industry* 5: 13.
Reischauer, E. O. (1977) *The Japanese*, Cambridge, Mass.: Harvard University Press.

Chapter five

The structure of industry

Picture yourself, on a clear day, peering from the pinnacle of New York's World Trade Center, Singapore's Westin Stamford Hotel, or the famous Tokyo Tower. What you would see is a microcosm of each country's industrial structure. From whatever vantage point, the mosaic of factories, corporate offices, government ministries, embassies, banks, department stores, and small shops is seen as a composite of separate – yet somehow connected – pieces of a huge jigsaw puzzle of industry. They all fit together and their synergism provides a total driving force far greater than the simple sum of the parts.

In this chapter we shall look at Japan's overall industrial structure. But first a popular myth must be discarded. This is the deceptively simple concept of 'Japan, Inc.' – of Japan as one vast, monolithic economic machine in which all major parts (business, government, labour, and the general public) work in perfect harmony toward common goals. Somehow, this ultra-simplistic notion of Japan will not go away, but there is little truth in it.

As we shall see in the discussion which follows, Japan is very much a pluralistic society, with very different values and ideologies characterizing each major sector. Business and government often do cooperate, but they frequently go in quite different directions. Labour unions are much less adversarial than in the United States. But there are occasional strikes and slowdowns in Japanese industry, and not all workers show total loyalty and dedication to their companies. Japan, after all, is one of the most democratic nations in the world, and democracy is by no means synonymous with singleness of purpose or action.

Instead of Japan, Inc., it seems wise to substitute what has been referred to as Japan's 'integrated national system (INS)'. This system binds together the following forces: a unique management style; advanced technology; abundant capital; supportive government; an incredible international network for intelligence and coordinated action; effective vertical and horizontal links among companies; and a strong sense of national mission. Following a brief overview of Japan's employment structure, each of these critical elements will be examined.

The structure of employment

Japan, since the early 1970s, has been a 'post-industrial society'. This title is bestowed upon countries which have crossed the threshold of having more than half their workforce engaged in tertiary, or service, industries. This no longer is an exclusive club, since a number of upper-middle income countries (for example, Argentina, Israel, and Singapore) and the majority of upper income, industrialized countries (for example, United States, Switzerland, and Canada) are members.

However, it is particularly interesting to note in Table 3 that almost half of Japan's workforce in 1950 still was engaged in agriculture and other primary employment. Today, this figure is considerably below 10 per cent. When one considers the small size of individual farm holdings, the shift truly is impressive.

Table 3 Structure of employment: Japan (1986)

| | | Composition (%) | | |
Total Employed (1000s)		Primary	Secondary	Tertiary
1950	35,626	48.3	21.9	29.8
1960	43,716	32.6	29.2	38.2
1970	52,042	19.3	33.9	46.8
1980	55,360	10.4	34.8	54.8
1986	58,530	8.5	33.9	57.6

Source: Bank of Japan, Comparative Economic Statistics

Although US employment in primary industry is less than 3 per cent, it does not seem likely that Japan will attain this level. Mechanization of farming on Japan's tiny farms is reaching its limit. Furthermore, an extensive fishing industry tends to maintain the ranks of workers at the primary level. However, one careful study does forecast that employment in primary industries will continue to decline until, by the year 2000, such workers will account for only 5 per cent of the labour force. The same source states that the number of people engaged in tertiary industries will continue to increase, particularly in the service activities, where productivity increases are relatively difficult to achieve. As a result, the study predicts that 'one out of every two people employed will be engaged in the service industry in the year 2000' (The Economic Planning Agency 1983: 85).

The expanding service sector already is apparent in the patterns of household expenditures in Japan today. As the Japanese have become more affluent and have acquired all the gadgetry of modern life, they have begun to spend more time and money on leisure activities, international travel, education, and social activities. In addition, demand predictably continues to build for such supportive industries as public utilities, transportation, finance, insurance, and a wide variety of repair and service activities.

The gradual shift from primary to secondary, and then to tertiary employment is a universal trend in developing nations. At the post-industrial level, there is little doubt that most future growth will come in the service sector. This is happily consistent with the Japanese consensus to move into a 'knowledge-intensive era'. Particularly rapid growth is expected in the field of computer data processing and a wide range of information services.

Such changes are both the cause and effect of changes in values and lifestyles. Already evident is a growing desire for cultural and social satisfaction, and for a better balance between work life and personal life. History indicates that what the Japanese want, the Japanese get. Much of their success can be explained by the tremendous strength and drive of the integrated economic, social, and political forces to which the discussion now turns.

Japan's industrial system

Returning to the earlier listing of seven critical elements which together make up Japan's integrated national system (INS), it may be worthwhile to take a closer look at each. Together these vital elements comprise a system which works very effectively.

Management

The unique character of the Japanese management system itself is a significant factor in the nation's powerful INS. Much has been and will be written about this subject, and it provides the major substance of the present volume. Few people have not heard of the four 'sacred treasures' of Japanese management – lifetime employment, seniority-based wages and promotions, consensus decision-making, and enterprise unions. All are under some pressure due to recent years of slow growth and the drastic changes inherent in restructuring the economy. But each is a part of the heritage of the post-war economic miracle, and each may be more durable than some doomsday journalists would have us believe.

These four 'treasures' will be revisited in later chapters, and a more detailed assessment of their present and future importance offered. But reference here to management as a cornerstone in Japan's INS goes beyond these notorious characteristics. Its importance lies also in the quality, the vitality, and the cohesiveness of a disciplined and professional management team. The expertise of this team, except in highly specialized fields such as engineering and science, is not acquired during high school or university education. Rather, it is at least partially the result of a lifetime of hands-on training in almost all of the functional areas of business. Job rotation, usually every three to five years is an expected part of every manager's career development. The result is not just a management force of generalists, although such a claim often is made. More accurately, the result is a scope and depth of know-how which is difficult to match. Perhaps we can refer to Japanese managers as neither pure generalists nor narrow specialists, but as 'multi-specialists', with sufficient knowledge of all aspects of the total management process to be highly effective leaders.

It is important, too, to appreciate that Japanese managers are relatively sheltered from stockholders' pressures. The president of Nissan Motor Company, Ltd, has referred to this separation of ownership and management in an article dealing with management style. He says that this allows managers 'to make decisions based on long-term company interest, free from the narrow self-interest of owners'. He adds: 'Managers are therefore free to manage as they see fit, concentrating on long-term company growth' (Ishihara 1983: 6–7).

Mention should also be made again of the extremely high ranking of work, the company, and one's work group among the priorities of Japanese employees. Work itself, and work-related activities, consume almost all of a businessman's time and energy. Working either five and a half days or six days a week, with ten-hour days common, a singleness of interest and purpose develops which encourages total concentration and dedication to a job. Almost reluctantly, some Japanese managers accept a needed break on Sundays. As one executive puts it, 'On Sunday we are able to recharge our batteries and be ready on Monday for another samurai duel.' But if golf or other social activities are scheduled, it is likely they will be with company co-workers or clients, and business will be the major topic of conversation.

So it is not just the unique policies and practices of the Japanese management system which make it a cornerstone of the INS. In addition, the spirit and vitality, the 'heart' of management, must be considered a part of its strength.

Technology

The history of technology has been aptly described as 'the history of the human race'. And at least since the 1950s, the development of technology seems to run parallel with the remarkable development of Japan. It has often been claimed that the Japanese are not creative and tend to be copiers. Perhaps it is true that until recently the main thrust of Japanese technological development has been taking, refining, and upgrading foreign technology. But the 1980s tell a different story. As one authority writes, 'Now, Japan has absorbed about all that Europe and America have to offer in this line. For the first time, Japan has no choice but to create its own new technology' (Moritani 1982: 19).

New 'firsts' now seem to be coming from Japan with impressive regularity. Examples include fibre optics, voice recognition systems, computerized language translation, and anti-pollution technology. Robotization offers another example of creative design and application. At present, some 70 per cent of 'steel-collar workers' in use throughout the world are in Japan. Dramatic breakthroughs can be expected from Japan by the turn of the century in such fields as genetic engineering, superconductors, and nuclear fusion.

A comparison of R&D expenditures as a percentage of national income in the major industrialized countries of the world shows Japan well up among the leaders. The Science and Technology Agency in Japan reported that in 1970 Japan spent only $5 billion on R&D, which amounted to 1.96 per cent of national income at that time. But by 1986, the amount spent had jumped to $49 billion and was a healthy 3.18 per cent of the nation's income. This percentage compares with 3.06 per cent in the United States, 3.25 per cent in West Germany, and was surpassed only by the Soviet Union with 4.95 per cent. The total amount spent by the United States, however, was more than double that spent by Japan.

In a sense, the whole argument of copying versus original creation has been overdone. As is true with all nations trying to catch up with the leaders, America started off as a copier in her attempts to surpass Great Britain. As one writer reminds us, 'American history schoolbooks remember this copying as a good example of Yankee ingenuity. British history schoolbooks see it in another light – as theft – Americans stole British technology' (Thurow 1986: 1).

Japan has impressed the world with products that have exquisite design, superior packaging, and outstanding quality. A senior researcher at Nomura Research Institute draws an interesting parallel between Japan's leading products and the traditional *makunouchi*, or lunch box. This traditional Japanese lunch box with its 'neat rows of rice balls, the orchestration of garnishments, and the plain yet handsome box', shows the Japanese skill in beautiful modelling, unification of disparate elements, and in meeting a multiplicity of human senses (Moritani 1982: 192–3).

The uncanny ability of the Japanese to combine the best of technology with the best of aesthetics is likely to continue to flourish in combination with ambitious programmes of R&D. As such, we can say that technology qualifies as an important component of her powerful integrated national system.

Capital

The only problem Japan has concerning the supply of investment capital can best be described as 'an embarrassment of riches'.

Literally awash with money, the ever-present question is how best to use it. Many Japanese companies are answering that question by devoting major resources to *zaitech*, roughly translated as 'the money game'. That is, because of the surplus of funds, financial investment has become an important business for all kinds of companies. Toyota, for example, is said to have earned more than half its annual income in a recent year by successful investment management.

Japan, now the world's largest creditor nation, has invested much of her huge surplus abroad. As a result, in 1988, direct foreign investment amounted to almost $140 billion. This means that Japan has come to play a major role as a supplier of funds for international financing. Furthermore, financial markets have been liberalized, and in recent years many foreign investment firms have set up branch operations in Japan. While not yet the standard of international currency, the yen increasingly is recognized as a medium for international capital transactions.

The size and scope of Japan's overseas investments have been outlined in an earlier chapter. Perhaps it is enough now to describe a cartoon seen in a newspaper which showed an enthusiastic US worker carrying a placard which read 'Buy American!' Next to him was an equally eager Japanese waving a placard which read 'Buy America!' This latter process is well underway, with strong feelings being expressed both for and against the economic invasion. The ironic fact is that Japan has become America's rich uncle and her chief source of foreign capital. With typical bankers' understatement, a vice president of the New York Federal Reserve Bank reminds us that since foreigners now own more than a trillion dollars of assets in the United States, 'they will expect to have some influence'.

A huge surplus of capital in Japan comes not only from selling more to the world than she buys but is also the result of the extremely high propensity among the people to save. According to a recent report by the International Savings Bank Institute, the Japanese are the world's top savers. The Institute reports that there is an average of $27,303 in savings for each resident of Japan while in the United States the comparable figure is $9,733. Recent trends in Japan, however, such as the ageing population and the removal in 1987 of tax incentives to save, lead most observers to expect a reduced propensity to save in the future (Kyoku 1985: 232).

Why do the Japanese show such a high rate of savings? Provision for educational expenses and as a hedge against natural disasters used to be cited as major reasons. Today, however, concern about financial security in an ageing society, and the need to accumulate large sums for home ownership or rental, are high on the list. In any event, it seems safe to say that an oversupply of savings, and hence capital for investment at home and abroad, will continue to be a key ingredient of Japan's INS for the foreseeable future.

Government support

A further ingredient is a close working relationship between government and business. The reader will recall, from our earlier discussion of the years immediately following the Meiji Restoration in 1868, that the government of Japan owned and managed the hurriedly developed basic industries which Japan needed so badly at the time. Then, after several decades, these industries were sold to prominent family groups on very favourable terms. These families, in turn, became the centre of the powerful industrial cartels known as *zaibatsu*.

In contrast to the United States, where government has always been considered by business people as an unwelcome intruder, the Japanese government has been perceived as a source of guidance and support. There is a high degree of cooperation between Japanese business and government, though the two parties do not always agree on key issues and strategies.

Since early formation of the *zaibatsu*, the growth of powerful monopolies and cartels has not only been sanctioned, but actively encouraged, by government. The Japanese have no fear whatever of cartelization and, in fact, see cartels as an element of competitive strength. Despite the passage of an anti-monopoly law, and the abortive attempt of the American Occupation to purge the *zaibatsu* leaders, there is more rather than less concentration of economic power today than in pre-war years.

The government bureaucracy, the ruling political party (LDP), and the private sector combine to create a three-legged stool of enormous strength and support. The education system funnels Japan's best and brightest into positions of leadership of key ministries and big companies. Graduates from the elite universities tend to keep in touch and to pursue mutual interests. Under a system known as 'administrative guidance', the two most important ministries, the Ministry of International Trade and Industry (MITI) and the Ministry of Finance (MIF), can encourage favoured companies and discourage those they see as dysfunctional. Businesses, in turn, perpetuate the close relations with the bureaucracy by providing lucrative jobs for retired government VIPs who are known as *amakudari*, or those descended from heaven.

Within the government bureaucracy there is a strong sense of public service and a dedication to the public good. Because laws passed by the Diet are notoriously vague and skimpy, the operation of government is left to senior bureaucrats who wield enormous power and influence. Furthermore, the powerful Ministry of Finance, through the Bank of Japan, can funnel investment and working capital to those companies whose activities and goals conform to national policy.

Finally, there is a strong link between big business and politics in Japan. Big business has effectively, through informal communication links with the LDP leadership, influenced the political process and the selection of political leaders. Money is lavished on those candidates most favourable to business. And once-a-month meetings are held in the most expensive Tokyo restaurants to discuss issues of mutual concern. Though lobbying in the American sense is practised in Japan – and by the Japanese abroad – such intimate 'club meetings' may actually have more influence. It is the Japanese way, and we shall later see the same approach used to coordinate the activities of individual companies in the large corporate groupings.

The international network

In this writer's opinion, the network of Japanese business and government offices throughout the world may be the most important component of the integrated national system. There is not a business centre in the world thought to be of present or future commercial importance that does not have a number of Japanese representatives living and working within it. They are there for an extended period of time, they speak the language, and they know the culture and customs of the host country. Most important, they are able to relay on a daily basis vital economic and political intelligence back to the home office in Japan. It is an intelligence network of which any governmental security agency could be justly proud.

Every major group of Japanese companies has its bank, general trading company, and other operations. Through branches, agencies, and representative offices, these industrial oligopolies straddle the globe. It is true that the Japanese tend to be socially clannish when abroad and congregate in plush cultural islands such as the Japan Club in New York City. But during the work day they are in the mainstream and carefully collect and document every shred of business intellience which could be of possible interest in Tokyo. In addition to the many corporate offices, outposts of such government organizations as the Japan External Trade Relations Organization (JETRO) also flourish throughout the world.

Though the normal tour of duty for overseas personnel is three to five years, the offices themselves are there to stay. Long before the United States formally recognized the Peoples Republic of China (PRC), special subsidiaries of major Japanese corporations had already established beachheads in this tempting future market of a billion consumers. In contrast to US latecomers, who move in and out in an incessant game of musical chairs, the Japanese have dug in for the long pull. The important point to be stressed is that the entire international network permits Japan to be proactive in its relationships with other countries. Unfortunately, the United States thus far has been only reactive – and often with too little too late. This proactive ability is a tremendous Japanese strength which other countries will find hard to duplicate.

Horizontal and vertical organization

From the vantage point of Tokyo Tower, you would also see spread out beneath you thousands of business organizations, large and small. Most of these are not totally separate companies operating independently of each other. Rather, they are tied together by a complex web of horizontal and vertical linkages. Big companies are linked with other big companies, and big companies have close ties with many small companies. Together, these groupings become constellations which, in turn, fit into a cohesive national pattern.

Here is further evidence that Japanese management truly is a system – that is, a web of interrelated and interdependent parts which together form an effective, systemic whole. In this section, we shall focus upon horizontal links that bind together large companies, and vertical links between the large companies and their many small *kogaisha* or 'child companies'.

Once again, the dual structure of the Japanese economy should be mentioned. As with other industrialized countries, if all types of business establishments are included, most are very small in size. In Japan, these tiny businesses are said to be in the lower part of the dual structure. According to an advance announcement of the 1986 Census of Establishments, 67.1 per cent of Japan's private establishments employed only between one and four persons. At the upper end, a mere 0.2 per cent of etablishments employed more than 300 persons. There are, of course, many distinctions between the relatively few stable and prosperous large companies at the top and the millions of small, struggling establishments at the bottom. If only the manufacturing sector of Japanese industry is considered, however, we find the establishments about equally divided between small–medium-sized companies employing fewer than 300 and the large firms with more than 300 employees.

Horizontal groups of large companies.

It is safe to say that almost all large Japanese companies are members of some form of grouping. Today, however, many of these groups have little to do with the powerful, pre-war *zaibatsu* and have grown around successful independent post-war organizations which are surrounded by their own subsidiaries and affiliates. A few examples of these more recent groupings are those surrounding Toyota, Honda, Shiseido, Matsushita, Sony, Canon, and Seiko. On the other hand, the traditional groups still exist. These are centred either around former *zaibatsu* or around the major city banks. Today these groups are most frequently termed *keiretsu*, though the old term *zaibatsu* often tends to persist.

Looking first at the 'Big Six' of the *keiretsu*, we have three organized around the former *zaibatsu* – these are Mitsubishi, Mitsui, and Sumitomo. In addition, there are three centred around the country's largest banks – Fuji, Daiichi Kangyo, and Sanwa. These six groups together account for a quarter of total Japanese assets. Each group is comprised of between twenty and thirty major commercial and industrial firms and may have as many as two hundred less-important members of the industrial family.

Most of the group's member companies are easily identified by the group name – for example, Mitsubishi Bank, Mitsubishi Electric, or Mitsubishi Warehouse. Others, however, are not as easily recognized – Asahi Glass, Kirin Beer, and the NYK Shipping Company are also members of the Mitsubishi family. These groups are loose federations of independent companies bound together over a long period of time because of mutual interests and the many benefits of cooperation. They have no top holding company or controlling stock interests, though cross holdings are common. Instead they coordinate their activities through a continued interchange of information, primarily by means of monthly meetings of presidents and other top officers of each company.

While it is assumed that members of a *keiretsu* will patronize and support each other, this is not always the case. Only if the terms offered by a group member – price, quality, and delivery – are at least equal to those coming from the outside will the family member get the business. Needless to say, this is most often the case. Similarly with bank-centred groups, the capital needs of members will usually, though not always, be met by the group's bank. In an economy with a typically heavy debt–to–equity ratio, long-standing and friendly relations with one's bank are essential, particularly in times of stress. However, in recent years the coffers of most large Japanese companies have been overflowing with cash, and dependence upon their banks has somewhat diminished. Recent data from the Ministry of Finance show bank borrowings and bonds, as a percentage of corporate funding, declined from 88 per cent in 1975 to 69 per cent in 1987 (Mitsui Bank 1989). More specific information about these groups and the individual companies composing them will be given later in this chapter.

Vertical groups of large and small companies.

There is also a complex network of ties between large parent companies and their medium- and small-size affiliates. These smaller companies usually are subsidiaries or subcontractors of the parent organization. Most large Japanese companies, whether independents or members of a grouping, will have a hierarchy of such affiliated companies.

While the legal relationship and degree of control will be different for subsidiaries as opposed to subcontractors, some of the same reasons exist for their proliferation. Perhaps most important are the financial advantages inherent in farming out labour-intensive operations. There is a substantial difference in wages paid by large and small companies. Therefore, it pays to separate such operations from the parent company. Furthermore, links between parent and related firms tend to be relatively long-term and involve a considerable degree of control through equity ownership and representation on the boards of smaller units. As a result, parent companies can shift such costs as inventory storage to their subcontractors and insist upon a 'just-in-time' delivery schedule.

Sometimes there is a problem of 'fair' capital allocation to specific divisions within a parent company, particularly to those with outstanding growth potential. A clear illustration of this is provided by Abegglen and Stalk as follows:

> Fanuc, the world leader in numerical control equipment and a leader in robotics, was a division of Fujitsu until 1972. The division that became Fanuc was, and still is, growing at a spectacular pace. The competition with the other high-growth divisions of Fujitsu for financial resources had become too great. The management of Fujitsu spun the division off into what is now a 43 per cent owned Fujitsu subsidiary that has fended for itself very successfully in Japan's capital market.
>
> (Abegglen and Stalk 1985: 180)

Not all the advantages of multiple vertical links are financial in nature. There are a number of human resource benefits as well. The *kogaisha* have long been an element of flexibility – in a sense, an escape valve – which allows the company to protect its elite of permanent, largely male employees who enjoy lifetime employment. These privileged employees are limited to a number that can be maintained during moderate cyclical fluctuations. If greater swings in the need for workers is encountered, adjustment can be made at subsidiary or subcontractor firms where the commitment to career-long employment is less binding.

Another personnel-related reason for extensive use of *kogaisha* is to provide transitional employment for employees between the ages of 55 and 60 who are forced to retire from the parent company. The case of a manager for a large electrical manufacturer illustrates this practice. After thirty-two years of employment with the parent company, he retired at age 57. At that time, he was assigned as president of a small, but long-standing, subcontractor which supplied transformers to the larger company. After three years in this post, full-time employment was terminated. But a part-time consulting arrangement was worked out for an additional two years before all ties were severed. With mandatory retirement by age 60 at least still prevalent in most Japanese companies, and with greatly increased life expectancy, such transitional employment is appreciated by workers who have devoted their entire career to a single company.

In recent years of slow growth, the hierarchy of small companies has served another purpose. It has provided a source of jobs for employees who have become redundant at the parent organization but who may be absorbed at one of the many subsidiaries or subcontractors. Though such moves are referred to as 'loans', they increasingly tend to be permanent as many large Japanese corporations face the need for 'paring the rolls' due to drastic restructuring and diversification.

Of course the practice of subcontracting is found in all countries. But it is in terms of numbers and layers in a pyramidal structure that Japan is unique. An example has been cited from Mitsui Toatsu Chemicals and its more than fifty related companies. These companies are described as being 'Under the personnel as well as the financial control of the parent company' (Sasaki 1981: 21). In the case of one such smaller company, Toyo Gas Chemical, 50 per cent of the stock is owned by the parent company, and five out of eight directors are from the parent organization.

The automobile industry provides another example of extensive subcontracting, with as much as 65–70 per cent of the products and parts used to produce a finished car being supplied by small and medium-size related firms. Some subcontractors supply a variety of larger firms. Most, however, maintain long-term and exclusive relations with a single parent company. In the latter case, the degree of dependence of the 'child' upon the parent understandably is very high.

National mission

The final and extremely important component of Japan's integrated national system is a powerful sense of national mission. Springing at least partially from the insularity and fragility of Japan as a nation, and the inevitable survival mentality which has resulted, what is seen as good for Japan usually is readily accepted as being good for each and every Japanese citizen. The outcome is a unity of purpose and a strong achievement motivation which are truly impressive.

The surprising effectiveness of this powerful consensus on national goals during the conduct of the Second World War need not be emphasized here. During the post-war era, Japan's unified attack upon all kinds of pollution is another case in point. Twenty years ago, even on a clear day Mt Fuji often could not be seen from Tokyo, the Sumida River was a mass of black sludge, the din of car horns was constant, and the streets were littered with trash. For each pollution problem, the government issued a call for action to remove these sources of national shame and to restore pride in their country among Japanese citizens. The response was overwhelming and today the view of Mt Fuji is enjoyed whenever weather permits, children once again swim and fish in the Sumida, horns are sounded only when needed, and the streets are remarkably clean.

In the past few years, the Japanese sense of national pride and purpose has been shown again. This time it is in the nation's total dedication to such goals as restructuring of industry and assuming the responsibilities as well as the rewards of true internationalization. Such a strong feeling of national mission is possible in a small, compact nation with a long history and strong traditions, and boasting of one of the most highly educated, homogeneous populations in the world.

Principal business players

Within Japan's integrated national system, three categories of organizations in the business sector play a major role. First, the extensive cartels of large firms, and their multi-layered families of small and medium-size firms, exert tremendous influence. Second, of particular importance are the Japanese general trading companies, or *sogo shosha*. Finally, added to these are the several prestigious management associations, sometimes referred to as the *zaikai*. The net effect is an industrial engine of unprecedented strength which, more than any other force, directs and drives the country. Brief case histories will help to illustrate each of these three major categories.

The Mitsui case

Looking first at one of the 'Bix Six' *keiretsu* mentioned earlier in this chapter, the Mitsui Group may serve as a good example. Based upon a former *zaibatsu* grouping, the name 'Mitsui' has been linked with commerce for more than three centuries. Today, the Mitsui Group is proudly described in a company report as 'the largest commercial entity in Japan and one of the mightiest economic/industrial/financial forces which has ever existed'. This does not seem to be an overstatement, though Mitsubishi and Sumitomo are not far behind.

Almost 2,000 companies make up the Mitsui Group, with activities ranging from steel and shipbuilding to banking and insurance; from petroleum and warehousing to tourism and nuclear energy. The Group's major enterprises alone employ almost a quarter of a million people and report annual sales of trillions of yen.

The origins of the Mitsui Group extend back to Japan's feudal age. Starting as a small family of wine sellers, the Mitsui name grew to prominence by the beginning of the Meiji period in 1868. Expanding during the next century of rapid industrialization, Mitsui became a conglomerate of enormous economic and political power. Though the Mitsui empire was scattered after the Second World War, the core of the Group was soon reassembled and cooperative ties once again established among the hundreds of Mitsui-related enterprises. As a company spokesman explains, this reincarnation was brought about by 'the natural affinity of many of these firms, and by the economic imperatives of capital investment and the need for a central organization capable of holding its own in the international business world'. As a result, Mitsui has become a powerful organization of separate but cooperating enterprises.

The Mitsui Group does not exist in any legal or formal sense.

The most visible evidences of collaboration are three policy-making bodies. The Second Thursday Club (Nimoku-kai) is perhaps the most prestigious of these bodies and comprises presidents or chairmen of the twenty-four most important (and Mitsui-est) of the enterprises. In addition, the Monday Club is a weekly luncheon meeting of high executives of major units, while the Public Relations Committee includes PR managers from both central and some less-strongly linked members of the Group.

Other large company groupings tend to be surrounded by similar constellations of big and little enterprises. Cooperation and patronage seldom are 100 per cent among members of each group. But through open channels of communication and wide acceptance of the conviction that 'united we stand, divided we fall', Mitsui and other long-established *keiretsu* continue to be dominant forces in Japan's industrial structure. A recent study finds that '17 per cent of all sales in Japan are accounted for by six horizontally integrated business groups known as *keiretsu*' (Katz 1989).

The C. Itoh & Company case

While there are general trading companies in other countries, none match in size or influence the Japanese *sogo shosha*. In a recent year, Japan's general trading companies together handled 80 per cent of total exports and 48 per cent of all imports. Major commodities involved in this tremendous trade included fuels and chemicals, metals, machinery, foodstuffs, textiles, and many others.

A point often overlooked is that the *sogo shosha* are not exclusively involved with foreign trade. In 1985, more than 41 per cent of their total transactions were domestic, 19 per cent were exports, 22 per cent imports, and 18 per cent involved offshore trade among countries other than Japan. Further evidence of their sheer size can be seen from the fact that the total number of subsidiary or representative offices of the major *sogo shosha* is about 1,700 and employment is almost 82,000. Clearly, these trading giants qualify as 'major players' in the Japanese industrial structure.

Japan's leading *sogo shosha* is C. Itoh & Company Ltd. Since its founding in 1858 by Mr Chubei Itoh, the company has grown

101

from a small wholesale textile firm to a worldwide general trading corporation. By 1987, the company reported having a fully integrated network of 180 offices in 87 countries. In addition, it had 502 affiliated companies, and more than 10,000 employees located throughout the world. In the same year, C. Itoh's annual revenues amounted to a staggering $103.6 billion, and its capitalization totalled $590 million.

In line with Japan's current thrust to expand domestic markets, it is interesting to note that 55 per cent of the company's business was domestic. With respect to type of commodities traded, the top three categories were machinery and construction, metal and ore, and energy and chemicals.

C. Itoh has attained its leadership position by a policy of aggressive expansion throughout the world. For example, it was the first major *sogo shosha* to engage in direct trading transactions with the Peoples Republic of China (PRC). Since its initial entry into this vast market in 1972, the company has built its China trade to more than $15 billion per year.

After almost ten difficult years, referred to as the 'winter' of the *sogo shosha*, C. Itoh has embarked on a new wave of expansion and diversification. Under a new ten-year plan, the company is being transformed into an 'international integrated corporation' (*kokusai sogo kingyo*) with a full range of activities including manufacturing and services as well as trade. At present, C. Itoh is especially active in expanding into the following three areas: electronics and advanced communications media; new technology, especially bio-technology; and investment activities in the world's money markets. The company's goal, as expressed by its president, is 'to span the full range of human needs, from satellites to instant noodles, and thus contribute to improvement of living standards in countries around the globe'.

A question frequently asked in recent years has been, 'If the *sogo shosha* work so well for Japan, why doesn't the United States develop some general trading companies of its own?' An answer was provided by former President Ronald Reagan in the Export Trading Company Act (ETC) of 1982. This law cleared away legal barriers to the formation of general trading companies patterned after the Japanese model. More noteworthy than its practical results thus far, the ETC reflected a determination to alleviate the crippling effect of US anti-trust laws on the international competitiveness of American firms.

Such large firms as General Electric, Sears Roebuck, and Control Data Corporation, as well as several large banks, jumped into this new business arena. The sad fact is that the going has been extremely rough for these pioneer enterprises, most of which have either terminated or cut back their operations. In the opinion of Professor Ravi Sarathy of Northeastern University, 'Would-be US trading companies could best emulate Japan's special, rather than general trading companies' (Sarathy 1985). It is not legal barriers but the human factors which limit US success in copying the Japanese model. The competition is remarkably well established, and US managers simply lack the exposure and commitment to global trade. On the other hand, the ETC opens the door for companies whose leaders are willing to be responsive to the varying cultures and customs in different countries, to show patience, and to take a long-term view when entering the treacherous waters of global trade (Whitehill 1988).

The Keidanren case

Shifting to the third category of major players in the Japanese industrial scene, we may look at the *zaikai*, of which Keidanren is the most important example. Sometimes referred to as 'a nebulous community of big business organizations', or simply as 'the financial world', the *zaikai* probably would be thought of by Western managers as resembling most closely their management associations.

The 'Big Four' of these well-organized pressure groups are: Keidanren, or the Federation of Economic Organizations; Keizai Doyukai, or the Committee for Economic Development; Nissho, or the Japan Chamber of Commerce; and Nikkeiren, or the Japan Federation of Employers' Associations. All were formed in the decade following the Second World War, and all exert very substantial influence on the political process in Japan.

A brief description of the organization and activities of Keidanren may serve to illustrate the unique, central role played by these federations of big business. One writer goes so far as to state that the term *zaikai* 'may almost be replaced with Keidanren, which is a league of big business' (Sasaki 1981: 98). A survey of labour union members seems to back up his view. Asked where they thought that power lies within Japanese society, a startling

28.2 per cent identified Keidanren as the centre of power, while only 27.9 per cent named the ruling Liberal Democratic Party. The fact is, Keidanren holds a virtual veto over all important economic decisions. Few, if any, important economic bills are introduced by the government or passed by the Diet without approval from Keidanren. It is a debatable question as to whether Japan's Prime Minister or the President of Keidanren is most influential in shaping the course of the country's economic development.

As of 1986, Keidanren's membership numbered 121 associations, 877 corporations, and 31 other organizations. The association members are industrial federations and regional economic organizations; the corporate members are leading Japanese enterprises and large foreign companies operating in Japan. Its board of directors consists of the presidents of the most important companies and the elder statesmen of business, industry, and finance.

Keidanren began to be a major political force in the 1950s. It was influential in seating the conservative Liberal Democratic Party in 1955 and in thus turning back the advance of more liberal forces. By 1965, Keidanren had assumed a direct influence in drafting the government's annual budget. Key ministries now are said to route budget proposals through Keidanren before submitting them to the Ministry of Finance. Rather than lobbying as an outside interest group, Keidanren in a very real sense operates within the government structure as the spokesman for the business sector. The many 'white papers' and other statements of business ideology prepared by Keidanren and other members of the *zaikai* constantly promote the key role of managers as responsible economic statesmen whose collective wisdom can chart the best course for the nation to follow.

A list of America's leading management associations – the American Management Association, the Committee for Economic Development, the US Chamber of Commerce, or the National Association of Manufacturers – may seem to be comparable to the *zaikai*. However, while structurally similar, their power and influence do not begin to match that of their Japanese counterparts. The *zaikai*, just as the *zaibatsu* or *keiretsu*, seem to be unique to Japan and congruent with the pivotal role business plays in Japanese society.

This overview of the macro-level industrial structure of Japan has emphasized the integration and interdependence of its major components. The expanding role of the service sector in employment patterns, and the basic elements comprising Japan's highly successful integrated national system have been described. In addition, the key roles played by groupings of large corporations, the general trading companies, and the powerful management associations in the system have been stressed. Now it is time to focus upon the micro-level management process in Japanese corporations. It is to the various functions within the management process that the seven chapters in Part III are devoted.

References

Abegglen J. and Stalk Jr, G. (1983) 'Japanese trading companies: a dying industry?', *Wall Street Journal*, 8 July.
Abegglen J. C. and Stalk Jr, G. (1985) *Kaisha: The Japanese Corporation*, Tokyo: Charles E. Tuttle Company.
The Economic Planning Agency *Japan in the Year 2000*, Tokyo: The Japan Times, Ltd.
Ishihara, T. (1983) 'Japanese corporate vitality', *Liberal Star*, Tokyo: The Liberal Democratic Party.
Katz, R. (1989) 'Japanese investment in the US', *Venture Japan*, 1, 4: 27.
Kyoku, , K. K. C. (1985) *Nihon Keizai No Genkyo: Naiju Chushin No Antei Seicho O Meyashite*, Tokyo: Ministry of Finance.
Mitsui Bank (1989) *Tokyo Report*, November: 2.
Moritani, M. (1982) *Japanese Technology*, Tokyo: The Simul Press Inc.
Nikkei Business (1983) *Shosha: Fuyu no Jidai (The Age of Winter of the Sogo Shosha), Tokyo: Nihon Keizai Shimbunsha*.
Panglaykin, J. 'The *Sogo shosha* and ASEAN', *Euro–Asia Business Review* 2, 2: 44.
Sarathy, R. (1985) 'Japanese trading companies: can they be copied?', *Journal of International Business Studies*, Summer: 101.
Sasaki, N. (1981) *Management and Industrial Structure in Japan*, Oxford: Pergamon Press Ltd.
Thurow L. C. (ed.) (1986) *The Management Challenge: Japanese Views*, Cambridge, Mass.: MIT Press.
Whitehill, A. M. (1988) 'America's trade deficit: the human problems', *Business Horizons* 31, 1: 18–22.

Part three

The process of management

Chapter six

Organization and planning

The need to organize and to plan is a universal imperative whenever, and wherever, two or or more people embark on a cooperative venture. Even the small, nuclear family is engaged in such a venture and demonstrates every element of larger and more sophisticated corporate organization and planning. The family must set short- and long-term goals, establish priorities, allocate responsibilities and authority, assign living and work space, establish a system for sharing the rewards of success, and so forth.

Without skilful organization and planning, the family or the business enterprise can only react to conditions as they occur – or after the fact. But in these days of rapid change and global competition this is not enough. Successful organizations are those which look ahead, plan ahead, and develop a proactive stance for dealing with the future. Nowhere are these fundamental truths more significant than in present-day Japan. Far-reaching changes demand organizational restructuring and strategic planning. And Japanese companies are meeting this demand in many creative and aggressive ways.

Parts I and II of this book dealt with the 'big picture' – historical and current – of the external environment within which business enterprises must operate. Now our attention shifts to the internal environment and the process of management as it is practised in Japanese companies. Each of the seven chapters in Part III will deal with one or more major functional areas of management.

The present chapter will focus upon two such areas – organization and planning. While an endless, and largely futile, argument could be conducted as to which comes first – organization or planning – we shall deal with these two functions in the order just mentioned.

The simple rationale for this decision is that good planning should be a group process, and that until a group 'gets organized' cooperative effort is impossible.

Organization

Organizing, a major phase in the process of management, involves identifying and arranging human, physical, and financial resources in a way best suited to attain organizational goals. There are at least the following five steps in organizing. First, the various tasks which are necessary to attain objectives must be determined. Then these tasks will be allocated to form jobs, which may be thought of as sets of related activities and responsibilities. The grouping process continues by assigning jobs to departments, and departments to divisions. To make these organizational units operational, responsibility and authority relationships must be created. Finally, delegation of tasks, and of adequate authority to carry out these assignments, must be made to appropriate groups and/or individuals.

All organizations have two sides: formal, and informal. The formal, official side is reflected in organization charts, designated work units, job specifications, titles, rank, lines of authority, and other such evidences of what the organization is intended to be and to do. The informal, less precise side is identified by such terms as cliques, informal leaders, and the ever-present 'grapevine' as its channel of communication. This is the more nebulous, slippery side of organizations. Yet its importance, and the challenges it presents to managers, never should be underestimated. These two clusters of organizational structure and behaviour, as they relate to Japanese companies, provide the major focus for this section.

Formal organization

It is important to point out that two key words crucial to the understanding of Japanese corporate organization are flexibility and ambiguity. Though organization charts appear to be quite concise, there is in fact a great deal of manoeuvrability. Job titles do not necessarily reflect duties performed. And what officially can or cannot be done (*tatamae*) often is quite different from what actually will be done (*honne*). The fluid nature of Japanese companies is in sharp contrast to the rigid, 'clear' organization of American firms.

Legal constraints

Because business enterprises, whether Japanese or American, favour the corporate form of organization, they will be constrained by the relevant laws of the governmental entities within which they are located. The Japanese Commercial Code imposes certain requirements upon the *kabushiki kaisha*, or joint stock company, which is the legal entity most closely corresponding to the American corporation. These requirements, however, are neither extensive nor unduly restrictive. Basically they call for documentation and registration of the articles of association, statement of purpose, and other essentials regarding the company (Tsunehiko).

Two important requirements of the Code do, however, differ from Anglo-Saxon commercial law. One is the requirement that every company have one or more 'representative directors', chosen by the board, and legally authorized to sign company documents. The other is the requirement that a 'statutory auditor', also chosen by the board at its annual meeting, be authorized to monitor the activities of directors, and check on documents they present to shareholders. Though legally assigned these important duties, in most cases the auditors are not likely to influence materially the behaviour or decisions of directors.

Class structure

Another extremely important organizational distinction between Japanese and American companies is the division between broad categories, or classes of employees. In the United States, there are two basic classes: management and workers. Managers include all those who spend a major part of their time supervising others; workers are all the rest. The lowest managerial rank is the foreman, who increasingly is recognized as a key member of the US management team. After all, it is he who serves as the connecting link between management and the workers.

One of the famous books in the literature of American management is *Management and the Worker*, written by Harvard professors Roethlisberger and Dickson in 1939. The basic dichotomy they set forth in the title never has been seriously challenged. To further cast this distinction in concrete, the Taft–Hartley Act of 1947 specifically defines the foreman as a member of management. Thus, the lines are clearly drawn between a category of rulers and a category of those who are ruled.

There is no such distinction at the comparable level in the Japanese corporate hierarchy. Instead, the critical dividing line is drawn between 'top management' and all other employees. In the Japanese case, to be in top management clearly equates with being a member of the board of directors. Except for this elite group at the top, everyone is simply an employee. This dichotomy seems to reinforce the widely held feeling of homogeneity and common destiny so frequent among members of a Japanese company. A recent study offers this comment on the unity or cohesion of managers and rank-and file employees: 'The line separating white collar workers from blue collar workers is quite indistinct in Japanese companies, so much so that it is very difficult to tell whether the employee is blue collar or white collar on the surface, namely by way of dress, living style, and behaviour' (Kuwahara 1989: 3).

Several characteristics of this class system should be mentioned. First, there is a statutory as well as a customary distinction between directors and employees. The directors, under the Commercial Code, are specifically directed to represent the shareholders. Most members of the board, however, are 'working directors' and continue to perform their managerial duties as, for example, division or department head. This is in spite of the fact that when elected to the board they formally resign as employees and receive their retirement allowances.

In fact, then, directors usually are top managers who are supposed to represent both the interests of shareholders and fellow employees in the company. This can create some conflict of interests since, as one writer points out, 'Most of the directors have responsibilities for running part of the company, and are not in an ideal position to objectively review the performance of a management which includes themselves and their senior and junior colleagues' (Clark 1979: 100).

Furthermore, the conduct of legally required annual meetings does little to encourage meaningful representation of shareholders. Attendance at these general meetings is sparse, and their duration notably brief. In fact, several surveys indicate that the average length of most such meetings is less than half an hour (Clark 1979: 103). Minor shareholders have almost no opportunity to question the actions of directors and thus have little influence on company management.

An interesting aspect of the *kaisha's* annual meetings is the common presence of *sokaiya*, or 'general-meeting-mongers', who extort money from companies by threatening to ask embarrassing questions or cause other trouble for directors. Unless the company pays a 'fee' to these corporate blackmailers, they can effectively disrupt the stockholders' meeting. Most Japanese companies hold their annual meetings in June. Therefore, when 694 companies held their meetings in June of 1989, the Metropolitan Police Department mobilized 2,400 officers to stop harassment by *sokaiya*.

At times there are somewhat similar hecklers in US shareholders' meetings. But the important distinction is that these noisy dissidents are there to grill the management and to promote their special objectives. For example, at an IBM annual meeting in Delaware, an organization called 'Young Americans for Freedom Inc.', which holds only three shares of stock, attempted to block the company from all trading with the Communist bloc. In response, the board pointed out that only 1.7 per cent of the company's total sales go to the Communist countries. After heated discussion, the demand by the shareholder group was rejected. This whole debate was something that would never take place in the tightly controlled annual meetings of Japanese *kaisha*.

The corporate hierarchy

Of course there are a number of levels, or ranks *within* the broad class distinctions described in the previous section. Table 4 shows these levels, with their titles in both Japanese and English, which typically characterize the *kabushiki kaisha*. Since internal organization is largely a matter of policy, there are some variations among companies in the titles used, the number of levels, and the number of positions at each level. But the structure illustrated here is quite standard for a large number of leading Japanese companies.

These corporate ranks do not correlate closely with any specific duties. Rather like military ranks, they indicate status in the ranking system instead of clearly defined job assignments. At times, so-called section chiefs may have no section to lead.

Table 4 Japanese corporate ranks

	Chairman	Kaicho
	President	Shacho
	Vice president	Fuku shacho
Top management	Senior managing director	Senmu torishimariyaku
	Managing directors	Jomu torishimariyaku
	Directors	Torishimariyaku
	General manager	Bucho
	(Division or department head)	
	Deputy general manager	Bucho dairi
	Section chief	Kacho
Employees	Deputy section chief	Kacho dairi
	Subsection chief	Kakaricho
	Foreman	Hancho
	Ordinary employee	Hirashain

Or a lesser subsection chief may, in fact, direct an important organizational unit. And, as with military ranks, the titles have enormous social significance. Mr Honda, for example, a company *bucho*, will be introduced as 'Honda *bucho*'. Backed up by impressive name cards indicating rank, each person's place in the status system is clear to everyone. What he or she actually does in the company, however, may be quite vague and fluid.

There is an American saying that one must not 'send a boy to do a man's job'. Similar, but far more restrictive, would be the Japanese warning that one should not send a *kakaricho* to do a *bucho*'s job – or to meet with representatives in other companies who are far above one's own rank. Even the appropriate language used, in form of address and linguistic style, varies in dealing with persons at different levels of the organization. Because of this reverence for rank, it is not unusual for a Japanese salesperson to have several *meishi*, or calling cards, for use outside the company. Each will identify him as a person of comparable rank with the particular client upon whom he is calling. One astonished American executive is quoted as saying, 'We had no idea of the workings of the class system. Hiring a good man from the lower classes, for instance, could be a disaster. If he called on a client of a higher class, there was a good chance the client would be insulted' (Ricks *et al.* 1974: 21).

Progress up the Japanese corporate hierarchy is quite slow when compared with promotion in American companies. The impact of *nenko joretsu*, the seniority-based promotion system, will be discussed in the next chapter. Here, it is enough to say that climbing the ranks in a Japanese company depends upon a compromise between age–seniority and meritocracy. The compromise will be influenced by the size of the company, the nature of the business, the needs at different levels of the ranking system, and external economic conditions.

A full discussion of career planning is reserved for Chapter 8. It may be useful now, however, to outline in broad terms a rather typical career path for a university graduate selected to join a corporate family. For his first five to ten years, the new recruit will fill a variety of untitled clerical–administrative positions. Along with other members of his entering class, he will be given extensive on-the-job training and rotated among various sections and plants of the company. He will be a member of the company's union, and his leadership abilities in the union will be watched very carefully. To be elected by one's peers to be a union officer is considered to be evidence of good potential for future managerial success. The typical company board of directors often includes one or more former union officers.

After perhaps ten years of broad exposure and training, a man may be ready for a title – usually that of *hancho* (foreman) or *kakaricho* (subsection chief). The typical age of such young managers would now be about thirty-five. At this point, competence and job performance gain in importance, though age–seniority is still a major criterion for further promotion to *kacho*. The *ka* (section) is the basic organizational unit in a Japanese company, and to become a *kacho* is considered an important step in career development.

The next ten years or so as *kacho* are important ones in which the individual's experience is further broadened by several quite different job assignments. Through job rotation, he becomes, if not a true generalist, at least a multi-specialist. With broad experience, and a growing list of impressive contacts throughout the organization, he may then be promoted to *bucho* (general manager or department head). This is the top of the ranking system before entering 'top management' and membership on the board of directors. If elected to the board in their early fifties individuals will assume the directorship while maintaining their *bucho* position and responsibilities. They may continue as a director so long as their health and energy permit, since total retirement is not mandatory for directors at any age.

Of course, not all *bucho* make it into top management ranks. For those who do not, their position none the less is secure and they remain highly respected leaders in the company. They will retire from their parent company at the mandatory retirement age of 58–60 and then perhaps be hired back for a few years as a consultant or posted to a smaller subcontractor or subsidiary related to the parent organization.

Board of directors

The typical Japanese board of directors is both wider and deeper than the boards of US companies. That is, they include many more directors and there are several different ranks among directors. Boards tend to be quite large, often having as many as twenty-five to thirty members. The articles of incorporation of Nippon Steel Corporation, for example, state: 'The company shall have not more than forty-eight (48) directors.' A review of the board of directors for the Fujitsu Corporation in mid-1986 showed the following composition: president (1), who was also representative director; executive vice presidents (2); executive directors (4); managing directors (7); directors (16); standing auditor (1); and auditors (3); giving a grand total of thirty-four board members.

The usual three top positions – chairman, president, and vice president – are at least superficially similar to US organization structure. Closer examination, however, reveals some significant differences. The highest position, chairman of the board, is occupied usually by a former president and has little actual responsibility. If, however, the chairman should happen also to be a representative director, this would provide a clue that the duties are more than ceremonial. But in many cases the chairman is primarily a senior diplomat and roving ambassador of good will, with few operating responsibilities. Some companies have dispensed with this position entirely.

The most important operating office is that of the president, who typically is the firm's chief executive officer. As in the case of the Fujitsu Corporation, the president may also be the representative director. Reporting to the president will be one vice president, or at most a few. Japanese companies are far more frugal than American firms in their use of VPs. Even some of Japan's largest firms have only one vice president who is, in effect, an executive vice president.

Then there are several layers of directors, usually headed by one or more senior managing, or executive, directors. These men typically retain their responsibilities as head of a division or of an important staff department. Next in rank will be a number of managing directors, perhaps between ten and twelve, each of whom also heads an operating unit in the company. Finally there are the younger and even more numerous ordinary directors, who hold a variety of management posts throughout the organization. Supporting this core of directors, most companies have a number of committees, advisors, and counsellors to provide a top-level forum for discussion of policy matters.

As with the VPs, outside directors are used only spartanly in the Japanese corporation. There might be one member from an important firm within the corporate grouping or from the company's major bank. Another exception to the general taboo against outside directors is the frequent inclusion of important, usually retired, civil servants. Known as *amakudari* (descended from heaven), they are highly valued for their contacts and influence in ministries related to the company's business.

It should be clear that board meetings in Japan are closer in make-up and function to a meeting of senior managers than to a cross-section of stockholder representatives. This fact has been cited as both a weakness and a strength of Japanese corporate organization. In any event, the preference for inside directors, for keeping company affairs within the 'family', seems consistent with a general cultural distaste for discussing sensitive matters with strangers. The practice does, however, limit the infusion of new perspectives and ideas into policy-level deliberations.

Collective structure

Organizations in Japan are structured in collective units rather than in terms of individual positions. It is to these organizational units, rather than to specific individuals, that authority and responsibility are assigned. As one expert emphasizes, 'The basic unit in the organization is a collectivity, not an individual. Herein lies one of the fundamental differences between American and Japanese management' (Yoshino 1968: 203).

This feature of organizational structure clearly reflects the group orientation so characteristic of Japanese society. The individual's success is measured by the success of a group – the individual's

117

work group, the company, oι Japan herself. An effective leader is not always a top achiever. Rather, he is a catalyst, coach, and source of inspiration for his team. A popular, though often neglected, definition of management is 'getting things done through people'. Nowhere is this more true than in the Japanese business organization.

Most of the departments, both line and staff, are roughly comparable in Japanese and US corporations. Staff departments might include personnel, finance, accounting, public relations, legal, and so forth depending on the nature of the business. Line departments might reflect major product lines, functional categories, or geographical locations. There are, however, several notable differences. For example, an important department in Japanese companies is the General Affairs Department (Somu Bu). As the name indicates, this department handles a variety of administrative matters. Greeting visitors, maintaining official documents, coordinating interdepartmental communications, and handling the mail and telephone switchboards are but a few of the myriad duties performed by General Affairs. Another example is the so-called President's Office (*Shachoshitsu*). This is a staff group whose duties might include planning and coordination as well as secretarial work. As we shall see in the next section, however, corporate planning has become such a critical responsibility in today's hard-pressed Japanese corporations that frequently a separate department has been created.

Physical lay-out

A final, and very meaningful, aspect of the formal organization of Japanese companies is the physical arrangement of offices. While often the subject of casual comment, it is not widely discussed as an integral part of the complex Japanese management system. One experienced Japanese observer aptly describes the unique physical layout as 'people in boxes' (DeMente 1981: 69). The 'boxes' to which he refers are the clusters of desks, facing each other in rectangular form. The supervisor sits at the head of the 'box', usually with his back to a window. Higher-ranking subordinates sit near the supervisor, while junior members are strung out along both sides. Here, cheek by jowl, the members of a work group spend their days.

When visiting a Japanese *kacho* recently, this writer was

ushered into a huge room which appeared to be about half the size of a football field. Clusters of 'boxes' formed departments, and at the head of one such cluster sat my friend, the *kacho*. He could survey the activities of all members of all sections reporting to him and was readily available to them. There were many such departments, composed of one or more sections, filling the large room.

In most companies, only the senior managing director and above will have private offices. And cases can be cited in which even the president does not enjoy this perquisite. For example, in an interview with the president of Honda America Motors (HAM), the question was asked, 'HAM doesn't have a president's office separate from other offices. Why?' The president replied, 'I share a spacious office area with other administrative staff members. When we work together in one big room, we can talk casually to one another. There are a lot of suggestions and ideas exchanged in these conversations' (JAMA 1987:2).

In general terms, what does this physical arrangement signify? Surely it indicates the Japanese manager's strong preference for open, oral communication. It also emphasizes the 'all for one and one for all' togetherness of Japanese employees. And it may not be going too far to say that this close personal proximity, which most Westerners would find intolerable, is a comforting antidote to the loneliness felt by so many Japanese in their social and personal lives.

Summarizing this section's treatment of the formal organization of Japan's *kabushiki kaisha*, it can be said that behind the superficial similarity to American corporations there are many significant differences. These differences run the gamut of structure, relationships, and behaviour. Now attention is shifted briefly to the informal side of Japanese corporate life.

Informal organization

Even more important in Japanese than in US companies, the informal side of organizations is of continuing concern to management. Informal leaders, groups, and channels of communication are particularly needed to supplement a hierarchy which puts tremendous stress upon vertical ranks. The informal organization enriches and extends the vertical structure and, at the same time, opens channels for important horizontal communication and relationships. In a sense, the formal organization is a company's 'official' side; the informal organization is its undocumented 'working' side.

In corporations where long-term employment is anticipated, new recruits enter the company and begin their careers together. Promotion tends to be steady but slow and personal contacts take on tremendous importance. A person's *jin miyaku*, or 'web of human beings', is a network to be constantly cultivated and forever cherished. Many of these contacts are made through the workings of the informal organization within the company.

Perhaps the most significant component of the informal organization is the *habatsu* – the Japanese version of an American clique. It is true that in most US companies there are a number of informal cliques. These groups may be based on a common interest in sports, hobbies, or community activities. Sometimes employees in a special category – such as old timers, newcomers, or singles – form a club or clique. But such informal groups are transitory in the sense that their membership is purely voluntary and frequently changes. While they provide an enjoyable social outlet for employees, such cliques seldom are a powerful driving or restraining force on management.

Japanese *habatsu* are quite different from American cliques. Most important, membership typically is based upon certain unchangeable criteria – graduating from the same university (*gakubatsu*), coming from the same prefecture (*kenbatsu*), or having a common hometown (*kyodobatsu*). Therefore, belonging to a clique is both involuntary and permanent for the individual. Such groups tend to have their own internal, vertical hierarchy.

These *habatsu* may be a constructive, or a disruptive, force in management. In decision-making, for example, a powerful *habatsu* can assure the success of a proposal or doom it to failure. The leader of such an informal group usually is a person with considerable prestige and seniority in the formal organization. The loyalty of *habatsu* members to the leader is often as intense and unswerving as their loyalty to their formal boss. Bound by highly emotional and personal ties, the member–leader relationship has been likened to the traditional *oyabun–kobun*, or patron–client, relationship in Japanese feudal society.

Clearly, the informal groups in Japanese organizations are a force to be reckoned with. Gaining the support of the dominant *habatsu* is essential for top management decision-making. Deference to influential informal leaders is necessary to avoid serious morale problems. The critical difference between the informal groups within Japanese and American companies is the permanence in the former. They are fixed components of organizational life which must be dealt with and will not go away – though top managers may at times wish otherwise.

Planning

Radical changes have occurred in the role of planning in Japanese management during recent years, particularly since the 1985 Plaza Accord and the resulting appreciation of the yen. Today there is little doubt that corporate planners have become the new heroes of Japanese industry. Among the external pressures on Japan at present, the yen appreciation has been the most effective in forcing structural readjustment from a primarily export-led economy to one more balanced between external and domestic markets. This far-reaching, and often painful, adjustment puts a heavy premium upon creative and aggressive planning.

The capstone of all business planning is top-level, company-wide, corporate planning. Corporate planning is referred to sometimes as strategic planning, since it deals with the overall organizational mission. It maps the future directions for growth, and identifies the strategies to be followed to achieve intermediate and long-term goals. Illustrative of the questions relevant to this important process are: 'Why is our company in business – what is our mission?' 'What goods and services should we be producing in the future?' And, extremely important today, 'How can we respond most effectively to changes in the environment – social, economic, and political?'

Pre-oil-shock planning

The questions just posed are those which are being raised daily in all major Japanese firms. However, this was not always the case. In the immediate post-Second World War days, exposure to Western management methods fuelled a surge in Japanese corporate planning. Usually this was performed by a staff group in the president's 'office'. Yet, most of the plans were highly quantitative and showed little regard for external conditions. Furthermore, companies relied heavily upon the government's macro-level forecasting which, at the time, totally ignored such qualitative aspects as the reaction of foreign nations to Japan's assault on worldwide markets.

In a sense, the period of phenomenal economic growth, which lasted until the first oil shock in 1973, led many Japanese executives to believe that growth was easily possible without recourse to planning. Little real market research was being done, and the affluence of America was presumed to be insatiable and everlasting. Corporate and government planners were so busy revising their forecasts upward that they failed to see what was going on in the world around them.

Post-oil-shock planning

The disruption caused by the 1973 oil embargo by the oil-exporting countries of the Middle East triggered a serious loss in confidence among Japan's corporate planners. Guidance from the government had proven useless in a time of crisis, and many Japanese companies temporarily gave up all planning, simply reacting to changes as they occurred.

With the realization that Japan had entered an era of stable or low growth, a new breed of corporate planners gradually emerged. Reliance on government plans was minimized, and companies were forced to re-examine their goals and the strategies most likely to achieve them. The highly sales-oriented, quantitative plans of the past were of little or no value in the more complex and demanding environment of the late 1970s and 1980s.

A more professional, qualitative approach to corporate planning was emerging prior to the drastic revaluation of the yen instigated by the Plaza Accord. From the time of that historic agreement, as the yen climbed to 180, then to 150, and to a peak of 120 to the US dollar in 1988, Japanese companies were ready with a new breed of planners, a new set of criteria, and a vastly expanded perspective in the corporate planning process. Many large firms have established separate corporate planning departments and assigned to them a vital role in shaping the future – even the survival – of former export-driven organizations.

New challenges – new plans

Let us now return to the illustrative questions mentioned earlier, which today's corporate planners must face. To determine how leading Japanese companies are preparing for the 1990s and beyond, the author met recently with executives in more than a dozen such companies. An interesting point is that in almost all cases, though not requested, the company representative leading these discussions was from the corporate planning department. Most were senior managers and directors, all of whom had spent their entire careers with the company. As mentioned earlier, current pressures on management have catapulted these men to powerful positions of leadership in shaping the future of their organizations.

What is our mission?

A statement of mission, or overall philosophy, is particularly significant within the Japanese management system. It is this broad policy declaration which establishes the corporate culture within which regular employees will spend their working lives. Becoming 'socialized' within the corporate culture, and internalizing the company spirit (*shafu*), are important foundations for building the Japanese employee's remarkable loyalty and dedication to the company.

These sweeping statements of corporate philosophy can be illustrated by the following example from Toshiba Corporation:

Toshiba contributes to a richer and healthier life and to the advancement of society through creation of new values based on human respect. In particular, Toshiba:

1. is consumer (customer) oriented and pursues a policy of consumer first.
2. wants to continue as a world enterprise and to carry out its business from an international standpoint.
3. gives emphasis to community activities and cooperation in its worldwide operations.
4. provides its staff members with the opportunity to realize their full potential and cultivate their abilities to the utmost.
5. is in the vanguard of progress through its traditional stress on systems engineering.
6. utilizes resources effectively.

7. works in harmony with nature and seeks to eliminate all forms of pollution.
8. strives to earn reasonable profits in ways that are beneficial to its stockholders, employees and society.

(Toshiba Corporation 1987:1)

The last point made in the above statement is of particular interest because it reflects a subtle shift in philosophy. In earlier days of uninhibited growth, Japanese companies seemed to neglect all claimants other than their own employees and managers. This inner-directed and limited sense of responsibility clearly is not appropriate in the present-day environment. The need for greater social responsiveness, internationalization, and environmental preservation has forced companies to look beyond their own boundaries.

Recognition of the complex demands made upon a corporation by different groups of claimants has long been a characteristic of US management. For example, as early as 1975, GTE Hawaiian Telephone Company was a pioneer in anticipating – and satisfying – the conflicting demands that diverse social forces place upon a modern business. According to a company corporate planner at the time, 'There are basically four concerns – those of our customers, employees, shareowners, and general public'. It was made clear that the company needed a comprehensive planning system to care for the particular needs of each group that had a stake or interest in the business (Matsunaga 1977). Recent Japanese declarations of corporate mission tend to reflect this more balanced sense of responsibility.

Goals and strategies

While general statements of mission are important, it is necessary to plan for more specific mid-term (two to five year) and long-term (over five year) goals. For many years, governments throughout the world have developed ambitious 'five-year plans' on a national basis. Though not always successful, these plans at least provided a blueprint for action. Private companies also need such plans as guidelines in reaching future goals.

Japanese corporate planners during the 1950s and 1960s tended to be highly quantitative and to focus upon a constantly greater market share as the main priority. Few companies felt the need to map plans and strategies for several years or more in the future. But today, leading firms have established top-level planning departments charged with a clear mandate to plan ahead!

An excellent example of such advance planning may be seen at Nippon Steel, the largest steel company in the free world. In the wake of the oil crises of the 1970s, dramatic changes were necessary to ensure the future survival and prosperity of the company. Keeping abreast of the times, Nippon Steel formulated an ambitious plan to rationalize its steel business, to develop new products and processes, and to implement energy-saving measures. First, extensive deliberations were conducted by a top-level Corporate Policy Committee composed of the chairman, president, six vice presidents, the general manager of corporate planning, and other key executives. Two basic thrusts were identified for future action: (1) rejuvenation of steelmaking, and (2) diversification into new businesses. The corporate planning manager and his staff members were given primary responsibility for setting targets and developing plans to move in these two directions.

The ensuing blueprint for rationalizing the steel business was creative and ambitious. In 1987, 80 per cent of Nippon Steel's sales were derived from steel. But the steep rise in the yen severely affected the company's production and earnings. Against such a background, the company announced a bold plan to close five blast furnaces and to cut steel production to the point where, by 1995, steel would account for less than half of its sales.

The company found that of its 65,000 employees, 19,000 would be surplus by March 1991. However, by that date about 9,000 were expected to reach retirement age or retire voluntarily, while new lines of business were to absorb about 6,000. As for the remaining 4,000 workers, the company announced that it 'intends to keep its long-standing principle of lifetime employment to avoid lay-off or dismissal at any cost'. These redundant employees will be transferred to affiliated firms or reassigned on a company-wide basis. Under the circumstances, this clear statement should provide a clue that lifetime employment (*shushin koyo*) is still alive and well as a 'sacred treasure' of Japanese management.

In addition, in 1990 Nippon Steel will open, as a joint venture with Inland Steel, what has been described as 'the world's most advanced cold-rolling steel mill', at a cost in excess of $400 million.

The new plant will reduce the processing time for cold-rolled steel sheet from twelve days to less than one hour – and improve the quality at the same time. Such initiatives do not just happen; they reflect strategic planning at its best as practised by Japan's leading corporate enterprises.

Turning to Nippon Steel's second major thrust – diversification – the company has devised a unique and forward-looking Multiple Management Plan. In its medium- and long-range plan announced in 1987, a decision was made to expand into non-steel fields such as new materials and chemicals, engineering, electronics and communication systems, social and cultural development, and biotechnology.

The planned distribution of Nippon Steel's total business in 1990 is shown in Table 5. While no specific target had been set for biotechnology, it is significant that this new field was mentioned by every firm in which interviews were conducted as a definite area for diversification.

Table 5 Nippon Steel: business structure in 1990 (turnover: ¥4 trillion)

Materials (steel, new materials, chemicals)	60% (steel under 50% of total)
Engineering	10%
Electronics (Information and communication systems)	20%
Social culture development (Urban development, etc.)	10%
Biotechnology and other	–

Source: Nippon Steel News, May/June 1987

In summary, corporate organization and planning constitute two of the most basic functions in management. In one sense, they are universals. Yet, as with any such function, they are interdependent parts of a total management system and must reflect the broad environment within which the system operates.

In this chapter, the important differences between Japanese and US organization and planning have been described. Examples have been drawn from some of Japan's leading corporations. It is time now to turn, in the next chapter, to a third and tremendously important function – developing the crucial human resources which are the heart and mind of management everywhere.

References

Clark, R. (1979) *The Japanese Company*, New Haven: Yale University Press.

DeMente, B. (1981) *The Japanese Way of Doing Business*, Englewood Cliffs: Prentice-Hall Inc.

Japan Automobile Manufacturers' Association (1987) *The JAMA Forum* 5, 2.

Kuwahara, Y. (1989) *Managerial Staffing in Large Japanese Companies*, Honolulu: Industrial Relations Center, University of Hawaii.

Matsunaga, L. H. (1977) 'Hawaiian Tel's planning program has something for everyone', *Telephony* 192, 21: 18.

Mitsubishi Corporation (1988) Tatamae *and* Honne: *Distinguishing between Good Form and Real Intention in Japanese Business Culture*, New York: The Free Press.

Ricks, D. A., Fu, M. Y. C., and Arpan, J. S. (1974) *International Business Blunders*, Columbus, Ohio: Grid Inc.

Toshiba Corporation (1987) *Toshiba in Brief*, Tokyo: Toshiba Corporation.

Tsunehiko, Y. *'Kabushiki kaisha no seisei to teichaku'* ('The formation and establishment of joint stock companies'), *Chuo Koron Keiei Mondai* 61: 326–32.

Yoshino, M. Y. (1968) *Japan's Managerial System*, Cambridge, Mass.: MIT Press.

Chapter seven

Staffing

Business leaders in Japan, perhaps more so than in any other country of the world, fervently believe that employees are their most important asset. In a small country with few resources other than the skills and energy of her people, this seems a natural conviction. As a result, personnel management, currently referred to more often as human resources management, plays a far more important role in Japanese than in American companies. The Personnel Department in Japan tends to be much larger, and the personnel director typically has more authority and responsibility. Though traditionally located within the amorphous general affairs department the trend today is to create a separate staff personnel department reporting directly to top management of the company.

In Japanese firms employees find that their careers are planned and implemented by the personnel department. Line managers and departments are in more a receiving than an initiating role, particularly with respect to non-production employees. This greater authority of the personnel group seems consistent with the fact that most employees are not hired for specific jobs but, rather, are brought into the firm as lifelong members of the corporate family. Therefore, it is considered appropriate for a top-level, company-wide staff department to plan and guide their entire careers.

It may be useful to preface the following discussion of the staffing process with some general comments concerning recent changes in the labour market. In the 1950s and 1960s, Japan's labour market was best described as 'closed'. That is, there were only a limited number of channels through which university graduates seeking employment and companies searching for young management employees could meet. Basically, there were only two such channels in wide use: university placement offices; and important, informal contacts. In effect, the candidate had to be recommended by the university of the firm's choice or by a responsible 'connection'.

A 1958 survey of graduates of all universities in Japan showed that the university and the private connection represented 48.5 and 43.4 per cent respectively of the employment channels used by new graduates who found employment (Azumi 1969: 54–5). The tremendous importance attached to connections, both inside the university and within one's social groupings, could not be stressed too much. Career success, and the future social standing of one's family, would depend upon the quality of the recommendations obtained from one or both these sources.

At that time, no job seeker would make direct application to the firm of his choice. This simply was not done and, if it were, the application would have been discarded. Nor were there any private employment agencies or professional associations to bring graduate and company together. The mass media were rejected as an appropriate channel by prestigious firms because they were considered too formal and impersonal. The Japanese do not like dealing with strangers, and the applicant responding to a company's advertisement would be a total stranger. A relevant, and extremely important general principle was stated many years ago by one expert on Japanese culture. He cautioned that in Japan 'The distance between strangers is great' (Azumi 1969: 54). This is a basic value orientation that is well to keep in mind when attempting to understand many aspects of Japanese social behaviour.

However, changes during the past two decades have drastically altered the nature of the labour market. No longer a closed system with few channels and many taboos, recruitment and selection of employees has become quite open and free of restrictions. There is a growing number of private employment agencies. Headhunting in Japan has become big business, though clients of such recruiting companies tend to be the smaller and medium-size organizations and foreign firms. The Japanese call these recruiters *heddo-hantas* and their role has been increasing in use and acceptance during recent years. Even some of the largest firms will turn to such specialists when they simply cannot fill a vacancy through traditional channels. In addition, professional associations have proliferated and serve as important recruitment channels. And there no longer is any real prejudice associated with an individual approaching the company of his choice.

While being aware of these important changes in job-seeking and hiring patterns, it should be realized that there are strong forces supporting continued use of the more familiar channels. Most important is the fact that lifetime employment remains the hope and expectation for at least the male sector of Japan's workforce. As two experienced observers of Japan's management system point out, 'In the ideology of Japanese management, this employment pattern is held out as the proper one, as the ideal model to be emulated. As the pattern of employment of major Japanese corporations, it is the pattern that the Western firm operating in Japan is expected to adhere to (and deviations from which will prove costly)' (Abegglen and Stalk 1985: 201).

It is useful to distinguish between recruitment and selection as two quite distinct processes. The former involves building a roster of potentially qualified applicants. As such, it may be thought of as a 'positive' process. The latter, in contrast, is a 'negative' process in the sense that it refers to the weeding out, and final acceptance, of a limited number of applicants on the roster. As we shall see, the perceived goals of and the resulting procedures for recruitment and selection are quite different in Japanese companies to those in Western countries.

One of these differences is that Japanese managers recognize, and discriminate among, a number of different categories of workers. For convenience in this discussion, we shall deal with two major groups: (1) regular, male employees; and (2) special employees, including women, part-time and temporary workers, mid-career recruits, and foreigners.

Regular employees

Regular, or standard, employees are those hired directly from the high schools and universities who intend to work for the same company for their entire working career. Only males are classified as regular employees, and the larger the company the higher will be the percentage of such favoured workers. A study by the Japan Institute of Labour indicates that firms with 1,000 employees or more may have as many as 73 per cent of their employees classified as regular employees. But small companies, particularly those hiring largely blue-collar workers, may have only 20 per cent or less of their employees in this category (Inagami 1983).

Regular employees enjoy special privileges, and in many ways are treated differently, when compared with other employees of a company. Their high degree of job security, and the considerable social prestige accorded to them and their families, set them apart from other groups. Such special treatment would not be permitted under US Equal Employment Opportunity legislation, but in Japan it is an essential part of the human resources management programme.

Lifetime employment

It is only this elite, favoured group of employees that enjoys total employment security for their entire working careers. But it must be remembered that lifetime employment, whether actually experienced or not, remains an ideal norm to which all companies, large and small, aspire. Western journalists have seemed to derive some pleasure in predicting the early demise of this 'sacred treasure' of Japanese management. For example, *Business Week*, a leading American business weekly, as early as 1978, predicted 'The end of lifetime jobs' (17 July 1978: 82–3). Five years later, the same publication hopefully announced once again that 'Lifetime employment may be on its last legs' (5 September 1983: 98).

For a more reliable review of the development of the lifetime employment system from 1954 to 1980, the Japan Institute of Labour points out that 'The lifetime employment system has become more and more widespread since World War II without once regressing' (Inagami 1983). Since 1980, the system has been under considerable pressure as Japan's growth rate has slowed and the problems of an export-driven economy have multiplied. As one Japanese writer cautions, 'lifetime employment as practiced in Japan is no more than a general guiding principle. It is by no means a guarantee' (Hasegawa 1986: 11).

But lifetime employment is a psychological contract between company and regular employees that is not taken lightly. Therefore, every possible effort continues to be made to honour this commitment. It seems fair to say that career-long employment remains alive and well in Japan today, and is likely to remain an important 'sacred treasure' for many years to come.

None the less, several important limitations of career employment should be emphasized. First, it applies almost exclusively to male, regular employees. These individuals are hired directly from high schools or universities and, in most cases, once each year. Such workers usually are not employed for a particular job but, rather, as a new member of the corporate family. Second, especially in small firms, career employment may be a hollow expectation if the company simply can not survive without paring the rolls. As the size of company decreases, it is true that the proportion of regular employees tends to fall, and the real possibility for enjoying lifetime employment lessens.

From the corporate viewpoint, a commitment to lifetime job security is not without its costs. Many large companies admit that 10–15 per cent of their workforce may be redundant. It is likely that Japanese firms make fewer mistakes than American companies in selecting new employees. After all, the stakes are very much higher since they will be on the payroll for thirty to thirty-five years. However, mistakes are made and some incompetent persons are hired. These unfortunate selections are treated as management errors rather than as shortcomings of the individual.

A commitment to avoid lay-offs or discharge of permanent employees means that some redundancy in the workforce is inevitable. The trade-off, it is hoped, is in employee loyalty and dedication to the company over the years. Redundant workers, rather than being laid-off, frequently are assigned to the *madogiwa-zoku*, or 'window-watchers' tribe', with few responsibilities and their career development seriously impaired.

A good question is: 'What happens when economic conditions are so bad that some shrinking of a company's employment is unavoidable?' Recent years have provided some examples of this dire situation in such hard-pressed industries as shipbuilding and steel. It is tempting for Westerners to answer that Japan will then have to become 'more like us'. But this is a trap that should be carefully avoided. It has been this writer's observation over many years that when dealing with a particularly difficult problem, Japanese managers are likely to devise a uniquely Japanese solution.

When forced to do the 'unthinkable' and cut the number of

employees, Japanese firms curtail hiring and encourage early retirement, just as do their Western counterparts. Appealing to senior employees' concern for company welfare, management engages in 'shoulder-tapping' (*kata-takaki*), as they urge such individuals to resign voluntarily.

But there are several strictly Japanese-style options available as well. For example, some employees may be lent to other companies in happier circumstances. The hard-pressed company may even subsidize a part of the salaries of the transferees. Or, surplus workers may be sent to a subsidiary or subcontractor, often with a more prestigious title but harder work and less pay. Another alternative is to send redundant employees home 'on call,' and to continue to pay about 60 per cent of their base pay for a fixed period of time. In all these cases, the expectation is that such workers will return to their earlier positions when conditions improve.

Direct recruitment

Another advantage enjoyed by prospective regular employees is that company recruiters actively seek applicants graduating from universities and high schools. As in most countries, the most prestigious companies tend to rely upon the most prestigious universities for their future management employees.

In some cases, a company's entire need for 'fresh' graduates will be met at one university. Perhaps this has been true over a number of years, and the company has been well-satisfied with the quality and quantity of recruits. As a result, close relationships develop between the corporate recruiters and university faculty and staff.

Most important among the university contacts are the director of the placement service and the student's senior seminar professor. The placement officer does a good bit of screening of applicants before the recruiters arrive. Tests and interviews with seniors determine who will have priority in interviews with leading companies. In contrast with US university placement offices that provide only a liaison between company and student, Japanese offices perform an important pre-selection service. The crucial role of placement officials is indicated by such student expressions as: 'When I see a staff member of the placement office, somehow I find myself bowing to him' (Azumi 1969: 63).

The senior seminar professor, too, plays a unique role in placement of graduating seniors. Although most classes in Japanese universities are large lecture sessions, up-coming graduates may take a senior seminar which tends to be rather small and focused on the research interests of the professor. Very close relationships are established between the professor and his seminar students. And when a corporate recruiter visits the campus he will invariably seek out this professor for recommendations. As one business executive explains, 'We try to cultivate our relations with universities and professors. One peculiar aspect of the problem is that before approaching the prospective employee, you have to meet his professor, who sort of distributes jobs for the students' (JETRO 1981a).

Finally, most companies contain one or more important *gakubatsu*, or university cliques. These are elite groups which are extremely cohesive and tend to be self-perpetuating. The resulting 'old-boy network' seems even stronger in Japan than in England. If a company already has a strong *batsu* from Tokyo, Keio, or Waseda University, it will prefer to return to these institutions each year to fill its management-track vacancies. The importance to the graduate of being in the right university at the right time can not be stressed too much.

The 'official' recruiting season in Japan is a short one compared with the almost continual process in many other countries. Under a gentlemen's agreement, signed by more than 200 leading companies and followed by many others, between 20 August and 4 September recruiters may meet only with groups of prospective graduates to explain the opportunities their companies offer. Then, on 5 September, they are allowed to meet with applicants on an individual basis.

This suggested time-frame is designed to prevent eager employers from making offers to students long before their anticipated graduation date. As one would suspect, it is not universally observed, especially with regard to top graduates from choice universities. It was the Nippon Recruit Company's questionable efforts to protect this agreement from pressures by employers to void it that brought down the Takeshita administration in mid-1989. However, the agreement survived, and it does inject some order into what otherwise could be a chaotic procedure. This selection process continues for about six months, with new employees entering their companies by 1 April.

Student preferences

Just as corporations have their preferred sources for prospective employees, so students have their favourites among the companies for which they would like to work. In this ranking process, one writer points out, 'Recruits do not choose a firm for the job or the monetary rewards, but they choose *a place to live in*' (Sato 1981: 31).

Japanese students still are essentially conservative. Most are looking for the stability and prestige of large companies. A survey by Nippon Recruit Center, for example, found that 59 per cent of males and 50 per cent of females wanted to work for large firms. Only 10 per cent of both sexes specifically preferred smaller companies. Since most graduates of leading universities are hired directly and do not use the services of recruiting firms, these percentages no doubt are quite conservative. When asked what qualities they think are important in choosing an employer, they opted for qualities found primarily in large companies: steady growth, stability, good atmosphere, and high salary (JETRO 1981b).

As for the specific kind of organization preferred, a survey by Recruit Research found that males chose banking and finance first, then general trading companies, with third choice shared by computer/communications and transportation/travel. Females gave first place to publishing and reporting, followed by civil service and trading companies. Among the most popular individual firms in 1988 were such giants as Nippon Telephone and Telegraph, Nippon Electric Corporation, Japan Air Lines, and Asahi Beer. It is of interest to note that IBM was the only foreign company appearing in the Top Thirty list (*Japan Times Weekly* 1988:16).

Because employment with a choice firm is so eagerly sought, most university graduates are not adverse to working long hours or being required to relocate frequently. Only one in five male seniors polled by Nippon Recruit Center objected to working on Saturdays, while just one in four rejected the idea of frequent transfers (JETRO 1981b). In spite of their eagerness to join leading companies, only about 30 per cent of college graduates actually found employment at the large firms listed on the Tokyo Stock Exchange. About 10 per cent entered government service, and the balance had to settle for joining the million or more smaller Japanese firms.

Recruiting criteria

What are Japanese companies really looking for when they contact universities, recruiting firms, and other sources of regular employees? The criteria, or desired qualities, clearly reflect the company's commitment to lifetime employment. They tend to emphasize personal, rather than technical, attributes.

For example, a personal philosophy compatible with the corporate climate, or *shafu*, is considered essential. So, too, is a lack of restlessness, and a deep desire for a stable life. Perhaps the most damaging barb that can be thrust at any prospective Japanese salaryman is that he is an 'unstable' individual. Furthermore, the ability to work with members of a group, and to teach others, are considered of prime importance. Finally, an 'appropriate' social and political philosophy will be required. As one corporate recruiter remarked, 'We don't want any night-chanting religious types in our organization.'

Little emphasis is put on job-related criteria. Detailed knowledge in a functional area such as marketing, finance, or accounting is not considered essential. Grade-point average (GPA), which is often the first and most sacred cut-off device used by US recruiters, is of little interest to Japanese talent scouts. After all, they are seeking a total human being to live and work within a corporate family for his lifetime. According to one keen observer, 'The most desirable employee is not a specialist trained in a particular *What*, but a generalist who can fulfill a collective need within a particular *Where*' (Ballon 1979).

There is, however, an exception to this recruiting norm which is of growing importance. In the electronics and telecommunication industries, highly trained specialists frequently are needed before the company can develop them. Therefore, such applicants, especially engineering graduates, are screened on the basis of their specialized academic background. But even in such cases, nontechnical qualifications are given serious consideration. If Japan moves, as planned, into an 'information era', we can expect more recruiting from universities and technical institutes on the basis of specialized training.

The selection process

When a sufficient roster of prospective regular employees has been identified, the next step is to determine which of the applicants to employ. To provide the necessary background for these important decisions, the Japanese company assembles an array of formal documents from each applicant. These include a personal *vitae*, photograph, an official family registry record (*koseki tohon*), physical examination report, and letters of recommendation.

When these documents have been thoroughly examined, the next step in most companies is to administer the entrance examination, usually in early November. A problem is encountered sometimes when several companies schedule their examinations on the same day. In such a case, the applicant must choose the company for which he would most like to work, losing the chance even to be considered by the others. Should he not be selected by the company of his choice he will have to settle for a less desirable, and probably smaller, employer.

While some firms are dropping the written examination, most still use it as an important screening device. The examinations, quite general in coverage, give some indication of the applicant's academic qualifications. Furthermore, some recruiters have confided to the author that the tests also provide a reasonably objective basis on which to reject an unqualified candidate who may enjoy strong support from outside connections.

The final, and most important, step is the formal interview conducted by a panel of examiners. This is an extremely stressful situation for the applicant and, as many agree, these are the minutes that decide one's future life. The questions are aimed at discovering the applicant's personality and compatibility with other members of the corporate family. Emphasis is placed upon such matters as political orientation, family background, finances, home ownership and related questions.

Such matters would be illegal, or at best considered irrelevant, as topics for discussion in an American interview. But in Japan, the total person must be evaluated in an effort to avoid hiring anyone who will not meet company expectations over a long period of time. Indeed, many firms check on the truthfulness of the applicant's claims and on his general lifestyle. In some cases, private investigators are sent to the applicant's neighbourhood to talk with friends and shopkeepers to make sure this individual is worthy of employment.

Because each new regular employee is expected to be another jewel in the corporate crown, the final hiring decision rests with top management. In many cases, the president himself has this prerogative. It is consistent, therefore, that when a new employee fails to meet company expectations it is considered a mistake of management, and the employee will be given every opportunity to prove his worth.

It is important to understand that the recruitment and selection procedures described thus far apply only to candidates who are being considered for lifetime employment as regular, standard employees. Now it is time to see the quite different attitude and procedures involved in hiring other types of workers.

Special employees

The care lavished on recruiting and selecting regular employees is severely curtailed when hiring special workers. Few of the benefits enjoyed by elite, male applicants are available to the considerable numbers of expendable workers recruited by Japanese companies. Yet, in a sense, these are the 'troops' who make possible the generous treatment accorded the elite corps. From a Western point of view, these less-favoured members of the organization are the targets of blatant discrimination.

To the Japanese, however, discrimination is perhaps too strong a term. Differential treatment of special groups of people is an accepted aspect of Japanese society. There is, for example, a proper role for men and an equally proper, though seemingly inferior, role for women. In addition, part-time and temporary workers 'naturally' do not enjoy the same treatment as do lifetime members of the corporate family. Nor should mid-career recruits – those who are hired at any time other than upon university graduation – be given the same deference as those who start and end their careers with the company. In the sections which follow, we shall discuss the differential treatment that is accorded each of four important categories of non-regular employees.

Women

A brief review of the status of Japanese women in the workplace is necessary before dealing directly with their recruitment and selection for employment. It will soon become clear why the procedures discussed above for hiring regular male employees do not apply to females.

In Japan, April 1986 was considered to be the turning point in the treatment of women in industry. At that time, the Equal Job Opportunity Law, passed by the Diet in the previous year, became effective. Though the law was enacted in response to international pressures rather than any strong domestic convictions, there was hope that exploited women – referred to in a business weekly as 'Japan's secret economic weapon' – finally would be given equal treatment with men in hiring, work assignments, and pay. Now, with several years' experience under the Act, opinion is divided over its impact. This is not surprising, since the law merely asks companies to 'make efforts' to treat men and women equally, but does not impose serious penalties on those who do not comply.

In a survey taken by the Prime Minister's Office a year after passage of Japan's version of an EEO law, almost two-thirds of the respondents said men and women still were not on the same level in the working world, and half doubted if they ever would be. Most of those surveyed felt that women should stick to 'women's work', with 64 per cent saying women should advance only in 'suitable fields'.

This is not to say that Japanese women have no opportunities to enter male-dominated professions or to advance to leadership positions. But the actual numbers remain very small. In 1984, for example, 12 per cent of all doctors were female. And, according to the Japan Attorney's Association, in 1987 there were 692 female lawyers, or about 6 per cent of the total. There are, at present, 29 women members of the Diet, but they represent only 3.8 per cent of all Diet members.

There are several well-known stories of successful Japanese women reaching executive positions in such prestigious companies as Takashimaya Department Store and Japan Air Lines. But it seems these same stories are told and retold each year. The plain truth is that women continue to find only limited opportunities to share in Japan's prosperous business environment. More women, it is true, are working than ever before. But their work experience typically is limited to the few years before marriage and to the years after their children are grownup. When they do return to the workforce, most often it is on a part-time basis. Women still dominate in menial jobs with low pay and little chance for promotion. The average monthly salary for females in 1986 was 52 per cent of men's and shows few signs of improving.

A key question is whether these rather dreary statistics reflect blatant discrimination in the workplace. The author was severely reprimanded by a highly intelligent Japanese woman when, in a lecture, he referred to the weakness of the EEO law and to continued 'discrimination' against females in Japan's workforce. Discrimination was, she said, not a proper word to use in describing the different roles assigned to men and women in life and at work. These roles are 'complementary and synergistic', she pointed out, and should never be competitive as in the United States.

Indeed, there does not seem to be widespread resentment and unrest among most Japanese women regarding their present role in society. In a government survey of 7,200 women in six countries, 71 per cent of Japanese women said their lives after marriage should centre on husbands and children. In sharp contrast, the US figure was 17 per cent. As one woman expressed it, 'Differentiation between men and women is only natural and does not necessarily mean discrimination or segregation.'

For those women who do succeed in climbing to responsible positions in the executive suite, life continues to be a struggle. Good advice, quoted earlier in this volume, is given by one female retail executive to women who want to avoid the usual pattern of marriage, childcare, and death. Her motto: 'Think like a man, act like a lady, and work like a dog.' In too many cases, even the brightest college graduates find themselves in the traditional role of *shokuba no hana*, or office flowers, whose main function is to smile, serve tea, and generally support and motivate male workers.

In spite of the persistent difficulties, however, substantial progress has been made in bringing Japanese females into the mainstream of industry. More than 16 million women were employed in 1987, accounting for over 36 per cent of the working population. Nearly 800,000 more women hold jobs than stay at home. But the real question, according to a spokeswoman for the Labour Ministry, is how well they are faring in a society that views them as somehow inferior to males. In Japan, newspaper boys (not girls) still collect bills in the middle of the day, expecting to find a housewife at home. Parent–teacher meetings are held during the day, and mothers are expected to attend. But it is true that women now have access to a variety of jobs, including such formerly male-dominated positions as bus drivers, police officers, airline and helicopter pilots, ship navigators, and security guards.

Japanese wives traditionally have assumed almost entire responsibility for maintaining the home, managing family finances, and seeing to the education of the children. The problem facing the increasing number of working women is that they still carry these responsibilities plus the added burdens of working outside the home. They usually receive very little help from their husbands or children. A multinational study conducted by the Prime Minister's Office showed that over 90 per cent of Japanese wives cook the meals, wash the dishes, do the house-cleaning and laundry, shop (usually every day), and care for elderly family members. Of the six nations studied, Japanese husbands gave their wives the least help. Nor were children required to do household chores. While only about 1 per cent of American children claimed that they did no housework, a startling 47 per cent of Japanese boys and 26 per cent of the girls claimed complete freedom from such chores.

Recruitment of Japanese women by Japanese companies is far more casual than for men. Junior high schools and high schools provide the majority of candidates to fill the many retail and service positions available to women. Those women who work in manufacturing are viewed as short-term, and often part-time, employees. Few of the commitments and benefits accorded males are extended to females. Their length of service with the company tends to be much shorter, and their opportunities for promotion severely limited. In securing jobs, most women either are sent to prospective employers by school counsellors, or simply apply on their own to companies advertising vacancies.

The selection procedure also is more informal for women than men. Written examinations either are eliminated or shortened, one interview usually suffices, and letters of guarantee from a third party seldom are required. Women workers constitute one of several groups which are considered expendable, and hence provide the flexibility in numbers required to protect the elite corps of permanent, male employees. Typically in the age-range from 19 to 26, they are expected to leave for marriage and children. If they return to work after their children are independent those in routine jobs are apt to be part-timers with few benefits and little security. Training women for higher-level positions is not considered cost-effective since their tenure will be short.

Even the few women who do not marry and who move up to responsible positions often are encouraged to leave the company long before the normal retirement age. For example, in a large joint venture company in Japan, a very effective director of marketing found this to be true. She was shocked and hurt when, on her fortieth birthday, she was asked by the president if she was 'thinking of retiring'. Another case involved a female announcer at a TV station who was asked to retire at 30 because, her boss told her, 'the voice and face of a middle-aged woman would make the audience uncomfortable'.

It is likely that sex–role differentiation will continue as the norm in Japanese corporations for the foreseeable future. On the other hand, there is a slow but steady trend toward greater equality in treatment and opportunity between the sexes. At the present time, however, the majority of female employees continue to be considered 'transients' in an otherwise stable and secure work situation.

Part-time and temporary workers

The term part time, or *parto timu* in Japanese, is a vague term which sometimes applies to women and men who actually may be working full time or more. However, the official definition of a part timer is one who works fewer than thirty-five hours per week. The average workweek for women part-timers is thirty-three hours, and their average age is 42. But nearly half of these women actually work from thirty-five to forty-eight hours per week at low wages and with few, if any, benefits. In a typical case, a 50-year-old woman part timer is described as 'working part time for twenty years, nine of them at a plant where she spends eight hours a day, six days a week' (Parengaux 1986). As in most such cases, she has no social insurance, no pension, no union, and no paid holidays.

If we accept the official definition of part timers, then approximately 25 per cent of all female workers are in this category. Though fewer are currently employed in manufacturing, the slack has been more than taken up in wholesale and retail operations and the service industries. Although most companies do not guarantee employment for a fixed period, a recent study shows that 70 per cent of part-time workers had been employed more than a year and 30 per cent for five years or more.

Both from necessity and for convenience, many women prefer part-time employment in spite of its many shortcomings. Their pay, though low compared with full-time employees, helps with family expenses. Most important, if they do work fewer than thirty-five hours, their work imposes minimum conflict with household responsibilities. From the company viewpoint, part-timers reduce labour costs and provide needed flexibility when there are seasonal fluctuations. For companies recognizing their commitment to regular, male employees, part-timers provide a welcome escape valve when it becomes necessary to cut back operations.

Since the use of part-time work meets little resistance from workers or management, their numbers are likely to continue to rise. Most housewives who currently are unemployed but would like to work want part-time work. These women are said to represent 3.5 times the number who would like to work as full-time employees.

Temporary contract employees (*rinjiko*), who work full-time for limited periods, are another pool of so-called 'non-ordinary' workers available to Japanese companies. These individuals usually are not recruited on the open market but are sent from subcontractors and subsidiaries. Low wages, unskilled work, and lack of union protection are all characteristics of such temporary employment status.

In a large steel company, for example, ordinary employees wear silver helmets while subcontract workers wear yellow helmets. During busy times, yellow helmets may outnumber silver ones. Regular workers observe operations, check dials, and operate highly automated machinery. Men in yellow helmets, on the other hand, do the dirty, difficult work and endure noisy and unpleasant working conditions. Needless to say, when business slackens, these temporary workers are the first to go. As a company executive explained to the author, 'We pay them *almost* as much as we pay ordinary employees, and we try to give them job security.' But he admitted that they really are second-class family members and work longer hours than regular employees for no extra pay.

An interesting method for recruiting temporary workers has developed during recent years of low growth in Japan. This new strategy involves companies with surplus workers 'loaning' them to other organizations with temporary shortages. This system of loaned employees (*haken*) has been useful in a number of cases. For example, a major automobile company that had cut back employment found itself with a labour shortage as conditions improved. Steel and shipbuilding companies which were in serious economic difficulties were happy to dispatch their redundant workers to the automobile firm. Such loaned employees are preferred to the usual temporary workers because they already have excellent basic training and tend to remain for the full term of the agreement.

It can be seen that part-time and temporary employees provide an important resource for Japanese corporations. Direct recruitment, simplified selection, and a flexible element in the otherwise rigid structure are some of the advantages they offer. We now turn to another special group of workers increasingly utilized in Japan.

Mid-career recruits

Though most large Japanese companies follow the norm of once-a-year hiring in the spring, there is a trend towards adding a few highly specialized individuals as needed throughout the year. Since they are a special group, these mid-career recruits (*chuto saiyo*) are considered irregular entrants. They often are recruited on the open labour market or from companies that are retrenching. Hiring such employees from competitors is considered 'pirating' in Japan, and generally is avoided.

In the past, mid-career recruits often were discriminated against by both managers and fellow employees. In a sense, they did not 'fit', since they departed from the regular path for joining a corporate family. In recent years, however, because of the high value placed on their special expertise, more tolerance has been shown.

In interviews with executives of large companies in a variety of industries, the author found varying degrees of use of mid-career employees. A large steel company, though cutting back on regular university graduates, none the less was hiring ten to twenty *chuto saiyo* a year in highly technical fields. A major electronics company did not hire any midcareer applicants. On the other hand, one of Japan's leading information systems companies in a recent year hired 100 mid-career applicants, mostly with experience in software engineering.

In one of two large trading companies visited, no *chuto saiyo* were employed. The other, with more than 9,000 employees, hired three to five each year. A major life insurance company, which hired 140 regular graduates in 1987 (selected from 2,000 applicants) hired 'several mid-way persons' with experience and specialized know-how. These non-ordinary recruits were placed in systems engineering or in security analysis.

In general, it can be seen that hiring experienced, older employees remains an exception to the general recruitment pattern in Japan. Creatures of necessity, mid-career employees seldom are fully accepted members of the corporate family. Theirs is a classic case of status ambiguity in a social system which demands clear and unequivocal status identity.

Foreign employees

According to data published by the Ministry of Justice, the number of foreigners registered in 1986 was 867,237, or only 0.7 per cent of Japan's total population. Of these, 78 per cent were from Korea, while a mere 3.5 per cent were from the United States. As emphasized earlier, Japan is a country reserved almost exclusively for the Japanese.

Yet, there have been noticeable increases in the number of foreigners employed by Japanese concerns. In addition, registered *gaijin* include more than 20,000 students and some 10,000 singers, dancers, and other entertainers. Some restrictions on the employment of foreigners have been eased, and the high-value yen continues to attract foreign workers at all levels. At the management level, proposals have been made for increasing the number of external directors and for actively promoting foreigners to high-level administrative positions. Foreign brokerage houses and investment consulting companies also have increased in recent years. In 1988, forty-four foreign brokerage firms and twenty-three investment companies were licensed to operate in Japan. When the number of memberships on the Tokyo Stock Exchange was increased by twenty-two, sixteen of the new members were foreign companies.

Perhaps the most important trend as far as employment of foreigners is concerned is their growing acceptance as regular, full-time company members with all the privileges and benefits accompanying this new status. In the past, most foreigners working for Japanese organizations were special employees, whose major role was to serve as a 'language machine'. A Japanese writer describes the new position of foreign employees as follows:

> Working as dedicated, full-time employees of Japanese companies, these people represent a 'new breed' of foreigner in Japan. They do not fit the typical stereotype – student, tourist, English teacher, missionary, American G.I., businessman sent here temporarily to represent his company – applied to foreigners in Japan. Rather, they have made the effort to learn Japanese and are interested in a professional career in Japan.
> (JETRO 1980)

Among the pioneers in regular recruitment of foreigners is the Seibu retail chain which has placed *gaijin* in fields such as merchandise planning, clothing design, and art curatorship. Fifteen such persons were hired during a recent year, and non-Japanese personnel now account for about 1 per cent of Seibu's total staff. The company plans to increase the quota of foreigners each year and to treat them as regular full-time employees under the same conditions as Japanese workers.

The same trend can be seen in Japanese universities. In the past, appointing foreign nationals to the faculty of national and local public universities was forbidden by law. Under new legislation, the procedure for appointing foreign nationals is exactly the same as that for appointing Japanese citizens. Furthermore, the government expects educational institutions to hire foreign nationals in all academic fields, and not just in languages.

Based upon this discussion of the policies and procedures governing the attracting and hiring of Japanese employees, it should be clear that there are two very distinct classes of corporate family members. The great care and exquisite attention to detail in seeking regular lifetime employees is noticeably lacking when the search is for more transient workers. The latter include almost all women, temporary and part-time workers, mid-career recruits, and the increasing number of foreigners.

To the Japanese, it is only natural to assign different status and roles to different categories of individuals. When pressed to justify this practice, one company's public relations manager explained that this is not discrimination. It recognizes that even special employees are part of the company family in 'an old sense of family'. This, he continued, is the traditional Confucian family, in which the superior members think it natural that they are richer and more powerful than their lesser relatives. However, it should be added that it is only because such 'lesser relatives' are in abundance that the 'superior members' can enjoy lifetime employment and other attractive benefits befitting their elite status.

In the next chapter, attention is once again focused upon the regular members of Japanese organizations. Specifically, we shall want to see what sort of person rises to positions of leadership – and why. Also, it will be helpful to trace the typical course for career development of a Japanese salaryman as he climbs the 'circular stairway' to higher organizational levels.

References

Azumi, K. (1969) *Higher Education and Business Recruitment in Japan*, New York: Teachers College Press, Columbia University.

Abegglen, J. C. and Stalk, Jr, G. (1985) *Kaisha: The Japanese Corporation*, Tokyo: Charles E. Tuttle Company Inc.

Ballon, R. J. (1979) 'Promotion of personnel in Japan', *Sophia University Socio-Economic Institute Bulletin 74: 6*.

Business Week, 17 July 1978: 82–3 and 5 September 1983: 98.

'Corporate Hit Parade.' *The Japan Times Weekly* (17 September 1988), p. 16.

Hasegawa, K. (1986) *Japanese Style Management: An Insider's View*, Tokyo: Kodansha.

Inagami, T. (1983) 'Labor-management communication at the workshop level', *Japanese Industrial Relations Series* 11:6.

JETRO (1981a) 'A foreign company tackles the Japanese market', *Focus Japan*, January: 31.

JETRO (1981b) 'Japan's job hunting season', *Focus Japan*, October: JS-A.

JETRO (1980) 'New breed of foreigner', *Focus Japan*, November: 3.

Parengaux, R.-P. (1986) 'Japan's six-day-week 'part-timers'', *The Guardian* 21 April: 13.

Sato, N. (1981) *Management and Industrial Structure in Japan*, Oxford: Pergamon Press Ltd.

Chapter eight
Leadership and career development

When a university graduate makes a decision to join a Japanese company, it is intended to be a commitment to stay with the organization for his entire career. The company, in turn, will if at all possible guarantee him secure employment until retirement. With this sort of long-term relationship, the matters of leadership and career development take on enormous importance. To what sort of leader does the new recruit look for guidance? When will he have a voice in the decision-making process? What pattern of leadership will he find prevailing in his new corporate 'home'? And what must he do to make steady progress up the corporate hierarchy?

Leadership

The effectiveness of a leadership style is a function of the cultural, socio-political, and economic framework of the manager and the people he leads. These contextual constraints do change, sometimes rapidly. Therefore, a given management style may not be effective even in the same country over time, and seldom is effective in another country without substantial modification.

This basic fact helps explain the shifting nature of leadership style in Japanese companies during the past several decades. Certain facets of Japanese culture have changed – the socio-political arena is different – and the economic framework has been altered drastically. Thus, in 1968 it seemed entirely correct to say that a commonly accepted approach in Japan was to assign a 'rather passive role' to leadership – to conceive of a leader as primarily a 'facilitator' of his group's achievements (Yoshino 1968:

206 and Okumura 1982). But today the situation and the needs are quite different. Therefore, the early post-war pattern of leadership in Japan has experienced substantial modification.

Nevertheless, many unique leadership patterns remain, and the old order has not been abandoned totally. When comparing Japanese with American management, the founder of Honda Motor Company was prophetic in saying that 'Japanese and American management are 95 per cent the same, yet differ in all important respects'. When examining leadership traits in the two countries there are some very important differences. One way to approach this subject is to identify the key characteristics of successful corporate leaders in Japan and to indicate how these differ from those of their American counterparts.

Emphasis on human resources

In both Japan and the United States, fervent statements of company philosophy constantly stress the top priority given to human assets in management. There is, however, a critical difference. The Japanese really mean what they say. Any accurate model of Japanese management, for example, puts primary focus upon human resource development and then develops general strategies and procedures for achieving this goal.

Innumerable statements by top Japanese business leaders could be cited to reinforce this point. Typical of such sincere expressions is that of Keizaburo Yamada, Mitsubishi Corporation's executive vice chairman of the board of directors: 'MC is a company of 10,000 people bound together by common destiny. The top must endeavour to understand the thinking of the bottom and vice versa.' Keeping in mind that regular employees are in a sense 'fixed assets' for the Japanese company, it is understandable that their well-being is given very serious attention.

American executives, too, speak of the central importance of people in their organizations. But too often such declarations are just at the verbal level. Many studies, as well as direct observation, indicate that participation in management decision-making is more often professed than practised. The fact is, employees in an American firm are considered 'semi-variable' assets and, within limits, can be hired and fired as needed. The popular scenario of the human relations movement of the 1950s and 1960s has faded in

149

recent years. US management priorities have shifted to mergers, takeovers, and rather desperate responses to international competition.

Hard-core evidence of this difference may be seen in the incredible success of QC circles in Japan as compared with their lukewarm acceptance in the United States (see pp. 238–40). This across-the-board approach to employee participation originated in the United States, but never really appealed to either management or workers. Managers did not feel the potential input of rank-and-file workers warranted the time and money required by a full-scale QC circle programme. Workers, on the other hand, felt such broad-gauge problem solving was not a legitimate part of their jobs. As one seasoned worker put it, 'Why should we worry about these problems? That's what the boss gets paid for. It's not in my job specs!'

There are, of course a number of showcase organizations such as IBM and the half-dozen others highlighted by William G. Ouchi in his popular book, *Theory Z* (Ouchi 1981). But these, unfortunately, remain the exceptions which prove the rule. In general, human resource management always has been considered to be a 'soft' area by most tough, hard-hitting US executives. When the chips are down, primary attention will be devoted to numbers and laws rather than to people. Luckily, the trend in recent years has been to reappraise priorities and to try once again truly to believe the old adage that 'management is getting things done through people'.

Future orientation

A Japanese steel executive insisted to the author that having a future orientation is the primary quality required of his country's corporate leaders. Similarly, a spokesman for Japan's largest life insurance company identified 'ability to see the future' as a 'must' for modern managers. It no longer is enough to make and sell the world's best product at the world's best price. Japanese leaders now realize that such success breeds the seeds of its own destruction. As a result, the restructuring of the Japanese economy from being export-driven to far greater dependence on the voracious domestic demand has been carried forward with remarkable success.

Leaders who have the ability to foresee and assess such forces as rising protectionism and the deadly competition of newly industrializing countries have become crucial to the survival of Japan's economy. As mentioned in an earlier chapter, corporate planners have become the new heroes of Japanese industry. During the boom years, when there was nowhere to go but up, preserving the status quo was sufficient. But today the ability to look ahead, to plan, and to shape corporate strategies to meet future challenges is an essential facet of successful leadership.

This quality of future orientation is not alien to Japanese leaders. Rather, it is simply an extension and elaboration of their customary long-term point of view. Corporate executives never have been bottom-line oriented to the extent typical of US leaders. With a higher debt–equity ratio, and a history of support from government, Japanese companies need not bow as deeply to the demands of dividend-hungry stockholders as must their American counterparts. A commendable patience – a willingness to accept ambiguity, uncertainty, and imperfection in the short run to achieve success in the longer term – has long been a characteristic of Japanese management. Today, patience must be combined with a keen ability to anticipate future events and plot a course to cope with them.

Group identity

Japanese management has been called *omikoshi* management. This term refers to the custom of having many young men carry a portable shrine in festival parades. It is impossible to identify the leader or even those who are carrying more than their share of the heavy load. But together they can accomplish what could not be done by a single individual. Submergence in a group, and satisfaction in being an anonymous contributor to group goals, are outstanding features of Japanese management.

Relative status – who outranks whom – is clear and important in the typical corporate hierarchy. One's status still depends heavily upon educational attainment and length of service. But the external symbols of status are noticeably lacking as leaders and followers strive to unite in one homogeneous, cooperative work-group. The lack of private offices, combined with the uniformity of dress, make it difficult for the uninitiated to distinguish leader from follower.

The Japanese like to say that 'the nail that sticks up will be hammered down'. In the American setting 'the nail that sticks up' is most likely to get a salary increase and a promotion. Thus while US managers tend to display rugged individualism, togetherness is the outstanding feature of management in Japan.

Another term frequently used to describe the fusion of managers and subordinates into a close-knit group is 'common-destiny management.' During the difficult early post-war years, the rebuilding of the nation required cooperative relations among all parties. Every person, without regard to position, was expected to 'share the fate' of the company – that is, all employees perceived themselves as sharing in a common destiny. The task of the leader, therefore, was to create an harmonious environment in which each member of his group would contribute effectively to group goals.

The mutual dependence of superior and subordinate in Japanese companies is stressed by social anthropologist Chie Nakane in this way: 'To counterbalance the dependence on the leader on the part of his followers, it is always hoped that the leader, in his turn, will be dependent on his men. The leader must have some weakness for which his men are always ready to compensate or provide support' (Nakane 1973: 68). This strong interdependence of a manager with members of his work group is another example of the broader phenomenon of groupism in Japanese society.

Intuitive leadership

Intuition may be defined as quick and ready insight concerning a problem which does not rely upon rational, studied procedures. In the context of leadership, this means that the supervisor sets overall objectives and then relies upon his subordinates to work out the details for themselves. Masaaki Imai, a prominent Tokyo consultant, provides the following example of this leadership style:

Kentucky Fried Chicken is reported to taste different from store to store in Japan. As in other countries, Kentucky Fried Chicken Japan uses the same store facade, the same color combination, chickens from the same farm, the same frying oil and sauce, and the same utensils in accordance with the same instruction manual. And yet, somehow, different stores' products taste different. . . . One would imagine that the management of a franchise chain would make doubly sure that manuals are followed closely and that all outlets offer identical products and services. ... In Japan, however, the people working at the stores apparently do not follow the instructions closely. Instead they innovate and try to improve on the recipes, which is why things taste different from store to store.

(Imai 1981a: 62–3)

Imai criticizes the West for providing manuals to salesmen, engineers, and accountants that often are 'as thick as the telephone directory'. He quotes one expert sales manager as saying that there was no need for lengthy sales manuals in Japan – all he needed was a single sheet of paper outlining the salesman's work. Once this is spelled out, it is up to each salesman to work out his own way of doing the job most effectively. Imai claims the justification for such intuitive management lies in Japan's homogeneity and uniformly high level of education. It may not be feasible in a multi-ethnic society with widely varying levels of educational attainment.

Close personal relationships tend to support reliance upon intuition in Japanese management. One such relationship is that of senior–junior, or *senpai-kohai*. Because most Japanese tend to have an extremely strong need for some person in whom they can have complete trust and confidence (*amae*), the selection of a senior confidant is a matter of great importance. In more general terms, all those who are superior in length of service and education are one's *senpai*. But in the present context we are referring to the specific and intimate relationship between two individuals.

It is one's office senior (*shokuba senpai*) who helps initiate a younger employee into the rituals of organizational life. The senior is expected to help his *kohai* in learning the social as well as the formal requirements of his job. The younger man has someone to whom he can come in times of trouble or confusion in both the work and personal phases of life.

Though this senior–junior relationship is not official, it does receive implicit organizational recognition and support. In discussing the qualifications of an effective *senpai*, one expert suggests, 'They must, of course, be the same sex as the newcomer, a little older, gregarious, and knowledgeable. Most importantly, they should be models of good work habits and proper attitudes' (Rohlen 1974: 130).

The support for a full measure of intuition in leadership is grounded in many aspects of Japanese management and the broader society in which it operates. Willingness to form and nurture an incredibly complex web of interpersonal relationships leads to a professional game of 'networking' in which Americans could never aspire to more than pure amateur ranking. With such a network, continuously oiled by frequent contact and open communication, the need for thick manuals and the 'rule of law' simply does not exist.

Private/work life integration

To this writer, one of the most fundamental characteristics of successful leaders in Japanese organizations is their impressive willingness to integrate personal and work sectors of their lives. In relative terms, it is fair to say that most Western executives insist upon a greater separation of these two sides of life. For example, the typical American executive tries to avoid external social relations which might require too much subjective involvement with subordinates. Both parties consider themselves to be private persons after normal work hours.

In Japan, all levels of employees see themselves as company representatives at all times. The strong identification of one's whole self can be seen in the sequence of terms often heard in introductions of business executives. If Mr Kato is employed by the Hitachi Corporation the company name is most likely to be mentioned first, and then the individual's name will follow. For example, '*Hitachi no Kato-san desu*,' or, loosely translated, 'This is Hitachi's Mr Kato.' In contrast, an American is almost always introduced along these lines: 'This is Joe Green of GTE.'

This subtle nuance in introduction may not be terribly important or even universally practised in Japan. But it is indicative of the unique role played by the company in the lives of employees, even at rank-and-file levels. In research conducted with Professor Shinichi Takezawa, the author surveyed workers in comparable industrial plants in Japan and the United States (Takezawa and Whitehill 1981: 57–62). Table 6 shows the choice offered in one question. As the results indicate, the extreme company role posed in item 1 had almost no appeal to Americans and attracted only 9 per cent of the Japanese respondents. The more balanced role portrayed in item

2, however, captured almost two-thirds of the Japanese votes. In contrast, items 3 and 4 together were selected by only 27 per cent of the Japanese, but were the choice of four out of five American participants.

Table 6 The role of the company

I think of my company as:

1	2	3	4
the central concern in my life and of greater importance than my personal life;	a part of my life at least equal in importance to my personal life;	a place for me to work with management, during work hours, to accomplish mutual goals;	strictly a place to work and entirely separate from my personal life
Japan 9%	Japan 64%	Japan 15%	Japan 12%
U.S. 1%	U.S. 20%	U.S. 42%	U.S. 37%

While the exact numbers are not crucial, the general message is clear: Japanese employees tend to support a healthy midground, equating work and personal sectors of their lives. Considerable fusion of life sectors seems to be a characteristic of most Japanese employees. Americans, on the other hand, prefer greater separation of work and personal life and have a more contractual view of the employment relationship.

Holistic problem-solving

When a problem arises in a Japanese company the high priority given to creating harmony and preserving good relationships influences how a manager will deal with the matter. Instead of embarking on an in-depth analysis to dissect the problem into specific parts, a systemic approach will be used. What was the situation that caused this problem to erupt? What can the company do to prevent its recurrence? How can the harmony and momentum of the group be preserved? These are the sorts of questions which will be dealt with in the typical Japanese problem-solving format.

An American manager faced with a problem in his department typically tries to isolate, define, and quantify the issue. There is a strong feeling that problems cannot be resolved until they are clearly defined. Instead of a holistic approach, attention is devoted to breaking the whole into parts, and submitting each part to intensive, rational analysis. After all, a manager's job is to cut right to the heart of problems and solve them as quickly as possible.

A related characteristic of the Japanese approach to problem-solving and to conflict resolution is the ready acceptance of blame at the highest levels of the organization. If there is a plane crash, the chairman of the airline will publicly declare his guilt and promptly leave his post. When the subsidiary of one of Japan's most respected firms was caught selling sensitive technology to the Soviet Union two top executives of the parent company resigned, accepting total blame for the incident. To be fair, it should be added that because such top executives are usually well along in years, retirement may be welcomed. Furthermore, they will be generously provided for by the company in recognition of their personal sacrifice.

In most Western countries, similar incidents are apt to trigger a massive 'search for the villain'. Who was to blame for the disaster? What punishment will fit the crime? How can we find the culprit and expel him from the organization for his grievous error? In important issues affecting the public the initial stage in dealing with a problem is likely to be followed by a deluge of lawsuits seeking reparations of mind-boggling proportions from the company.

One sees the Japanese holistic approach not only when dealing with dramatic problems of broad scope but also in handling everyday problems in the workplace. The following is an example from the service department of a Japanese firm:

Recently, an expatriate manager accompanied his service engineer on a customer call. Although it was customer negligence which had caused the machine to fail, the service engineer fixed it and then, to the expatriate manager's surprise, apologized for the trouble. Even though the engineer knew it was not his fault at all, he apparently put himself in the position of the inconvenienced customers and reasoned that the customers would not have had this trouble if they had not bought this machine in the first place.

(Imai 1981b: 13)

As with most Japanese management practices, this approach to problem-solving fits well with the rest of the system. Lifetime employment and lifetime training create employees with strong group consciousness and company loyalty. These valuable traits must be nurtured, and a manager must not upset the stability of relationships. The possible negative consequences of confrontation, of ferreting out the culprit, would outweigh the benefits. Therefore, apologizing and accepting full blame in problem resolution is important whether or not one is actually at fault.

Technical literacy

One of the most vocal critics of American business believes that a serious problem facing US managers is their 'technical illiteracy'. Pointing to the fact that many more Japanese than American executives hold science and engineering degrees, he goes so far as to claim that few Americans 'have the skills to solve real world problems' (Tsurumi 1983). The facts of world leadership easily prove this to be a gross overstatement. Yet, the development of greater 'number skills' – particularly at the high school level – is a recognized need in American education.

In this age of information systems, electronics, and biotechnology, increasing numbers of science and engineering specialists are needed to manage the technical side of industry. On the other hand, a company dominated by technical specialists is at a disadvantage in dealing with the important conceptual and communication challenges inherent in a global economy. There is no easy answer to this dilemma. But a sensible solution would seem to call for a balance between leaders who are 'technically literate' and those who have demonstrated conceptual, communication, and other human-related expertise.

Japanese companies depend heavily on their leaders' technical competence. The quality and reliability of Japanese mechanical products attest to their engineering prowess. And their considerable leadership in pushing ahead into the new information age is impressive. However, the great difficulty Japan has in understanding, and being understood by, other nations may indicate a shortage of broadly literate leaders essential to assure for Japan a permanent and responsible role in the international community of nations.

Courtesy in business

A basic, simple characteristic of successful Japanese executives is their commitment to courtesy in all business negotiations. This welcome trait has been described as 'the most subtle, but most powerful, weapon in Japan's management arsenal' (Cicco and Snyder 1985). It is certainly one of the aspects of leadership style most frequently commented upon by foreign businessmen returning from Japan.

This pervasive courtesy is obvious each day when dealing with sales clerks, waitresses – yes, even taxi drivers. But it is also a significant part of all business negotiations. Many a Western visitor, primed for a quick discussion and firm conclusion of the business at hand, leaves the initial conference in bewilderment. Business was not even mentioned. The conversation revolved around such matters as the weather, family members' activities and health, politics, baseball, and other 'unrelated' topics.

To the Japanese it is unseemly to jump into hard-core negotiations too quickly. Even a business letter requires some preliminary coverage of non-business topics before addressing its real purpose. The visiting executive who insists upon getting down to business too quickly may well find himself with no business to transact. There is a long and dreary record of disappointment, frustration, anger – and lost contracts – due to ignorance of this important side of Japanese business etiquette.

Once again, the Japanese put primary emphasis upon the precious and fragile relationship with another person. Whatever the problem, this relationship will be the basis for its solution and therefore merits any time that must be spent on its development. This really is a broad social, rather than strictly business, trait. It is not something that can be instilled through 'assertiveness training' or other behaviour-modification seminars so widely, and so futilely, conducted in many other countries. And it is one aspect of Japanese leadership behaviour which is very much worth emulating not only in Japan but in business negotiations everywhere.

Employee expectations

In concluding this summary of leadership in Japan, it may be well to turn briefly to the preferences and expectations of those being led. Referring again to the comparative studies conducted by the author with Professor Takezawa, Table 7 shows the choices offered in answer to a question concerning the nature and degree of decision-sharing desired by subordinates in Japanese and American companies.

Table 7 Decision-sharing

When changes in work methods must be made I think a supervisor should:

1	2	3	4
decide himself what the changes shall be and put them into effect since he is in charge of the work;	first decide on the changes, and then ask for the cooperation of the workers;	first ask workers for their suggestions regarding proposed changes, and then decide what to do;	allow workers to decide for themselves what changes should be made and how to make them.
Japan 3%	Japan 27%	Japan 67%	Japan 3%
U.S. 8%	U.S. 14%	U.S. 74%	U.S. 4%

Source: Takezawa and Whitehill 1981: 113

The message is clear. Respondents in both countries showed their strong preference for item 3, which describes a realistic degree of participative management. Basically, there seems to be a continuum of leadership style which ranges from authoritarian to participative. At the authoritarian end of the continuum, supervision is characterized by 'top-down' decision-making, unilateral action by management, and passive conformity by workers. The participative mode, on the other hand, is characterized by decentralization of authority, an emphasis on mutual dependence and cooperation, and active participation in the decision-making process.

The extremes of this continuum are, of course, seldom found in reality. The negligible responses to items 1 and 4 indicate that workers in both countries know this to be true. There is little doubt that employees prefer a consultative approach to decision-making. They would like their ideas heard, but then are quite willing to 'let the boss decide' what to do. With the 'bottom-up' (*ringi seido*) approach to decision-making in Japan, it is fair to say that the Japanese come much closer to meeting the preferences and expectations of workers in this matter than do their Western counterparts.

Decision-making

Before exploring the rather tortuous and lengthy path followed by Japanese salarymen in their career development, it may be valuable to take a closer look at the decision-making process referred to above. It is a unique aspect of the Japanese style of leadership. Much nonsense has been written about the *ringi seido*, and the following two misconceptions should be clarified: (1) Japanese style bottom-up decision-making means that all decisions are made at mid-management levels, and (2) consensus decision-making is a tedious process which is much more time-consuming than the top-down, more autocratic process found in other countries. Let us evaluate each of these claims.

Delegation or diffusion

It would be extremely naïve, given the extremely competitive environment within which Japanese companies operate, to believe that consensus decision-making implies outright delegation to mid-level managers to chart their own course and to decide on critical changes in direction. This does not happen in Japan any more than in other countries. It is true that the *ringi* system does provide for prior discussion and approval by all who are directly affected by an important change. The initial idea, however, probably was passed down from top-executive levels. It is then that the important discussions – often referred to as *nemawashi*, or preparing the ground – take place.

The Japanese decision-making process, then, is one of diffusion rather than outright delegation. Japan's top managers can be, and often are, as autocratic as any in the world. In a *Fortune* magazine article, the writer profiles half a dozen examples of so-called 'one man' management in Japanese firms. Powerful leaders are found at the top of such pace-setting companies as Sumitomo Bank, Suntory Ltd., Daiei Inc., Fanuc, and the Seibu Group of Retail Enterprises. It is a fallacy to believe that the authority to give final approval to decisions is delegated to lower levels by these top executives. Every important decision must be confirmed ultimately at the highest levels of management (Smith 1985: 56–65).

In this sense, the system may best be thought of as a confirmation–

authorization process. A proposal is written on a form called a *ringi-sho* by the initiator of the idea. It is then circulated to all affected individuals for review and confirmation by affixing their seals (*hanko*) to the document. Then it is sent to top management for final approval or, in some cases, veto. This process would seem to have advantages over a simple one-way method either from bottom up or top down. And it does seem to be quite consistent with the preferences of employees at all levels to have some input on decisions affecting their well-being.

The time factor

The second misconception concerning Japanese decision-making is that the time requirement is excessive and would never be tolerated by Western managers. This claim, I believe, misses the essential nature of decision-making as a process rather than as an event. Reference to Figure 3 may be helpful in explaining this critical difference.

Figure 3 Decision-making continuum

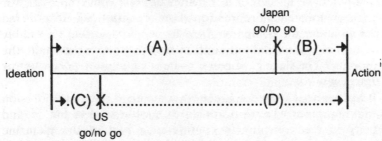

After an idea is formulated in the Japanese company it is explained, discussed, and confirmed by all those affected. This requires considerable time (A). When the 'go/no go' point is reached, however, very little time (B) is required to take action. In the US case, the 'go/no go' stage is reached rather quickly by top management (C). Then a massive 'selling job' must be mounted taking a considerable period of time (D).

In the final analysis, the total time span required by the Japanese and American approaches is not very different. However, in the Japanese system when a 'go' decision is reached all elements of disagreement have been eliminated, the responsible person assured of cooperation from top management and other departments, and the proposal turned into an immediate administrative assignment. In the American system the difficult problem persists of selling a change to managers who have had little or no input prior to the 'go' stage. Too often managers affected by the decision agree to go along with it but are not fully in agreement with the proposed change. What other choice do they have? The 'go' stage was determined at upper levels some time before the idea was brought to their attention. Providing for greater input from those affected *prior* to commitment to a change does not seem unduly time-consuming and will help to meet the basic human desire to have a voice in shaping one's destiny.

Career development

For the fortunate high school or university graduate who is selected to join a Japanese firm, financial security seems assured. Looking forward to perhaps thirty-five years of 'total immersion' in the social as well as the technical aspects of corporate life, the development of his career is a matter of great concern. What are the criteria for steady progression in the organization? How can he learn all about the company – and its people – so that he will be able to make a substantial contribution to company growth and prosperity? The stage has been set – he is an untested performer in a brand new role.

It has been said that the Japanese company is regarded as a *dojo* (a training place where one practises martial arts) of life. Every activity in the company is considered a part of the plan for developing individual careers. Included are not only on-the-job training and seminars, but also induction and orientation programmes which range from moral lectures by the president to gruelling endurance walks. Socialization into the corporate culture is an important and continuing process in the overall development of Japan's future business leaders.

There are basically two categories of training opportunities which provide direction and support for career development: (1) in-house, and (2) institutional. Each of these will be examined in detail in the sections which follow.

In-house opportunities

Japanese companies, far more than their Western counterparts, rely upon on-the-job experience and other internal programmes for management development. An individual's managerial career begins when, with other members of his entering 'class', he is welcomed to the corporate community which will be his 'home' for the next thirty-five to forty years. His career will end when he is forced to retire at perhaps age 60 or, if he is selected to become a director, at a much more advanced age. In between these career terminuses, many experiences hopefully will contribute to the development of a well-adjusted and totally integrated 'company man' with a single-minded devotion and loyalty to the organization often likened to the US Marine Corps.

The first ten years

Immediately upon entering the company the new employee will undergo a month or more of orientation exercises. It is likely that he will opt to live in the company dormitory so as to begin the development of the close personal relationships so necessary to business success. In addition, those in the entering class and members of their families may attend several meetings led by the president and other top-level executives. These meetings tend to resemble pep rallies, with strong moral and spiritual overtones. Team spirit is encouraged through singing up-beat company songs and reciting statements of company philosophy in unison.

At Tokyo's Matsuya department stores, orientation training includes the use of styrofoam triangles to teach new sales clerks the 'right angles' for bowing to customers. For 'May I help you?' the proper angle is 30 degrees; for 'Just a moment, please,' an angle of only 15 degrees is suitable. But for 'Thank you very much,' a full 45 degrees is required.

Professor Thomas P. Rohlen gives us an excellent example of two special training activities offered by the conservative Japanese bank in which he was a participant observer (Rohlen 1974: 203–7). The first was an experience called *roto* which, loosely translated, means bewilderment, isolation, and a sense of insecurity. Each trainee goes from door to door in a village offering to work for the day without pay. He is to do whatever his host asks and is forbidden to reveal who he is or why he is there. Several outcomes are expected from this exercise. The individual, acting alone and stripped of his company identity, learns the importance of group membership and the joy of serving others. Furthermore, in his awkward request for work of any kind, he is reminded that all tasks, no matter how menial, are honourable and can be the source of much gratitude and satisfaction.

The second special activity described by Rohlen was the twenty-five mile endurance walk around a large public park. The last seven miles were to be walked alone and in silence. This was to give the foot-sore and weary walkers ample time to call upon their spiritual resources to carry them through the ordeal. Furthermore, successful completion of the walk reminded the trainees that the more difficult the task, the more pride one could take in its accomplishment.

With completion of such orientation exercises, the new trainee then starts a series of practical on-the-job work experiences. If his company is in manufacturing, the work may be as a production worker on the factory floor. If joining a bank, front-line experience is likely to be as a teller. In a sales organization, working as a store clerk would be a likely initial job assignment.

The remarkable aspect of all this is that front-line experience is required not only of high-school recruits but of university graduates as well, some of whom have earned the MBA degree. Furthermore, it may continue for a considerable period of time. A young man must expect to spend years in a series of relatively low-level jobs before he can begin to assume managerial responsibility. By then he will have acquired not only a variety of technical skills but an intimate cadre of people upon whom he may call for assistance in the years ahead.

During the first ten years or so of his career, the trainee gradually will be introduced to increasingly responsible tasks. It is likely that he will move between functions, offices, and geographical locations. In the process, he gets to know the people, the problems, and the procedures of many areas within the organization.

In effect, there is no fast track in most Japanese companies. Critics claim that by following a non-specialized career path Japanese managers become broad generalists but have little specialized expertise. I would prefer to think of them as becoming 'multi-specialists'. Because new assignments under the job rotation system come only every three to five years, enough time is spent on each assignment to develop considerable expertise in a number of areas. Professor Ouchi, in *Theory Z*, sums it up well in his statement that 'Japanese do not specialize only in a technical field; they also specialize in an organization, in learning how to make a specific, unique business operate as well as it possibly can' (Ouchi 1981: 33).

The next ten years and beyond

After ten years or more of employment, the first real threshold is reached. This may be promotion to *kakaricho* (sub-section chief) or *kacho* (section chief). Because the *ka*, or section, is the basic organizational unit in Japanese companies, to be chief of a section is an important leadership position. For some, this is both an initial and terminal managerial appointment. For most, however, it is clear evidence that they are on the way up.

At the section-chief level, the still-young manager will be assigned every few years to new functions and geographic locations. His experience – and his contacts – continue to widen. Spring is the time of year when such new assignments are made. Usually the employee will be asked to complete a *jiko-shinkoku* (literally, a self-declaration) to inform his immediate superior and the personnel department of his preferences concerning a new position. But when he receives a *jirei*, a brief order telling the employee where he will go and what he will be doing for the next few years, there is little choice. If he refuses the assignment his career development may be blocked and he is likely to be relegated to a routine, dead-end job. Every effort is made in determining a reassignment to consider the worker's self-assessment together with his immediate superior's evaluation and the company's needs. However, the latter tends to be the controlling criterion.

For ambitious, upwardly mobile *kacho* the need now is to broaden their leadership abilities. It is in these years that the individual gains 'experience', the primary qualification for further promotion. This means that he will gain maturity, that with age he will become wiser, and that he will be sharpening his abilities and sensitivities in dealing with people.

After a total of twenty years or more of employment – perhaps at about age 45 – another threshold is reached. It is at this time that promotion may be made to *jicho* (deputy department head) or directly to *bucho* (department head). The latter is the top rank in the employee classification prior to a directorship. It is an important position carrying with it considerable responsibility and prestige. As such, *bucho* will have a liberal expense account, travel opportunities, and many other perquisites of high office. Because the pyramid narrows at this level and there is a limited number of director slots to be filled, many managers will remain in this position until mandatory retirement.

Those individuals who have built up impressive records of accomplishment through the years, at about age 52–5 will be promoted to a directorship. It is likely that they will maintain their *bucho* positions at least until they reach normal retirement age. For directors, as mentioned earlier, there is no mandatory retirement age. Board chairmen in Japanese companies frequently are in their seventies or even eighties, though their responsibilities may be few. At this pinnacle of their career, many assume the role of roving ambassador of good will for the company.

During the long career path from *hira-shain* (ordinary company member) to a directorship, a Japanese salaryman may have had as many as a dozen quite different work assignments. An important question is the relative importance of merit and seniority in deciding who will get the more important and challenging opportunities.

In the 1960s and 1970s, decades of record-breaking growth in Japan, promotion based solely on length of service (*nenko joretsu*) was common. There was plenty of room at the top as companies continued to expand. Reliance upon 'the merit of years' was acceptable and feasible as the basic criterion for advancement. As a former student and young businessman confided to me: '*Nenko joretsu* in Japanese companies takes ordinary, even incapable people who enter the company and make no serious blunders, promoting them to the head of departments and occasionally to the head of the company.'

Of the several 'sacred treasures' of Japanese management, primary emphasis upon length of service in promotion is under the greatest pressure. Already, most companies have shifted to a policy called *noryokushugi kanri*, or ability-based management. This does not mean that serious consideration of the Confucian age/wisdom equation has been abandoned. It does mean, however, that greater emphasis is being placed upon such 'meritorious' criteria as personal trust of colleagues, knowledge and skills, practical experience, contribution to productivity increase, and sense of responsibility.

A serious problem is that well-defined performance criteria have not yet been developed in most Japanese companies. In a discussion with Japanese personnel executives, the author frequently encounters a kind of 'Catch 22' dilemma in which they find themselves. When asked if they now base personnel decisions primarily on merit, they quickly answer 'Yes'. But when encouraged to be more specific concerning the meaning of merit, they often fall back on how long the employee has been with the company and what prestigious university he attended as indicators of merit. This is circular reasoning coming full circle.

There is little doubt that individual measures of performance must be developed further if merit is to become the leading indicator of qualification for promotion. But there are problems in pursuing individual evaluation in a group-centred work environment. To single out one person as being more productive, or as a better person, than other members of his group is considered not only wrong but can be personally humiliating to the individual so recognized. If the old adage mentioned earlier that 'the nail that sticks up will be hammered down' is honoured, then job evaluation and the whole concept of meritocracy will have difficulty gaining acceptance in Japan. In Chapter 12 we shall return to this dilemma when discussing efforts made to improve organizational effectiveness.

In comparison with Western management systems, the Japanese still give far greater weight to seniority in personnel decisions. Managers are dedicated to promoting harmony among their subordinates. *Nenko joretsu* is the safest way for everyone. With this system, nobody complains that promotions are unfair. But for companies experiencing moderate or low growth in the future, there seems to be no alternative to placing more emphasis on each individual's contribution to corporate goals and giving less credit for mere length of service.

External development programmes

An important difference exists between Japanese and American companies in their use of outside institutions for developing managers. While US firms rely heavily upon university executive programmes, Japanese companies tend to follow the European model in using special management institutes sponsored by government and industry. However, even this use is sparse since Japanese firms prefer to 'grow their own' executives.

Although in recent years a handful of Japanese universities have begun to offer both degree and non-degree programmes for executives, the numbers are still very small. Instead, young Japanese managers – especially those destined for overseas assignments – are sent to special training facilities either in Japan or abroad. An example of one such training centre in Japan is the Institute for International Studies and Training (Boeki Kenshu Center) located several hours from Tokyo at the foot of Mt Fuji. Both Japanese and foreign faculty teach courses at the Institute, and there are many opportunities for interchange between the Japanese students and foreign students selected from leading American universities.

An example of a training facility located outside Japan is the Japan–America Institute of Management Science (JAIMS) in Honolulu, Hawaii. Founded in 1972 by Fujitsu Ltd., JAIMS has been a pioneer in the area of cross-cultural (US–Japan) management training and executive development. Through its comprehensive core programmes – the Japan Management and American Management Programs – JAIMS addresses the highly sensitive issues of managing business across cultures. Other activities include shorter-term orientation programmes for executives moving to or from Japan, computer courses, and specialized Japanese and English language programmes.

Perhaps the reason that Japan has opted to follow the model of European management institutes, such as INSEAD in France and IMEDE in Switzerland, is the general lack of mutual trust and support between Japanese universities and the business community. Leaving their universities upon graduation, students are said to enter the 'real world' and seldom return to the campus. Businessmen tend to think of university professors as 'ivory tower' and radical in their views. Professors, in turn, consider businessmen to be too obsessed with daily operating problems to deal with broader political, economic, and social issues. With some outstanding exceptions, Japanese professors generally are not widely used as consultants to corporations.

In contrast, the degree of mutual trust between business and academia in the United States is amazingly high. Most state and private universities offer half a dozen or more special programmes, both degree and non-degree, for executives. In short, the bulk of responsibility for management development is shifted from the firm to the university. Additional evidence of these close ties and interdependence is the fact that many professors of business administration in the United States more than match their university salaries through corporate consulting assignments.

In concluding this discussion of career development, it is clear that even the perception of a career is quite different in Japan and America. The Japanese version depicts a life-long association with a single company in which slow and steady progress will be made up the 'spiral staircase' to the top. The company will, and can afford to, take primary responsibility for charting a satisfying career for each member of the corporate family. Because this is a 'family affair', most of the development opportunities are confined to within the organization. Broad experience, through job rotation, is the ultimate goal.

In US firms, employment typically is short-term and specialized. Studies show that university graduates tend to be very impatient, changing employers if they feel they have not been placed on a 'fast track' career path. It is said that MBA graduates, of which there are more than 40,000 produced each year, on the average work for three employers during the first ten years after graduation. Though there are some development programmes within the company, the range of special university programmes is staggering and more than meets the needs for continuous development of managerial abilities.

In any country, the 'ideal' for leadership, and the various paths for its development, are at least partially a function of culture and tradition. In addition, leadership must be congruent with the immediate needs of the organization and with the totality of the given management system. Which pattern – Japan's or America's – is best, few are prepared to say. Each seems to be meeting the need for corporate vitality and competitiveness within the broader social and economic environment of which it is a part.

References

Cicco, J. A. Jr and Snyder, R. D. (1985) 'Japan's secret weapon'. *The New York Times*, 13 June.

Imai, M. (1981a) *16 Ways to Avoid Saying 'No'*, Tokyo: The Nihon Keizai Shimbun.

Imai, M. (1981b) *When in Japan*, vol. 1, Tokyo: Hotel Okura.

Nakane, C. (1973) *Japanese Society*, New York: Penguin Books.

Okumura, A. (1982) *Nihon no Top Management (Japanese Top Management)*, Tokyo: Diamond Publishing.

Ouchi, W. G. (1981) *Theory Z*, Reading, Mass.: Addison-Wesley Publishing Company.

Rohlen, T. B. (1974) *For Harmony and Strength*, Berkeley: University of California Press Ltd.

Smith, L. (1985) 'Japan's autocratic managers', *Fortune*, 7 January.

Takezawa S. and Whitehill, A. M. (1981) *Work Ways: Japan and America*, Tokyo: The Japan Institute of Labour.

Tsurumi, Y. (1983) 'US managers often "technically illiterate" and out of touch', *Washington Post*, 31 July.

Yoshino, M. Y. (1968) *Japan's Managerial System*, Cambridge, Mass.: MIT Press.

Chapter nine

The compensation system

Pay, particularly relative rates of pay, has always been a topic close to the hearts of employees at all levels of any organization. While money is alleged not to be a primary motivator, a 'fair day's work for a fair day's pay' is accepted as a minimum requirement for compensation systems. Built around this bare-bones foundation is an incredibly complex package of payments and benefits which make up the modern reward system.

A company's compensation system must be congruent with the culture and values of the society within which it operates as well as with other facets of the management system. As a result, we find very substantial variations in the perception and practice of wage and salary payments in two countries as different as Japan and the United States. There are certain aspects of the Japanese pay structure which are certainly distinctive if not unique.

In this chapter, three major segments of the Japanese compensation system will be examined: (1) wages, salaries, and other payments; (2) employee benefits and services; and (3) the closely related issue of hours of work. Where appropriate, Japanese practices will be compared with those in the United States.

Wages, salaries, and other payments

The wage policies of Japanese firms form a complex but balanced and flexible system. Composed of base pay, semi-annual bonus, and a variety of allowances, each component meets a particular need. On the whole, the composite wage system seems to be well accepted and to function smoothly.

The base pay component is linked primarily to length of service and provides a sense of security and stability for employees. Bonuses provide a somewhat flexible link with overall organizational performance and thus provide motivation for group and individual effort to improve market share and profitability. Finally, there is a wide variety of allowances (*teate*) designed to meet individual, personal needs.

Wage and salary criteria

It is essential to recognize the special blend of criteria, or important influences, which determine rates of pay. Six of the more significant of these criteria will be examined, and the relative importance of each in Japanese and American firms will be suggested.

Prevailing pay

A general rule in US wage administration is that a company must pay at least as much as do competitors for similar work. However, this is a matter of policy rather than law, except in cases involving government contracts. Of course a company may pay less than the prevailing rates if quality is not important and labour abundant. Or the policy may be to pay slightly more than prevailing rates and thus be able to attract better-than-average workers.

It seems likely that prevailing pay rates are not quite as important a factor in Japanese as in American firms. The size, reputation, and prestige of a company loom larger than differences in starting pay to a new recruit anticipating lifetime employment with a company. Furthermore, as we shall see later in the discussion, starting pay rates are quite standardized among leading Japanese companies for all entering employees. It is only in later years of one's career that the spread among individual's begins to widen.

Union bargaining power

In companies having a union, no final wage and salary figure can be reached without agreement from the union. However, the role and influence of labour unions is quite different in US and Japanese firms. Therefore, union impact on wage determination varies considerably.

In Japan, unions are physically and psychologically a part of the company. Located on company property and given various types of support by management, these so-called 'enterprise unions' generally play a cooperative role in company actions. It is also interesting to note that Japanese unions often provide an important source of company executives. Leadership in the union is considered excellent preparation for company leadership positions.

Contrast this with the long-standing adversarial role of US labour unions. Never physically or psychologically attached to the company, unions typically are viewed by management as the 'enemy'. Each side – labour and management – tries to contain the other in as small an area of influence as possible.

With these differences it should be clear that union bargaining power is a far less significant wage criterion in Japan than in the United States. There is a deep reluctance on the part of enterprise union members to harm *their* company by excessive wage demands. Furthermore, restraint is encouraged by the general feeling that all members of the corporate family must 'share the fate' together. More will be said about enterprise unions in Chapter 12, where the focus is upon improving organizational effectiveness.

Individual needs

The scale tips in the opposite direction, however, when the subject is recognition of individual needs – differences between Mr A and Mr B – in determining rates of pay. Concern for the whole person as a lifelong member of the organization is an important characteristic of the Japanese management system. US firms, in contrast, think of workers as only one, though an important one, of the several factors of production. And many employees conceive of the company as simply a place to work eight hours a day, forty hours a week.

In Japanese companies, each person's total situation will influence the amount of his income. The number of family members, his housing needs, the distance from his home to the plant, and other person-centred factors are given consideration. This leads to the payment of special allowances depending upon individual needs. Requests for such payments by US workers would probably lead to the boss replying 'Sorry. That's your problem.'

Job requirements

A fundamental principle in American management is to start with the job. American firms hire for a job, train for a job, pay for a job, and fire from a job. Job analysis, job descriptions, job specifications, and job evaluation are almost sacred procedures in US companies. After all, most personnel procedures rest firmly on this foundation.

Therefore, in setting pay rates, it is only natural that job requirements will be the most important of all wage criteria. Applicants for employment at an American firm will soon ask 'What does the job pay?' If they like the answer, they will start to work; if they do not, they will quickly leave and look elsewhere.

Seldom if ever would this question be asked in Japanese employment interviews. It really would have little meaning, since the applicant will be hired for the company and not for a specific job. The job does not pay – the company pays individuals for their length of service and contribution to the overall goals of the company with little reference to job rates *per se*.

It is clear that here is a significant difference in the whole approach to wage determination between the two countries. Job specifications in Japanese companies are notoriously vague. Even demarcation of responsibilities between sections and departments tends to be fuzzy. Thus flexibility and 'elbow room' are characteristics which are deliberately built into the Japanese organizational structure.

Seniority and education

These two criteria are combined, not because they are less important but because they have been discussed earlier in connection with career development and promotion policies. While seniority and education are given some recognition in US companies in setting wage rates, their importance in Japan is very much greater.

Though Japanese firms are trying to build greater concern for job performance in setting wage rates, it is difficult because of the traditional dependence upon length of service and educational attainment as the primary pay criteria. In addition, clear standards of job performance have not yet been developed widely in Japanese management.

Ability to Pay

Of course an organization's ability to pay certain levels of wages and salaries is conditioned by its ability to generate the means to do so. This is an important consideration in US collective bargaining sessions, as the management team 'talks poor' to its union rivals. In recent years, some troubled companies have even negotiated wage decreases by releasing their profit statements and proving that present levels could be a serious threat to company solvency.

Japanese companies, too, are well aware that wages are paid from earnings and, if earnings plummet, they may not be able to maintain even present levels of wage and salary payments. But a crucial difference is seen in the way the problem is dealt with. The first step will be to announce a 10–20 per cent cut in all management salaries right up to the top. Then, and only then, will workers be asked to endure a similar cut in their pay. This is in sharp contrast to recent disclosures of American auto executives getting generous bonuses for negotiating lower wage rates for workers.

The pay package

The pay package in Japanese corporations traditionally has been quite complex. First there are the various payments received in cash once each month. It is customary to pay all employees near the end of the month. The brisk business enjoyed by restaurants and amusement centres immediately after 'pay day' reflects this general custom. The monthly pay is made up of the individual's base rate plus a variety of allowances and incidental pay. An important supplement, paid twice each year, is the generous bonus. Finally, though not received until retirement, a lump-sum separation allowance is paid which, in a sense, represents a deferred salary payment. Let us look at each of these categories.

Monthly compensation

An individual's monthly base pay is set by a number of factors. Though merit is being given increased recognition, seniority still seems to be the major factor in setting base rates. For entering employees, pay tends to be rather standardized, with no great difference related to company size. Average starting salary (excluding bonuses) for male university graduates in 1988 was

¥153,100 (about $1,100 at prevailing exchange rates) per month at companies with ten or more employees. For male senior high school graduates it was ¥120,300 ($860).

Salary increases are rather modest in the first few years, but after a period of about seven years begin to increase more rapidly, peaking at about age 45–9. The average monthly salary (including overtime allowances, but excluding bonuses) in 1987 at companies with thirty or more employees was ¥251,298 ($1,800). Adding the two semi-annual bonuses brought the total to ¥335,944 ($2,400) – an average annual salary of ¥4.031 million, or about $29,000.

Across-the-board base rate increases are normally negotiated by national federations of unions and employers' associations in March of each year. This agreed-upon 'base up' merely sets a guideline for companies in determining actual increases. These negotiations are known as the Spring Wage Offensive (Shunto). Its influence in recent years has waned, however, as real differences in the ability of individual companies to follow the guideline have become apparent. The Shunto wage increase was 7.68 per cent in 1980, but slipped to only 3.56 per cent in 1987. Both employers and the unions are beginning to question the usefulness of this traditional spring ritual.

According to the Ministry of Labour, base pay amounts to roughly 75 per cent of monthly wages and salaries. This is the amount upon which bonuses and retirement allowances are calculated. Added to the base rate is overtime pay earned by ordinary employees for work beyond the normal work week and at night and on holidays. In addition, a position allowance typically is paid to employees holding formal supervisory posts in the firm. Additional work-related allowances paid each month may include those for special assignments and skills. Special assignments include overseas positions and other temporary assignments of a non-recurring nature. Together these work-related allowances average about 10 per cent of base pay.

Finally, monthly compensation includes a staggering variety of optional, person-centred allowances not related to the work performed. Best known among these are the family allowance, housing allowance, commuting allowance, and allowance for no absences. But there are many others, with several companies even reporting the payment of a 'dating allowance' for single, young, male employees in need.

Payment of a family allowance is fairly widespread, but declining in use among leading Japanese companies. Personnel surveys show that throughout the 1960s family allowances were paid by more than 90 per cent of the firms studied. But more recent studies in the 1980s indicate that slightly less than 25 per cent of companies reported payment of a special allowance for family dependants. Those firms that have continued this practice now are limiting coverage to a worker's spouse and first two children. The dramatic improvement in real wages, as well as increasing numbers of young, single workers, have contributed to the decline in importance of family allowances in the typical Japanese pay package.

Housing assistance provided by employers generally follows a three-tier system: dormitories for single workers, both male and female; low-rent apartments for young married couples; and a limited supply of rental housing available to staff workers and managers.

Because the housing shortage is Japan's most critical social problem, corporate assistance really is a must. Employment opportunities have grown faster than housing in all urban centres of the country. As a result, adequate housing for most urban workers has become 'farther away' – both in terms of physical distance and in price. The average time spent by workers commuting each day is at least one hour, with many spending more than two hours. Cases of some employees spending as many as three to four hours each way, from door to door, are not uncommon. Yet the 'my home' dream dies hard, and most Japanese continue to yearn for a home of their own.

Unfortunately, the most expensive land prices in the world are combined with a national obsession to compress all industrial and government activities in Tokyo, Osaka, and a few other crowded urban centres. Together, these factors have contributed to an acute and persistent shortage of affordable housing, and an equally acute necessity to spend a sizeable portion of the day packed into buses, trains, and subways. As a result, company assistance with housing and commuting expenses is both commonplace and expected by workers.

In our study of rank-and-file workers in Japanese and US factories, Professor Takezawa and I found that Japanese interviewees felt much more strongly than Americans that their company should pay family allowances and assist with housing. Table 8 summarizes the results concerning family allowances.

Table 8 Family wage allowance

Each worker's total pay should include:

1	2	3	4
a special allowance, with extra compensation for *all* family members;	a special allowance, with extra compensation for a limited number of family members;	no specific allowance for family members, but his wage should indirectly reflect size of family	no direct or indirect compensation for size of family.
Japan 32% US 16%	Japan 29% US 5%	Japan 28% US 14%	Japan 11% US 65%

Source: Takezawa and Whitehill 1981: 151

As the results indicate, almost two-thirds of Japanese workers approved of paying a family allowance for all, or a limited number of family members (items 1 and 2 combined). In the US, on the other hand, almost two-thirds felt size of family is not a concern of the company and no extra compensation is necessary.

When attention is turned to housing policies, an even more striking difference is seen. Table 9 presents the survey results. Clearly, more Japanese employees see company-provided housing as proper than do their US counterparts. Again, almost two-thirds of Japanese questioned felt the company should provide housing, either free or at low rent (item 1 and item 2 combined). But 92 per

Table 9 Housing policies

In regard to housing for workers, a company should:

1	2	3	4
provide company housing at no charge;	provide company housing at special low rent;	offer loans to workers for building or buying houses instead of providing company housing;	avoid direct financial assistance in housing.
Japan 17% US 1%	Japan 47% US 7%	Japan 35% US 52%	Japan 1% US 40%

Source: Takezawa and Whitehill 1981: 159

cent of American workers rejected company-owned housing, preferring either some help through loans or a company 'hands off' policy.

In the United States, as in England, 'a man's home is his castle', be it ever so humble. And he does not want the company to cross the moat of personal privacy. Japanese workers, by contrast, approve of a much more multiphasic involvement of the company in their lives.

In summary, the present discussion shows the Japanese monthly pay package to be a much more complex matter than monthly pay in the United States, which typically is just the job rate plus overtime. Attention will now be turned to the bonus – a twice yearly extra that is highly appreciated by employees at all levels of a Japanese company.

Semi-annual bonus

In addition to their monthly compensation, Japanese employees receive bonuses twice a year, in December and in July. The annual amount of the bonus in recent years has averaged the equivalent of between four and five months' pay. In other words, about one-third of annual compensation is paid as a bonus and is a very important part of the employee's total pay. Larger firms tend to pay more generous bonuses, though the practice is almost universal among all Japanese companies, large and small.

Furthermore, the bonus is paid to all levels of employees. The bonus is one feature of the Japanese compensation system that is favoured by both top management and ordinary employees. From management's viewpoint, it is really a deferred wage payment which provides a substantial amount of 'free' working capital for the company. Also, since retirement benefits are calculated on base pay, it is advantageous to keep the bonus a separate salary item. And the bonus is, of course, a flexible cost item that can be reduced in difficult times without cutting the total labour force.

The author has asked Japanese employees why they don't press the company to include the bonus in base pay. If this were done they, rather than the company, would earn interest on the additional money until spent. The suggestion has had absolutely no appeal. Extra income at the New Year's gift-giving season and again at summer recreation time has become a cherished part of the Japanese lifestyle. There is little doubt that the bonus as a part of total compensation is here to stay.

The amount of the employee's bonus is determined, at least in theory, by overall corporate profitability. As such, it should serve as a motivator to improve organizational effectiveness. But there is not a clear relationship between size of the bonus and company profitability. Furthermore, companies are extremely reluctant to cut bonus rates unless a strong case can be made to do so.

In addition, the bonus amount is tied to the employee's performance as an individual. This is the means by which superiors can reward extra effort and high achievement in a monetary way. The bonus is a discrete means of rewarding outstanding individuals without compromising the seniority-based wage system. While a bright young employee may not receive base-rate increases faster than his peers, one way in which the company can recognize his abilities is through boosting his bonus. Therefore, it serves as an individual motivator in a largely group-oriented work environment.

Retirement allowance

It has been customary for many years for Japanese corporations to pay employees reaching mandatory retirement age a single, lump-sum payment. Sometimes referred to as 'separation pay', the practice stems from several characteristics of the Japanese social and economic systems.

Mandatory retirement in Japan always has been at an early age relative to Western countries. Until the past decade, 55 was the generally accepted standard – this at a time when 65 was well-established as the normal retirement age in the United States. Recently, the Japanese norm has crept up close to 60 for retirement. In the US, however, mandatory retirement at any age is well on the way to extinction both in government and private organizations.

The lump-sum separation payment has served a number of purposes for the Japanese. With forced retirement at a relatively young age, and with life expectancy in Japan claimed to be the world's highest, there is a considerable span of years during which the retired person would wish to be self-supporting. The retirement allowance in many cases has provided the wherewithal for a small retail or service business, often with living quarters attached. The hundreds of thousands of such family-run enterprises still found throughout Japan attests to the popularity of this plan for financial independence.

The amount of the retirement allowance is a function of length of service and final salary. Generally, the allowance is calculated as one month of base pay for each year of service. For example, let us take an average office department manager (*bucho*). In 1986, average age of *bucho* was 50 years and average monthly base salary (including position entitlement but not including overtime) was ¥565,905. At the then prevailing exchange rates, this would be a monthly salary of approximately $4,000. Bonus, of course, is not included since it is not a monthly pay item, nor are non-work-related allowances.

Let us assume our average *bucho* started in the company at age 25 and will be required to retire at 65. At his present salary, he would receive a lump-sum retirement allowance of ¥22.6 million, or about $161,000. This is a substantial sum and can be the basis for an investment which will be an important financial aid in retirement. It does, however, further assume that the company does not put a cap on service years at 55, an increasingly prevalent practice as retirement allowances become burdensome with higher mandatory retirement age.

There is a trend among large Japanese companies toward dividing retirement benefits between a lump-sum separation payment and a monthly pension payment. Private pension plans vary widely at this early stage of development, both in terms of amount and number of years of payments. But, as a supplement to Japan's Employees' Pension Insurance (old-age, survivors' and disability pensions), private pension plans fill an important niche. Pension Insurance and other legally required benefits will be discussed in detail in a later section of this chapter.

Salary distribution

The spread in salary between president and new employee – between top and bottom of the college-educated class – is far less in a Japanese company than in a comparable US firm. It is no news to anyone these days that there are some extremely wealthy individuals in Japan. But these members of the 'income elite' tend not to be top corporate executives. Rather, they are farmers selling their land for housing developments and golf courses,

TV stars, speculators in the booming stock market, or sports heroes.

While Japanese executives enjoy generous fringe benefits and services, their salary income is modest compared with the United States. Much publicity has been given to the fact that some US chief executives earn from $3–5 million a year. In contrast, the annual pay for Japanese top executives ranges from $100–300,000, depending on size of company. With the tremendous emphasis upon egalitarianism and togetherness in Japanese organizations, it would be unseemly for a chief executive to receive an exorbitant salary compared with his fellow employees. The considerably lower levels of executive pay in Japan mean much less spread (or greater compression) in the salary structure than in the United States.

Minimum wage legislation

In Japan, minimum wages are mainly set at the prefectural rather than the national level. Therefore, in contrast with the single US minimum wage, Japan has a patchwork collection of many different minimum rates. Regional minimum wages may be applicable to all workers in the prefecture regardless of industry or occupation. Or they may be in the form of industrial minimum rates applicable to specific, major industries in the area.

Collective bargaining will, of course, influence minimum rates set within each of the forty-seven prefectures of Japan. But in most instances the government sets rates based on studies by the regional Minimum Wage Council, a tripartite body composed of representatives of the public, management, and labour. Because of the diversity of minimum wage rates in Japan, their impact probably is greater – that is, more workers are favourably affected – than under the 'one size fits all' policy in the United States. In Japan, minimum wages tend to be about 50 per cent of the average wage in the industry. In general, they are equal to the starting wage for junior high school graduates (Japan Institute of Labour 1979).

Benefits and services

Turning now to employee benefits and services these are, in a real sense, an important part of the total reward system. Though many are expressed in money terms, they are not a part of the wages, salaries, and other payments made to employees in return for their services. Most are contingency payments – that is, payments contingent upon the occurrence of some event, such as illness, job loss, work-related accident or, more happily, the entertainment of business clients. Others are in the form of facilities and services, often free or at low cost to employees.

To facilitate this discussion, we shall look at two major categories of benefits and services: (1) those legally required; and (2) all others.

Legally required plans

Japan has a comprehensive and highly sophisticated set of social insurance programmes. Health insurance, pension insurance, employment insurance, and worker's accident insurance are required for all employees. In addition, the national health insurance and national pension plan cover all Japanese citizens who are not employed or not dependants of covered employees.

Because contribution rates and benefit amounts are varied and constantly changing, they will not be reported here. However, a general description of the nature and coverage of each plan follows.

Health insurance

Provision of health insurance for employees and their dependants is mandatory for all Japanese employers. The insurance covers all medical (including dental) expenses incurred due to injury or illness not related to employment.

In addition, the insurance pays a portion of basic wages for the period the employee is not working. Health insurance is financed by a monthly premium, a percentage of standard regular pay, shared equally by employer and employee. Everyone in Japan is covered either by private or national health insurance.

Medical care in Japan is excellent. Physicians are well trained – and well paid – and enjoy a position of great prestige in Japanese society. The hospitals and other facilities, however, do not always meet Western standards in terms of patient comfort or maintenance. Also, some of the medical practices do surprise foreign patients. One is the widespread custom of giving generous tips to the doctor on completion of treatment. Another is the provision of prescriptions and other drugs by the physician's own pharmacy. Both practices, of course, serve as supplemental sources of income for doctors.

Pension insurance

Employees' pension insurance is provided through eight plans, the most important of which are the Employees' Pension Insurance Plan – sometimes called the Welfare Pension Plan – for employees of firms having five or more employees, and the National Pension Plan for the self-employed and all others. As with health insurance, everyone in Japan is covered by some form of pension insurance.

Most relevant to this discussion is the private sector Employees' Pension Insurance. Benefits under this plan include old-age, disability, and survivors' pensions. The old-age annuity is paid to workers with twenty years of coverage, with the qualifying age set at 60. The premium is a percentage of standard regular monthly pay and is shared equally by employer and employee. Pension benefits are adjusted annually to reflect changes in the nationwide consumer price index.

In addition, a disability annuity is paid to those with mental or physical handicaps caused by injuries or diseases. To be eligible for this pension, a person must have had the handicap and been insured for at least six months. Finally, survivors' pensions are paid on the death of a worker who has been covered for six months or more. Eligible survivors include spouse, children, parents, grandchildren and grandparents, who were dependent on the worker at time of death.

Employment insurance

This insurance scheme covers all employees and is designed not only to pay unemployment benefits but also to assist in finding work. Costs of the insurance are borne by both employer and employee, with the former paying a slightly larger share.

Unemployment benefits are classified into job applicant benefits and employment promotion benefits. The former include a basic allowance, skill acquisition allowance, boarding allowance, and sickness and injury allowance. Employment promotion benefits include moving expenses as well as a clothing allowance for full-time employment.

Workmen's compensation insurance

This insurance plan, administered by the Ministry of Labour, is designed to compensate workers for injuries, diseases, disability or death due to occupational causes. In addition, coverage is extended to commuting accidents on the way to and from work. Formally called Workmen's Accident Compensation Insurance, this plan covers all employees in the private sector. Other plans provide similar protection to civil servants, seamen, employees of public corporations, and several additional special groups.

Various types of benefits are paid under workmen's compensation, mainly in the form of medical care and cash payments. Medical care accounts for more than one-third of all payments, with disability and survivors' pensions accounting for most of the balance.

This plan is funded by employers under an 'experience rating' scheme, with a small subsidy provided by the government for administrative costs. Each employer's contribution rate is determined by the type of industry and the frequency of accidents and injuries during the preceding three years. In recent years, contribution rates have ranged from about 0.5 per cent to 8.9 per cent of gross wage payments, including bonuses.

In summary, legally required benefits in Japan follow closely the pattern set in the United States. Benefits in Japan, however, tend to be slightly more generous both in duration and amount. As in the United States, concern over adequate funding is evident. This is true particularly with respect to the Welfare Pension Insurance Plan which is comparable to old-age and survivors' insurance under the US social security system. Rapid aging of the population, combined with the Japanese claim of the highest life-expectancy in the world, means that the percentage of pensioners in the population is growing by leaps and bounds.

The Ministry of Health and Welfare forecasts that people aged 65 and over will account for one-quarter of the total population by the year 2005. The plain fact is that Japan now faces the same problems already encountered by most Western countries in funding their social security programmes. It is clear that a far larger portion of national income will have to go to support the growing population of senior citizens in the near future.

Other benefits and services

We already have discussed the various allowances (family, housing, commuting, and others) that are paid on a monthly cash basis, and the legally required employee benefits. However, there are a number of additional benefits which are neither a part of monthly pay nor legally required. These include a wide variety of programmes to enhance the work lives of Japanese employees. Because so much of the employee's life involves work and work-related activities, provision of services to satisfy the 'whole person' is a natural goal of the company.

Perhaps most impressive to outsiders are the many recreational, educational, and cultural programmes offered by Japanese corporations. Company seaside and mountain resorts provide very inexpensive vacation sites for workers and their families. A staggering variety of general courses offered by the company include everything from foreign languages to flower arranging. Company-sponsored softball, volleyball, and bowling teams are commonplace. Overnight excursions to resort areas are an expected annual event in most companies. There are few employees of Japanese firms who are not constantly involved in one or more such group activities.

Most companies have cafeterias providing low-cost meals for employees. Many maintain barber shops and beauty salons, as well as nursery and other child-care facilities. It is common for a company to make supplementary payments, in addition to those legally required, for health insurance, or to offer monetary gifts to employees at times of personal celebration or grief.

Top managers in Japanese firms enjoy another layer of special benefits and services which often are the envy of their Western counterparts. It must be remembered that the regular salaries of such executives tend to be quite modest. However, it is true that top-management perks in Japanese corporations include very generous expense accounts. Company limousines with white-gloved drivers, lavish executive 'retreats' both in town and at resort areas, travel and housing benefits are additional amenities.

Most notable is the Japanese executive's expense account to

support the long-standing tradition of lavish entertaining and long nights on the town. While American executives spend more time and money on two-martini luncheons at smart restaurants, the Japanese prefer to do their entertaining after the workday is over. One writer estimates that in 1981 Japanese corporations spent more than $13 billion on entertainment for clients (Deutsch 1983: 84). That is about $37 million a day, and goes largely to support the famed *mizu shobai* – literally 'water business' – referring to the thriving entertainment trades that employ more than 5 million people throughout the country. There are hundreds of thousands of bars, cabarets, clubs, hot spring spas, and restaurants catering to Japan's *shayozoku*, or 'expense account tribe'.

When entertaining important clients, Japanese executives spare no expense. A night on the town for even a small group will cost a minimum of several thousand dollars. Many small, exclusive bars serve as private clubs for regular patrons, and are 'for Japanese only', as an unaccompanied foreigner will be told at the door. The true mark of distinction is for the host not to display cash, credit card, or even his *meishi* (business calling card). He is so well known, trusted, and affluent that the bar simply will present his tabs to his corporate accounting office at the end of the month.

Company car and driver, for personal as well as official business use, is another top-management perquisite far more common in Japan than in the United States. The author, with a few minutes to spare one morning before giving a lecture at the building housing the Tokyo Stock Exchange, wondered at the chauffeur-driven limousines stretching for blocks in every direction. The occasion turned out to be a monthly meeting of the top executives from companies forming one of the large *zaibatsu* groupings described earlier in Chapter 5.

A *Fortune* magazine writer sums up the complex reward system in Japan candidly in her warning that 'What you see isn't all of what they get' (Mesdag 1984). When the whole package of base salary, overtime, allowances, benefits, and services are considered, total compensation of regular employees is usually quite comparable to that received by similar US workers. But it is difficult to make exact international comparisons because there are substantial differences in components of the total pay package and in the statistical methods of reporting.

Hours of work

A persistent complaint from the United States and European countries is that Japan is a nation of hopeless workaholics. Implicit in the complaint is that the hard-working Japanese are 'unfair', and that they should work less and play more – like the rest of us. Because Japan takes such criticism seriously, steps have been taken to bring working hours more in line with foreign standards. But progress has been slow, and future trends are not entirely clear. The Labor Standards Law was revised in 1987, and an ultimate goal of a standard forty-hour workweek, with all hours above forty requiring overtime pay, was established. However, companies which meet certain criteria in terms of scale and type of business will be allowed to continue their present longer workweek until March of 1992.

Average working hours

Studies by the International Labour Organization (ILO) compare actual hours worked per week in manufacturing for various countries. Weekly hours of work in 1986 were: Japan, 46.0; United States, 40.7; West Germany, 40.4; France, 38.6; UK, 41.6; and Korea, 54.7. Shifting to an annual basis, excluding overtime and absenteeism, the Japanese worked 2,192 hours, compared with 1,850 in the United States and an average for fifteen Western countries of 1,691. While international statistics are at best risky (the Bank of Japan reports weekly hours for the same year at only 43.2), the message seems clear: the Japanese work substantially more hours per week, and each year, than do workers in Western industrialized nations. But when compared with even harder-working Korea, their most aggresive Asian competitor, they are laggards.

Pressure from Japan's Western trading partners has resulted in a slow but steady decline in hours of work during the past decade. And the government, with the revised Labor Standards Law behind it, is now engaged in an ambitious crusade to bring work hours down to Western levels by instigating a nationwide two-day weekend. If this were accomplished, the theory goes, exports would fall and the Japanese worker, with more time on his hands, would save less and spend more. By forcing the nation to work less, the government hopes to stimulate domestic sales, particularly in the leisure industries.

This is a rational point of view, but one which not everyone shares. The powerful management associations, such as Nikkeiren, the Japan Federation of Employers' Associations, are against any shortening of hours since that would mean higher labour costs. Even workers themselves are not all in favour of the movement, many saying that they are unhappy when away from the company for long. A Japanese salaryman often refers to his company as *uchi no kaisha*, meaning 'my home company', and feels a deep sense of responsibility to it. As a result, he will work long and hard within the company, and feel lonely and without purpose when not among his co-workers.

Younger people, particularly those who see themselves as *shinjinrui*, or 'new human beings', scoff at such old-fashioned views and claim they are solidly behind the move towards more leisure and less work. But in many cases once a coveted position with a prestigious company is won, the individual becomes a typical 'good company man' whose life focuses around the company.

Progress thus far towards the full two-day weekend has been patchy. Employees of banks and other financial organizations, who have had one Saturday off each month for several years, began a full five-day workweek system in February of 1989. All public servants were given a five-day workweek, but only twice each month, starting in January 1989. As the financial institutions and the public sector move towards the two-day weekend every week – the government's ultimate goal – private corporations will be under pressure to do the same. But opinion continues to be divided, and full attainment of that goal will take additional time.

Days off

The author once asked members of a Japanese management seminar how many days vacation they were allowed – not how many they actually took – each year. The answers were astounding, ranging from 85 to 120. Obviously, there had been a breakdown in international communication.

After some discussion, we discovered that the problem was the fact that they included any Saturdays they might have off plus all Sundays in the year. Weekends, then, were considered 'vacation' days. When they asked what Americans considered weekends to be, the only answer that came to mind was their 'basic human rights'.

Eliminating weekends and annual leave, we can identify the most common days off given to Japanese employees. According to the Japanese Institute of Labour, most firms offer an average of 16.1 days off a year. The breakdown is 9.2 days for national holidays, 3.9 days for year-end and New Year holidays, 1.9 days for special summer holidays centred around the 'Buddhist All Souls' Day', and 1.1 other days off (Mesdag 1984). The last figure might well include time off for the anniversary of the company's founding or for some local festival. National holidays include such uniquely Japanese celebrations as Coming-of-Age Day (15 January), Respect-for-the-Aged Day (15 September), and Culture Day (3 November).

Annual leave

Annual paid leave ranges from a legal minimum of ten days a year for workers in their second year of service, to a maximum of twenty days per year for more senior employees. The average number of annual paid vacation days offered to Japanese workers in 1986 was 14.9.

However, it is a well-known fact that few employees take their full vacations. The average number of days actually taken in 1986 was 7.5. But many employees settled for just three or four days of vacation. These few days often are combined with 'Golden Week' in May which has three national holidays (1979).

The Japanese government has launched a campaign to persuade workers to take their annual paid holidays. Most take less than one-third of the time off to which they are entitled. They believe that full use of holidays would reflect disloyalty to their boss and peers, or show a lack of interest in their work. Failure to take vacations is considered such a serious problem that the Ministry of Labour has distributed a series of pamphlets urging workers to get out and relax – pointing out that all work and no play adds up to stress and fatigue. This sort of campaign is not one likely to be mounted by American or European governments. In most European countries, both in the East and in the West, workers are given – and take – a full month of paid vacation each year.

Leisure-time activities

What do Japanese workers do in their limited leisure time? For male workers, the quick answer is that they head for the golf courses and driving ranges. The national obsession with golf means that courses are crowded and the better clubs incredibly expensive. Furthermore, the distance from home or work to a golf course is often great. Two hours in a car, or on a crowded bus or train, is not considered prohibitive, because playing golf is seen as a prerequisite for one's successful career development.

Other sports, especially skiing and tennis, are popular among women office workers. Every winter weekend the night trains are jammed with young people, both male and female, on their way to the many ski slopes in the 'Japanese Alps'. Also popular with women in their leisure time is going out with friends for dinner. This is especially true after payday near the end of the month. Restaurants are packed with groups of single women ordering fine wines to accompany their gourmet meals. French, Italian and other foreign restaurants are particularly favoured and considered to be very chic and 'now'.

Overseas travel is another activity which has grown rapidly during the past decade. The number of Japanese going abroad, including those going for business purposes, jumped from less than 3.9 million in 1980 to 8.4 million in 1988, a 23 per cent increase over the previous year. This compares with a total of 2.4 million foreign travellers going to Japan in 1988. Foreign vacation travel is especially popular with single women office workers and with honeymoon couples. Popular destinations are Hawaii, Guam, Hong Kong, Italy, France and England. Among young unmarried women, the population group with the largest discretionary income, shopping while abroad is as important as sightseeing. They attack a Tiffany counter of fine gems in much the same way a Frenchman pushes and shoves to buy his daily loaf of bread.

After golf, the most popular leisure activities of male employees would include tennis and fishing, and the less athletic pastimes of drinking with co-workers, playing mah-jong, pachinko (vertical pinball machines), or *go* (a kind of Japanese checkers). Of course, watching TV and reading books are additional relaxing activities to fill leisure hours.

In conclusion, in this chapter on the Japanese compensation

system we have seen that the total package of employee rewards includes far more than a basic salary. The semi-annual bonus, various allowances, and a full range of benefits and services all contribute to meeting the full range of employees' needs. In general, rewards are generous. Little wonder that survey after survey finds the typical Japanese salaryman confident and secure in his work, and quite satisfied with his life in general. In the next chapter, attention shifts to the important topics of motivation and the evaluation of performance within the Jaspanese *kaisha*.

References

Deutsch, M. F. (1983) *Doing Business With The Japanese*, New York: The New American Library Inc.

The Japan Institute of Labour 'Wages and hours of work' (1979), *Japanese Industrial Relations, Series* 3: 19–25.

Mesdag, L. M. (1984) 'Are you underpaid?', *Fortune* 19 March: 22.

Takezawa, S. and Whitehill, A. M. (1981) *Work Ways: Japan and America*, Tokyo: The Japan Institute of Labour.

Chapter ten

Motivation and evaluation

During the 1950s the author visited a factory operated by one of Japan's leading pharmaceutical manufacturers. In the long corridors connecting work rooms, a strange device had been installed in the ceilings – two continuous ropes moving in opposite directions with knots tied at regular intervals. When asked what purpose the ropes served, the company's personnel director replied: 'They keep our people walking at a good pace. When in the corridors they are expected to keep up with the knots in the rope. It's a kind of motivation booster.'

Times have changed remarkably since those early post-Occupation days following the Second World War. Today, such a crude approach to 'motivation' would not be tolerated by management or labour. Instead, a number of subtle, yet powerful, elements of the Japanese management system itself have combined to produce one of the most highly motivated workforces in the world. In this chapter we shall attempt to discover the sources of this enviable dedication and productivity of Japanese employees.

A second objective of the present discussion will be to investigate what, if anything, is done in Japanese corporations to evaluate the performance of employees. If seniority really is the controlling factor in promotions and salary increases, is it necessary to have any systematic appraisal of performance? And how can employees be evaluated and compared without a serious loss of face? We shall attempt to answer such questions and to provide an understanding of the special way that interpersonal comparisons and evaluations are used in Japanese organizations.

Motivating employees

How most effectively to motivate employees remains the 'million-dollar question' for business leaders in most countries of the world. Why is it that some employees do an outstanding job, performing their work with diligence and enthusiasm, while others do barely enough to justify their employment? Why do some seldom miss a day of work, while others use every excuse to be absent? These are difficult – and vital – questions to answer. Furthermore, they must be answered within the total cultural context of each industrial society.

Let us first look at the work ethic, or general attitude toward work, prevailing today in Japan and the United States.

Work ethics

An issue affecting all members of any nation's labour force is the meaning of work. Such a concept reflects an individual's general philosophy and prioritized values, and is too complex to deal with adequately here. But a few comments may be useful as they relate to the general problem of employee motivation.

First, it is clear that both Japan and the United States enjoy a strong work ethic. Workaholism in Japan, as discussed earlier, has become an important national issue. Recently in America, however, doubts have been expressed that work still enjoys a high priority. But all one must do is visit some of the more southerly nations holding a *mañana* approach to work to appreciate the fact that the US work ethic is alive and strong.

It is true that Japanese and US attitudes toward work spring from quite different sources. The Confucian work ethic in Japan does reflect some of the doctrines espoused by that great Chinese teacher–philosopher many centuries ago. And the Protestant work ethic in America no doubt can trace its beginnings to the strict teachings of Calvinism. But in neither case today are these early roots of great significance. Current events and present values seem to be much more relevant in explaining the positive attitude toward work prevailing in these two such different cultures.

Perhaps most important in setting varying attitudes toward the meaning of work is a society's stage of economic development. Both Japan and the United States have passed through the highly industrialized stage when work ethics were at maximum strength.

Now, as post-industrial societies with their labour forces shifting from manufacturing to service and other tertiary industries, it is likely that some of the priority given to work, though still high, may tend to weaken. In Japan, for example, much greater interest in *ikigai* (a general term referring to satisfaction of psychological needs, or quality of life) seems to indicate some lessening of an almost fanatical work ethic.

Shifting to the corporate scene, Japanese executives now often express concern about the increasing demands of employees for *hatarakigai*, or work-related, inner satisfactions. And, of course, much has been said about the differences in attitudes toward work between the 'young' and 'old' as the generation gap widens. There is much concern these days among older Japanese that young people are changing the nation's traditionally strong work ethic. While many younger workers still are working very hard, there is fear that their loyalty to the company may be slipping. This can lead to concern that the younger generation lacks the values that built Japan's success: dedication, loyalty, selflessness, and cooperation.

It does seem that there is some increasing ambivalence among young people concerning traditional values. The author had a chance to see this inner struggle in action on a pleasant Sunday afternoon at Harajuku in Tokyo. Harajuku is one of the 'in' places for young people, and offers a dazzling array of trendy boutiques, theme coffee shops, and a variety of recreational facilities. It is also the scene on Sundays of uninhibited street dancing to loud American rock music by a number of *zoku*, or 'tribes' of young people.

A well-known example is the Takenokozoku (Bamboo Shoot Tribe), whose members dress in garish versions of Japanese peasant trousers worn under long, bright-coloured gowns. They dance in a style much like that of the Bon summer festivals when people dance to honour their ancestors – and to have fun. They move in controlled – and traditional – patterns, with names and ranks neatly pinned to their tunics.

How truly rebellious are such attempted demonstrations of individuality? In fact it seems to be a rather desperate attempt to show rebellion and still enjoy the security of association. Like other groups in Japan, the Bamboo Shoot Tribe is divided into several subgroups, each with its own leader. Rather than true rebellion, such demonstrations seem to be more an escape valve for the frustrations of youth in a tightly organized and controlled society.

In non-work-related activities, there is a clear trend among young people to want more freedom and individuality. But when that coveted job is found in a prestigious Japanese company, these same *shinjinrui* often fall readily into the mould of hard-working, dedicated salarymen. On balance, it seems fair to say that most Japanese, as well as Americans, continue to give work a high priority in their lives.

The meaning of motivation

Motivation is both the foundation and the ultimate measure of success of a management system. Indeed, the stimulation, direction, and control of a person's will to work is of vital importance in the progress of nations, industries, and firms. Its critical role in the stability of society was stressed by an eminent industrial psychologist more than thirty years ago in these terms: 'Upon work depend all other pursuits of man. Hence, permanence of a social system – of a civilization – is determined by its ability to maintain and direct to its desired ends the will-to-work' (Viteles 1953: 475).

At the corporate level, what are these 'desired ends' to which the will-to-work of employees everywhere should be directed? In very broad terms, increasing market share and maintaining profitability might qualify as desired corporate goals. But for the manager in his daily tasks of leadership, a more workable concept is needed. For management it seems best to interpret organizational goals as simply the idea of achieving desired worker responses. These, after all, constitute the behaviour patterns sought by management and, therefore, are the relevant outputs which employees must integrate with their own individual needs.

For example, one useful guide suggests that 'management desires three responses from workers' (Harbison and Meyers 1959: 48–9). These are: (1) subordination, (2) loyalty, and (3) productivity. Subordination refers to the willingness of workers to take orders and to recognize the need for certain management prerogatives, including that of maintaining discipline. Loyalty is used in the sense of a positive identification with the company and a willingness to share its fate. Productivity refers simply to the rather obvious requirement that workers produce efficiently.

The Japanese generally score high on these three valued responses. Employees enter, and work within, a rather rigid hierarchy of which subordination is a part. Loyalty, and a multiphasic lifetime involvement with a single company, is a well-known feature of the employment system. Finally, productivity must be considered satisfactory, though long-term diligence and steady output are more important than maximizing productivity in the short run.

Motivation, then, means the ability of management to create an environment in which employees are able and willing to demonstrate these desired responses and to work towards corporate goals. An essential ingredient is that corporate goals are seen to be identical with, or at least contributory to, the individual's own needs. Many sophisticated theories have been developed dealing with the complex subject of motivation. Let us now look at two such theories which are best-known to business executives.

Motivation theories

Unfortunately, theoretical discussions of motivation by Japanese scholars are not developed in language and form to be widely understood in many other countries. On the other hand, such Western theorists as A. H. Maslow and Frederick Herzberg are widely known and often quoted in Japanese literature. The fact is that such theories, with some modification, seem to fit quite well in Japan. For example, in such affluent societies as Japan and the United States, the Maslow theory of 'prepotency' of needs has equal application. In both countries, the lower-level biological and safety (security) needs generally are satisfied by the vast majority of citizens. Therefore, meeting higher-level ego, social, and self-fulfilment needs comes into focus as a driving force. These needs are quite universal, though the means to meet them may vary widely among management systems.

Similarly, if we look at Herzberg's two-dimensional motivation theory, only slight modification is needed to make it applicable and helpful in the Japanese situation. Several 'maintenance factors', such as peer and supervisory relations, are important enough to be shifted to the 'motivator' category. And some of the motivators, such as achievement, advancement, and recognition need only to be expressed in group rather than individual terms to fit the collectivism of Japanese corporate life.

The data in Table 10 from the author's study in Japanese and US factories tend to support this view. Note that those selecting items 1 and 2 accounted for 80 per cent of Japanese and 70 per cent of US replies. There was no significant difference between the two sets of responses. In both cases, money was not seen as a primary reason for working hard on the job.

Table 10: Motivation

I believe workers are willing to work hard on their jobs because:

1	2	3	4
they want to live up to the expectations of their family, friends, and society;	they feel it is their responsibility to the company and to co-workers to do whatever work is assigned to them;	the harder they work the more likely they are to be promoted over others to positions of greater responsibility	the harder they work, the more money they expect to earn.
Japan 34%	Japan 46%	Japan 7%	Japan 13%
US 17%	US% 53%	US 15%	US 15%

Source: Takezawa and Whitehill 1981: 55

As Professor Herzberg wisely reminds us, 'The latent values of all people through all recorded history have been the same. The joker is that the diverse *manifest* needs must be managed' (Herzberg 1929). These latter needs, he feels, are expressed in confusing code words such as tradition, rights, participation, and quality of work life. However verbalized, satisfying the basic human needs of employees must be accepted by managers as an essential prerequisite to reaping the benefits of a truly motivated workforce.

Sources of motivation

In direct questioning by this writer, a large number of Japanese managers have expressed their opinions regarding the factors in the company which motivate them to work long and hard to accomplish corporate goals. Some of the sources of motivation such as responsibility, challenge, interesting work, and recognition are familiar in Western nations as well as in Japan. But several factors perceived as prime motivators by the Japanese are rather surprising to foreign business executives.

For example, the single source of motivation mentioned most frequently was the seniority wage and promotion system (*nenko joretsu*). Though American labour unions emphasize seniority in making personnel decisions, most managers see it as a distinctly negative factor. The prevailing view is that relying too heavily on length of service will encourage laziness and complacency.

In the American context this may be true. Not so, however, in Japan. An executive from a leading oil company explained it this way: 'When our company follows *nenko joretsu* we can work hard at ease and without anxiety.' A great deal of insight is conveyed in this brief statement. Under a seniority system, struggles for power, building little 'empires', and destructive levels of interpersonal competition for promotion and pay can be put aside.

With lifetime employment every person can look forward to a secure career with normal progression and salary increases. Therefore, each employee may devote his or her full energy to achievement of group and corporate goals. And such achievement is, after all, the end product of motivation. This is an excellent example of the need for a systems approach to management. The vital interdependence of components in each system can mean that the impact of a factor such as seniority may be positive in one and negative in another.

Other intriguing responses were offered by Japanese managers in interviews. One said that the primary reason he worked hard was 'to make his goal so that upper-level goals could be achieved', and added that he did not want 'to cause trouble for other members of his group'. Such comments clearly indicate the importance of group harmony and cohesiveness in motivating all members of a Japanese corporate family.

Less frequently mentioned motivators still having a distinctly Japanese flavour included: drinking with fellow employees; personal, friendly leadership; an 'at home', friendly atmosphere; overnight excursions; job rotation; and company sports programmes. The quality of supervision, and the friendship and respect of one's peers, loom large among the factors contributing to the high motivation level of Japanese workers.

When Japanese employees are motivated, enthusiastic participants in working for company goals, they are sometimes described as *konjo ga aru*. They are people who have willpower and a 'fighting spirit' to get things done even against great odds. To their bosses, such subordinates can be trusted to carry out the most difficult assignment without complaint.

An important cornerstone underlying the high motivation of most Japanese employees is the fact that the principle of equality prevails in business. A well-known author and executive states it this way: 'Japanese business organizations paradoxically use the principle of equality to motivate employees to compete and simultaneously to cooperate with one another' (Takeuchi 1985: 18). A good point is made that individuals in the Japanese *kaisha* do compete. But such interpersonal competition is aimed at gaining the more desirable position assignments and special considerations in long-term career development rather than at getting an immediate promotion or salary increase.

To a Japanese, the dichotomy seen by American workers between competition and cooperation is a false one. The Japanese way to compete is through teamwork – by working with and through one's group in a way that gradually will be recognized by higher levels in the organization. Americans try to gain instant distinction on a fast track early in their careers; Japanese seek distinction twenty to twenty-five years into their careers. But teamwork is the vehicle, and recognition comes nearer the end of one's long career.

Does this blending of teamwork and competition work? At least to date it has seemed to be successful and is completely congruent with the general philosophy of the Japanese firm. As two authorities on Japan point out: 'The company can call for, and reasonably expect, levels of effort and quality of output that are only exceptionally available in most other employment systems' (Abegglen and Stalk 1987: 207).

A similar viewpoint has been expressed by Mr Takashi Ishihara, president of Nissan Motor Company, in discussing the enviable vitality of Japanese corporations. One of the two factors he sees as most important in contributing to that vitality is 'the thorough organization of all members of a company into an integrated group oriented toward long-term company growth. Rather than serving as mere corporate bodies, companies in Japan usually function very much as social entities – social bodies comprised of all employees' (Ishihara 1983).

The other source of corporate vitality this executive considers of prime importance is the separation of ownership and management. Individual shareholders in Japanese corporations have little interest in active intervention in corporate affairs. The bulk of most big companies' capital stock is held by a combination of financial institutions, insurance companies, business corporations, and a variety of public investors whose primary investment goal is long-term capital gains rather than short-term dividends. 'Managers,' Mr Ishihara concludes, 'are therefore free to manage as they see fit, concentrating on long-term company growth' (Ishihara 1983).

The Japanese do not have the complete and final answer to the complex problem of human motivation. There is however, much food for thought in the singular success of Japanese managers in creating an environment in which all employees identify their own interests with those of the company and are motivated to strive actively for the goals of the organization. Identifying each individual's contribution to attaining these goals requires evaluation. It is to this problem that attention is now turned.

Evaluating performance

The evaluation and comparison of individual performance is a difficult and frustrating task at best. In Japan it is particularly difficult because of the long-standing emphasis upon group activity and overall results rather than individual 'track records'. Most experts everywhere agree that performance evaluation is one of the least satisfactory procedures in management. Yet employees always will be compared, even if it is simply a rough-and-ready opinion that Imai-san is a 'better man' than Suzuki-san. The challenge is to find a reasonably objective appraisal system which will be most useful in a specific corporate climate for a particular group of employees.

To compare one human being with another, except in those rare cases when both are considered equal, means that one must win – and one must lose. To suffer this latter fate is to suffer a painful loss of face among one's fellow employees. Furthermore, to convey the bad news to the loser – the less competent subordinate – is a burdensome and distasteful assignment for most supervisors.

Nevertheless, the need to compare individual contributions to corporate goals remains. Effective employee development depends upon an ability to evaluate performance, to identify individual needs, and to provide opportunities for personal growth. How to meet this challenge remains an unsolved puzzle for executives everywhere. In this chapter we shall examine the attempts made to resolve the dilemmas involved in performance appraisal programmes in Japanese corporations. When appropriate, reference will be made to the far longer experience of American companies in dealing with this basic management problem.

Evaluation systems

Systems and standards for performance appraisal vary among companies in Japan as they do among companies of any nation. Based upon observation of a number of US and Japanese companies, the author has concluded that there is a continuum of appraisal methods ranging from the most subjective to the most objective procedures. At the subjective end would be an annual review by the supervisor in brief, descriptive terms. There would be no follow-up with ratees, and decisions concerning salary and position changes would be made unilaterally by management. Obviously, such an approach has many problems – questionable validity of factors considered predictive of future performance, lack of reliability among raters and over time by the same rater, personal bias and favouritism, and others.

Dissatisfaction and frustration caused by loose, subjective appraisals start the pendulum swinging toward the objective end of the continuum. Such devices as simple ranking, checklists of desirable behaviour, reference to critical incidents, and finally the use of a variety of graphic rating scales are likely to be tried. The scales themselves become more complicated and lengthy as attempts are made to standardize and validate each of the factors being rated and the degrees to which subordinates are judged to demonstrate each of the factors. A bulky manual often is compiled and supervisors are urged to study and use the complex procedures it contains.

At this point, the appraisal system may be more objective but the question now is whether it can be understood – and trusted – by subordinates or their superiors. In many cases the manuals are discarded and the pendulum swings once again toward the subjective end of this unhappy continuum.

Having made the point that there is no easy answer for managers to the challenge of interpersonal evaluation and comparison, it may be useful to see what employees – those being evaluated – think is the best procedure to use. Table 11 shows what response we got to this question in our study in Japanese and American factories.

Table 11: Performance

In order to maximize satisfaction of workers, the best management policy is to:

1	2	3	4
make evaluations and inform each worker of both his strengths and weaknesses so he will know where he stands;	make evaluations and comparisons, and encourage better workers by informing them of their strengths;	make evaluations and comparisons, but keep the results secret;	avoid, whenever possible, evaluation and comparison of individual performance.
Japan 30%	Japan 22%	Japan 31%	Japan 17%
US 70%	US 11%	US 4%	US 15%

Source: Takezawa and Whitehill 1981: 85

Several generalizations may be drawn from these responses. First, few employees in either country believe it is possible to 'avoid evaluation and comparison of individual performance' (item 4). The first three items accept the need for evaluation but offer different procedures. Full disclosure of both the 'good news' and the 'bad news' proposed in item 1 was chosen by fewer than a third of Japanese interviewed but by more than two-thirds of US workers. A second generalization, therefore, is that Americans like to 'know where they stand', while Japanese typically prefer a greater degree of ambiguity. Looking at items 2 and 3, a final generalization may be that a substantial proportion of Japanese employees do not want their weaknesses discussed. In fact, almost one-third would be happy if appraisal results were 'kept secret' and not discussed at all.

The spread among all items by Japanese participants clearly shows a lack of unanimity concerning the most satisfactory appraisal method. The response pattern reflects an underlying confusion among corporate personnel officers as to the best appraisal methods to be used. Until very recently, almost complete reliance had been placed upon *nenko*, or years of service, as the basis for promotion and salary decisions. But with the need for tighter controls and cost savings during recent years of low growth, there has been no escaping the need for evaluating individual performance and increasing efficiency. As a result, merit rating has assumed an important role in personnel management.

Table 12: A definition of qualification ranks

Classification	Definition
Shukan	1) Employees capable of performing the tasks requiring a high level of knowledge and a capacity to plan and make judgement in accordance with the normal business practices.
	2) Employees capable of performing the job of *sagyocho* (foreman); other jobs requiring a high level of skills, or a job similar in nature to that of foreman.
Shuji	1) Employees capable of performing a job requiring a considerable degree of work experience, knowledge, and judgement, in accordance with the normal business practices.
	2) Employees capable of performing the job of *kacho* (team leader) or the job requiring considerable skills, or a job similar in nature to that level of *kacho*.
Shumu	1) Employees with the potential to become skilful in their job and able to apply abilities already acquired while working within prescribed standards under the guidance of a supervisor or the superior.
	2) Potentially skilful employees able to work under the guidance of a supervisor or other superior, and capable of training workers in the Tanto rank.
Tanto	Employees capable of working within prescribed standards under the supervision and guidance of a supervisor or other superior.

Source: Nippon Kokan no Shain-seido ni kansuru Kyoteisho (A Collective Agreement on the Personnel System at Nippon Kokan), July 1981.

Qualification systems

According to Takeshi Inagami, Hosei University Professor and Research Officer for The Japan Institute of Labour, an ability-based appraisal system (*shikakuseido*) emphasizing employees' performance has become widespread among private enterprises in Japan. The evaluation plan, or qualification system, used in a major steel company is offered for illustrative purposes (Inagami 1983).

In this case, all employees up to the level of sub-section chief are classified into four ranks as shown in Table 12. Each rank is further divided into several grades. High school graduates are hired at the *Tanto* grade 3 level; university graduates enter at *Shumu* grade 1. The definitions given in Figure 15 justify this distinction in terms of differing capabilities and potential.

Different qualification points are awarded to new employees depending upon their educational attainment. In addition, maximum 'preparation periods' for advancement are set. Thus the hallowed criteria of education and length of service continue to be important. However, additional qualification points, on a seven-point scale running from excellent to very poor, are assigned on the basis of an annual performance review.

Without going into further details concerning the qualification system, we can see that there is a trend towards a combination of ability with seniority and education in making personnel decisions. Within this framework it becomes necessary to develop procedures for periodic appraisal of individual job performance. The following section will outline the criteria and methods typical of many Japanese evaluation systems.

Criteria and procedures

In any evaluation of performance the criteria, or factors considered to be relevant and valuable, must be selected. In other words, traits and patterns of behaviour must be selected which seem closely related to present and future job success. Furthermore, a decision must be made concerning the procedures to be used in the design and administration of a plan, and in the use to be made of results. Each of these matters deserves brief explanation.

Selection of criteria

In general, the list of criteria used by Japanese firms in evaluating employees is far broader and more comprehensive than that found in American firms. This is natural since job assignments in Japan are more fluid and general in nature. Let us not forget that educational level and length of service still weigh heavily in evaluating personnel.

There are three general guidelines which should be followed in selecting factors for any system of evaluation: first, they must be relevant to the level and type of work performed; second, they must be clear in meaning; and third, they must be valid in the sense that they accurately reflect good job performance.

An example of separation of employees according to level is found in a Japanese high-technology company with just over 1,000 employees. Although the firm has a total of eleven ranks under the president, it is considered sufficient for evaluation purposes to divide employees into three general classes: junior employees, senior employees, and managers. For all levels, criteria are divided into the categories of performance, attitudes, and general abilities. For junior-level employees, such factors as quality and volume of output, reliability, and the ability to follow directions are emphasized.

Senior employees also are evaluated on these same factors, but goal achievement becomes more quantified, creativity and motivation assume greater importance, and ability to instruct and influence subordinates is added to the skills required. For managers, decisiveness, the ability to identify and solve problems, and skill in foreseeing important future trends become high-priority criteria in performance appraisal. Unless otherwise specified, all levels of employees are rated with the following grades: S – superior; A – above average; B – average; C – below average; and D – inferior.

As mentioned earlier, the same criteria may not be relevant for different types of work even at the same general level. For example, junior-level employees in a bank may include tellers and maintenance workers. A relevant criterion for the former (for example, responsibility for funds) may have no bearing on the latter's job. For him, the ability to withstand uncomfortable working conditions may be a prime requirement and will be included in the evaluation. Experience indicates quite clearly that one approach, or one set of criteria, will not fit all employees. Therefore, different systems and forms must be used to fit the special needs of the organization.

In addition, a second guideline must be observed in selecting criteria. They must be clear in meaning so that raters will be consistent in their use. What do 'responsibility for funds' in the case of the bank teller, or 'physical stamina' in rating maintenance workers, really mean? Through training and the use of manuals, consistency is sought. But it is very difficult to get completely reliable interpretation of factors among different raters with different values and experiences.

A third guideline is that criteria must be valid. By this is meant that the measures used must truly reflect successful job performance at the employee's present level as well as be predictive of success at the next higher level of work. Validation studies take a great deal of time, and require the assistance of persons skilled in their construction and use.

From the discussion it is clear that selection of criteria is a necessary, but extremely difficult, first step in evaluating performance. Japanese executives are struggling to select criteria that meet the tests of relevance, clarity, and validity. But the heavy hand of tradition keeps the importance of education and length of service foremost in the minds of those responsible for performance appraisal. It is true that half a century of experience in American firms has produced a vast amount of experimentation and volumes of research. Unfortunately, however, this has not resulted in a great deal more confidence or satisfaction with present evaluation programmes.

Who does appraisals?

Though the immediate supervisor is the most likely person in a Japanese company to conduct appraisals, additional sources of evaluation sometimes are sought. For example, in the high-technology company described above, junior workers are rated only by their immediate supervisor. A senior employee, however, is interviewed by his boss and then asked to evaluate his own performance. His boss adds his own appraisal to this self-evaluation and passes the documents on to the next higher level for completion of the final evaluation.

A similar procedure is used at the management level. Managers are assumed to be quite familiar with the purpose and practice of the evaluation system. At this stage, they are given the opportunity to write brief paragraph statements in answer to three key questions, and then to pass the evaluation forms to their superiors. The superior writes out his comments about the manager's performance and then grades him on various criteria. The opinion of a second superior is then added. Multiple ratings of this sort at the managerial level are not uncommon.

There has been some experimentation in the United States with peer rating – that is, everybody in a department rates everybody else. The results have been unsatisfactory in most cases, and disastrous in several instances with which the author is familiar. In Japan, the idea of rating one's co-workers and turning the results over to a superior would be totally unacceptable behaviour and is not likely to be tried in the forseeable future.

Rating frequency and use of results

Paradoxically, Japanese companies rate their employees' performance more frequently than US companies, but usually delay explicit use of the results for several years or more. For example, in the high-technology company referred to earlier, all employees are rated twice a year. This is not unusual, and some companies go through evaluation three times a year.

In the vast majority of US firms, performance appraisal is an annual event. Though done just once each year, it is considered an extremely time-consuming and distracting procedure. For several weeks before 'appraisal time', work suffers as employees attempt to gather evidence to impress their supervisors – or to behave in a way that will draw favourable attention to themselves. The appraisal procedure itself may take a month or more depending upon the number of people to be rated. Then the agonizing post-appraisal interviews begin, with the usual frustrations among those not receiving the highest rating. In a very real sense, this is non-productive time, and a period of anxiety and tension for all concerned. Little wonder that American companies seldom attempt to suffer more than one performance evaluation each year.

The same high level of apprehension does not seem to characterize job evaluation in Japanese firms. One reason is that post-appraisal interviews seldom are conducted. When supervisors do discuss results with subordinates the talks tend to be supportive, rather than threatening, in nature. Most important, they are not directly related to any immediate salary or promotion decisions.

Evaluation results in Japan become a part of the individual's personnel file. A single evaluation seldom is used as the basis for any immediate action. Instead, over a period of years the appraisals provide a useful profile of each employee's maturity and growth in becoming a useful, productive member of the corporate family. Perhaps five to ten years later, when important decisions will be made concerning new job assignments or promotion to a managerial position, this record of career development will be carefully reviewed.

Is performance evaluation necessary?

With the almost universal complaints and dissatisfaction associated with performance evaluation programmes, it may be appropriate to ask 'Why do it?' Thus far, with the important differences noted above, most large Japanese and American companies have a formal appraisal system. Most feel that evaluation and comparison of individual performance are an essential feature of efficient management.

One notable dissenter to this conventional wisdom is W. Edwards Deming, an American statistical expert who has become a national hero in Japan. Deming, who had pioneered statistical quality control for a largely unappreciative American audience, was invited to Japan in 1950. The invitation came from a prestigious group, the Union of Japanese Scientists and Engineers (JUSE).

Dr Deming's success in Japan was little short of miraculous. Within ten years, almost 20,000 engineers had been trained in statistical methods, and Japan was well on her way to another economic miracle – this time, quality products that would astound the world. In 1951, the Japanese established the Deming Prize for outstanding success in statistical analysis and application. To further show their profound appreciation, in 1960 the Japanese awarded Deming the Second Order of the Sacred Treasure – the first American to receive such an honour.

It was not until he reached 80 years of age that Deming was

'discovered' in his home country. But discovery did not mean universal acceptance. Deming and his doctrines continue to be the subject of heated debate among American engineers and business executives. Many agree with a Minnesotan executive who, after a Deming seminar, argued, 'We can't adopt an unrefined Japanese approach. We don't lockstep!'

Directly relevant to the present discussion is the fact that, over and over again, Dr Deming has preached that performance appraisal is wrong because it focuses on short-term results. Rating employees, whether by rating scales or by the popular management by objectives (MBO) programmes, is referred to by Deming as 'management by fear', which he is convinced can only have devastating results. In fact, he accuses all annual performance reviews of destroying teamwork, building fear, and leaving people 'bitter, despondent, and beaten' (Walton 1986: 36).

Many reasons could be given, most of which go far beyond the scope of this discussion, for Dr Deming's incredible success in Japan compared with his lukewarm acceptance in the United States. His arguments seem persuasive, but the real need for measuring individual contributions to organizations simply will not go away.

In concluding this discussion of performance evaluation, it seems fair to say that most Japanese companies will listen to, and learn from, the Deming management method. At the same time, they will continue their low-key, long-term approach to performance evaluation as an essential element of the Japanese management system.

Motivation and evaluation continue to be two of the most perplexing areas of business management. Yet they hold the key to improving organizational efficiency, an objective prominent in the 'wish books' of business leaders everywhere. While the present chapter has raised more questions than it has answered, there are few really good answers presently available. On this inconclusive note we now turn our attention in the next chapter to the fascinating, and equally challenging, topic of communication.

References

Abegglen, J. C. and Stalk, Jr, G. (1987) *Kaisha: The Japanese Corporation*, Tokyo: Charles E. Tuttle Company.

Harbison, F. and Meyers, C. A. (1959) *Management in the Industrial World*, New York: McGraw-Hill Book Company Inc.

Herzberg, F. (1929) 'Herzberg on motivation for the 80s' *Industry Week*, 1 October: 58.

Inagami, T. (1983) 'Labor–management communication at the workshop level', *Japanese Industrial Relations Series* 11: 15–18.

Ishihara, T. (1983) 'Japanese corporate vitality,' *Liberal Star*, 10 January: 6.

Takeuchi, H. (1985) 'Motivation and productivity', in L. C. Thurow (ed.) *The Management Challenge: Japanese Views*, Cambridge, Mass.: MIT Press.

Takezawa, S. and Whitehill, A. M. (1981) *Work Ways: Japan and America*, Tokyo: The Japan Institute of Labour.

Viteles, M. S. (1953) *Motivation and Morale In Industry*, New York: W. W. Norton and Company Inc.

Walton, M. (1986) *The Deming Management Method*, New York: Dodd, Mead & Company.

Chapter eleven

Communication

Every writer approaches the topic of communication with some uneasiness. The word itself means so many different things to different people. There is, of course, a technical meaning when we speak of telecommunications, management information systems, smart buildings, intelligent robots, or computerized translation capabilities. It is difficult to visualize the interdependent global community we inhabit today without the wizardry of such state-of-the-art communication facilities. However, this technical concept clearly is beyond the scope of the present volume.

Instead, the focus of this discussion will be upon communication as a uniquely difficult and challenging aspect of the Japanese management system. Communication in Japan, whether in-company, between companies, or on an international level, is a particularly hazardous affair both because of the language itself and the inner-directed orientation of the people.

One of Japan's keenest observers comments on the latter problem as follows: 'It is time that Japan learned to communicate in ways that enable the world to understand it better . . . Very few people in Japan have made an effort to make themselves or their country understood' (Ohmae 1987: 43). As for the inherent difficulty of the Japanese language, St Francis Xavier, the sixteenth-century Jesuit missionary, is said to have described it as 'the devil's tongue'. For those few foreign executives in Japan struggling in early-morning language classes the description is as apt today as it was four centuries ago.

The president of one of America's largest household products companies once defined communication simply as 'the process of sharing information and understanding among people'. There are several reasons why this is a particularly good definition for our purposes.

First, it emphasizes the fact that communication is a process, not merely a single event. The process begins with an idea which must be put into language which the intended receiver can understand. Then it must be conveyed to the receiver. While receiving the information, that person will interpret it in terms which are most meaningful for him or her. Based on this interpretation, the receiver is then able to respond or take some other action. This process may be diagrammed as follows: ideation–encoding–transmission–reception–decoding–action.

Second, our simple definition makes the point that communication is a two-way process. The word 'sharing' makes this clear. In fact, the word communication is derived from such roots as 'common', or 'communion', both of which imply the quality of sharing. In short, one person alone cannot communicate; it takes two or more people to share information and feelings.

Finally, the definition tells us that understanding is the ultimate goal of the process. Communicating is not just the use of words – spoken or written. Unless true understanding results, no communication has taken place.

Many years ago, one of Harvard University's most illustrious professors, Fritz Roethlisberger, said: 'I know of no human relations problem which is not in some way the manifestation of a breakdown in communication.' It is difficult to disagree with this evaluation. Whether a problem is related to business, finances, international negotiations, or intimate personal relations, the real cause typically lies in a failure to communicate effectively.

From management's viewpoint, there seem to be three major concerns in dealing with the development of effective communication: (1) promoting effective communication within the company – written, oral, and non-verbal; (2) assuring wise use of Japan's active and efficient mass media; and (3) surmounting the incredible problems in international communication. Each of these important areas will be discussed in the sections which follow.

In-house communication

It is useful to think of communication within a company as being of three types: written, oral, and non-verbal. Writing is, in a sense, a last resort for Japanese business executives. If at all possible, they will choose to talk directly with another individual or group. A great deal of time and attention, therefore, in a Japanese firm is devoted to oral communication, whether person-to-person or in groups. Finally, because non-verbal communication – communicating without words – is such a continuous, subtle process among the Japanese it, too, is an important part of the total communication process.

Written communication

In any company, Japanese or American, certain basic information and statistics must be reduced to writing. Annual reports to stockholders and to government agencies, compliance reports to regulatory bodies, letters which contain complex information to persons at a considerable distance from the writer, and notices to employees concerning important company policies and actions are just a few of the items which must be put on paper.

Preparing such necessary documents is a universal chore which managers everywhere cannot escape. But the veritable flood of letters, memos and reports circulated in most US firms constantly amazes Japanese managers. To the Japanese, written communication is considered cold, formal, and lacking in the reciprocal give-and-take they consider so essential to true sharing of understanding.

Short, terse letters are looked upon with particular disfavour by the Japanese. Strict traditionalists will not, for example, write a letter of only one page. A short, succinct letter of a paragraph or two – direct and to the point – is considered rude. It is far better to begin with a rambling introduction dealing with matters of general or personal concern before getting to the real purpose of the letter. Little wonder that 'business-like' letters received from foreign correspondents frequently are filed away, unanswered and forgotten, by Japanese managers.

This antipathy towards writing even extends to personal conduct in meetings. As Dr Kiyoshi Nagata, Research Director of Mitsubishi Research Institute, points out, 'Many Japanese businessmen won't take any notes during a meeting. Top managers especially are supposed to be good listeners, with no memo pads or pens.' Then he warns, 'Moreover, you are not expected to bring your steno or your secretary to take minute notes when attending meetings with the Japanese' (Nagata 1984).

Added to the general dislike of putting words on paper is the inherent complexity of the Japanese written language. With two phonetic alphabets of fifty characters each (*hiragana* and *katakana*), plus literally thousands of Chinese ideograms (*kanji*), Japanese typewriters resemble small printing presses. Fortunately, computers have come to the rescue, and software programs now allow quick reproduction of the many complicated, multi-stroke characters.

Thus far, however, the advent of PC's has had little impact on the communication habits of the present generation of Japanese managers. They still have little use for written documents no matter how produced. A Japanese friend told the author that he would not want to carry necessary written materials to a meeting. Instead, he delegates this menial task to a junior assistant.

It follows, therefore, that files in Japanese companies tend to be both haphazard and personal in nature. Secretaries often do not know the system or the substance of their bosses' files. Therefore, it is not considered good form for an employee to request a particular written item which has been filed by a fellow worker. The chances are good that neither he nor his secretary will know where to find it.

An American pastime that the Japanese simply do not understand is the continuous drafting of inter-office memos. They cannot believe that such notes are exchanged frequently between managers occupying adjoining offices. 'Why not,' they ask, 'just get up and go talk to the guy?' But the American obsession with putting everything in writing, and then making multiple copies to make sure everyone has the same information, continues to support the most prolific paper and copier industries in recorded history.

Oral communication

There are so many occasions for oral communication in the workplace that it is impossible even to list them all. One-on-one interpersonal communication includes providing instructions, exchanging work information, issuing orders, handling complaints, listening to suggestions, or counselling a troubled employee, to mention just a few.

There is an important difference in the perception of Japanese and American managers concerning the exchange of information. To the Japanese, secure in their jobs and confident of regular promotions, sharing information freely and openly seems a natural way to contribute to the success of the work group. Americans, on the other hand, equate information with power. Because of this, they tend to hoard any data which they alone might have, doling out only so much as is absolutely necessary at any given time. With such a storehouse of private information, individuals hope to make themselves invaluable to the company and to draw favourable attention to themselves at some future time.

As mentioned earlier, verbal interaction between supervisor and subordinate in Japanese firms is easy and natural due to the lack of private offices and the open layout of office space. The close proximity of all members of a work group encourages spontaneous conversation. Even senior executives usually are available to be talked to simply by walking up to them. Foreign visitors are amazed at the degree of 'togetherness' seen in the large, rather noisy rooms having as many as a dozen distinct work groups identified only by the cluster of desks in front of the supervisor. On the other hand, the Japanese have been found generally to prefer 'significantly greater conversational, inter-personal distance than Americans' (Barnlund 1989: 138).

All telephone conversations made by the supervisor or one of his subordinates are easily heard by every member of the work group. Therefore, everyone is kept up-to-date with what is going on. If an individual lowers his voice during a telephone conversation it is assumed that he is conducting strictly personal business on company time – a practice that is not encouraged.

To avoid distraction by the many activities going on in these busy workplaces, outside visitors are ushered into one of the small conference rooms adjacent to the large room. Since it is not customary to 'drop in' on business contacts without an appointment, conference rooms typically are reserved in advance. Supplied with ample reading materials and comforted by a cup of green tea, the visitor will wait for his contact to join him – usually ten to fifteen minutes after the appointed time as it is likely a desk-side conversation with a subordinate must first be completed. Since this is 'par for the course', no apology is offered or expected for the delay.

Face-to-face communication, whether with co-workers or outsiders, frequently is continued at a restaurant during long lunch hours or after the workday is over. In such situations, very little of the discussion will deal directly with the business at hand. But keen observation of others, and the exchange of subtle signals among colleagues, mean that this usually is not strictly a social affair.

Even between top-level executives and regular employees, attempts are made to establish the warmth of direct oral communication. In Japan's largest trading company, for example, the president talks directly to all employees several times a year. His New Year's talk, via the public address system, tells employees his hopes and plans for the coming year. In addition, he personally chairs special conferences for all managers twice a year, and meets with the presidents of smaller related companies (*kogaisha*) on an annual basis.

Turning now to the subject of group meetings, we see that there is a vast difference in the ways that Japanese and American managers perceive their jobs. Ask any American executive 'How was your day?' It is likely that the answer will be: 'Terrible! I was tied up in meetings all day.' Unless a day's work results in some written product – some visible evidence of productivity – an American feels the day has been wasted.

In sharp contrast, the Japanese executive feels the day has been an especially rewarding one if it has been spent interacting on a personal basis with other employees or visitors. Whether on the telephone or face to face, oral exchange of views is considered by far the most effective vehicle for conducting business. Meetings provide an excellent medium for sharing information, exploring alternative courses of action, and getting to know the strengths and weaknesses of fellow employees or clients.

Not all communication, however, requires the use of words. It is to the important strategy of communicating without words that attention is now directed.

Non-verbal communication

Because the Japanese have a common history, language, and culture, they have developed the act of communicating their desires and feelings without words into a fine art. This process of feeling one another out on an issue is known as *haragei* , which literally means 'stomach language' or, less elegantly, 'belly talk'. A smile, a raised eyebrow, or a gesture to the receptionist to replenish the tea, can convey special meaning to those who are 'in' on the game being played.

Perhaps the type of *haragei* with which Japanese business executives are most skilled is the prolonged silence. Extremely painful to Westerners, periods of silence are treasured by many Japanese as the most productive time spent in meetings. This writer's own frequent experiences in meeting with groups of Japanese managers has led me to agree that silence, even when accompanied by closed eyes, does not necessarily mean a period of rest. Rather, this is a time for mental summary, sorting out of relevant facts, and reaching a tentative conclusion – tentative because any decision will become final only when all those involved have concurred. Getting a consensus before taking action is the *ringi* system discussed earlier in Chapter 8.

This discussion of non-verbal communication may be a good time to explain a distinction which influences many negotiations in Japan – the distinction between *honne* and *tatemae*. In dealing with others, *honne* is what you really intend to do or say; *tatemae*, on the other hand, is the facade of what one should do or say because of one's position or current situation. Masaaki Imai offers the following excellent illustration of this subtle difference by recalling the following story of a researcher who was at a government office to collect some data:

> Although it was not classified information, the official was reluctant to give it out, since it was not meant to be made public at the time. Instead, he said, 'I am not in a position to provide you with this information. However, as a researcher you are free to pick papers up off the floor and look at them if you wish.' So saying, he casually dropped the sheet of paper with the statistics on it and left the room for a few minutes. In this case, the *tatemae* was that he could not disclose the information to an outsider, but his *honne* was that he wanted to be helpful.
>
> (Imai 1981: 13)

This is not an isolated incident. The author recently asked the director of a Japanese management institute if it would be possible to add reimbursement for travel expenses to his consulting fee.

The answer was, 'Sorry – that simply is not done here' (*tatemae*). But when future payments were received they did, in fact, include the extra amount (*honne*). Such an experience is quite common in Japan.

The mass media

With a functional illiteracy rate of less than 1 per cent, few people in the world are as well-equipped as the Japanese to get the most out of their mass media. Added to this is an insatiable curiosity and a basic commitment to lifelong personal development. Here you have the answer to why Japan is the most media-saturated country in the world. Japanese newspapers, weekly magazines, and TV are the major means for mass communication and they work extremely well.

Newspapers

Over 90 per cent of Japanese adults regularly read newspapers. In addition to numerous local and regional papers, Japan has three major national dailies – *Asahi Shimbun, Yomiuri Shimbun*, and *Mainichi Shimbun*. Together, these three newspaper giants sell more than 30 million copies a day. Total daily newspaper sales are estimated to be almost 70 million, and per capita newspaper sales in Japan are among the highest in the world (Tasker 1988: 110). This outpouring of news each day is devoured in the homes, on trains and buses, and even at work when time permits.

Because of their huge size, Japan's Big Three have almost unlimited resources. Each employs close to 10,000 staff, and reporters are an elite, high-status group. Company-owned limousines, planes, and helicopters back up the reporting staff. Their depth in foreign coverage is particularly impressive. Visiting Americans often claim that they learn more about the United States when they are in Tokyo than in New York.

With this sort of coverage and support, Japan's newspapers are among the best in the world. A reporter will spend years cultivating a close relationship with a rising politician, and the resulting insight contributes to an extremely high-quality product. Furthermore, each Japanese government office has its own press club, or *kisha kurabu*, to which all reporters covering the office belong. Needless to say, a politician sees to it that his relationship with his press club is carefully nurtured.

Unfortunately, foreign reporters find themselves quite isolated from prime sources because of the cliquish nature of the *kisha kurabu* and its ability to control access to its 'patrons'. A further criticism of the otherwise impressive Japanese press corps is the fact that its intimate relationship with the bureaucracy does put a damper on the sort of investigative reporting found in the United States. Even the Big Three sometimes allow themselves to be scooped by a weekly magazine to avoid revealing questionable activities of their long-standing close contacts. Except for these minor flaws, it is difficult to fault the Japanese daily press, perhaps the best trained and most productive in the world.

Magazines

In addition to their addiction to newspapers, the Japanese are avid readers of magazines. A recent count indicated that about 3,000 are published regularly. High in popularity are the weekly magazines with 105 titles available and sales of 1.7 billion copies a year. Vast supplies of these weeklies are delivered every morning to the train stations to satisfy the voracious appetites of commuters.

Weekly magazines have become so popular among young business executives today that they are called 'tickets to the new information society'. Most target a particular audience, though there are a number of general news magazines covering politics, economics, entertainment, and sports. In this general category, the Japanese-language editions of *Time* and *Newsweek* enjoy tremendous popularity. Then there are the women's magazines, targeting young office workers and housewives, which focus on fashion, cooking, and stories about famous personalities. There are even catalogue magazines to provide readers with guidelines to purchase the vast range of consumer goods on the market. Though some of the best-selling weekly magazines in Japan have been described as 'salacious, libellous, and utterly unreliable', the same source admits that the weeklies are 'the most vital of all information sources for anyone who wants to know what the Japanese are really thinking' (Tasker 1988: 118).

Television

Finally, mass communication in Japan today is dominated by the world's most highly developed television broadcasting system. Like Great Britain, Japan has both quasi-governmental and private channels. The majority of TV stations are operated by Nippon Hoso Kyokai (NHK), a public corporation largely financed by user fees paid by all owners of sets. The ample resources generated by these fees lead to an extremely high quality of programming. Some NHK stations devote themselves entirely to educational and cultural programmes, while others offer a limited selection of pure entertainment shows as well. NHK has its own symphony orchestra. Its dramatic productions are outstanding, and the many documentaries it produces are considered to be on a par with the famed BBC programmes.

Private TV stations specialize in pure entertainment programming with sumo matches, samurai duels, and hit-song programmes high in the popularity ratings. Regular classes in English and other foreign languages are also popular with the viewing audience. Whether watching a public or private station, one cannot help being impressed by the generally high quality of Japanese TV productions.

Considering their busy lives, it is hard to understand how the Japanese can manage to read everything in sight and still have time left over to watch TV. Numerous studies indicate, however, that the average Japanese spends more than three hours a day in front of the tube – as much time as that spent by Americans. With the excellent fare offered, it seems safe to say that television plays an important and constructive role in present-day Japanese society.

International communication

As the Japanese strive to become truly international people (*kokusai-jin*) in their view of, and relations with, the rest of the world, the need for new and improved communication skills can hardly be overstated. One management expert has concluded that communication is 'a bridge of meaning to safely cross the river of misunderstanding that separates all people.' To construct such a bridge to cross the vast oceans of misunderstanding that today surround Japan emerges as a tremendous challenge for the 1990s.

The usual problems encountered in written, oral, and non-verbal communication have a tendency to be magnified when on the international scene. As Robin A. Berrington, director of the Tokyo America Center, suggests, the most important source of difficulty is the different reasoning or thinking patterns of Japanese and Westerners. He illustrates such differences by recalling meetings at the Center during which Americans tended to be direct, asking questions that have an identifiable beginning and end. Japanese, on the other hand, tended to be more vague, posing questions which could only be implied from a statement. Berrington sums up by saying, 'The American wishes the Japanese could be more specific, more direct, and more challenging. The Japanese wishes the American would not be so specific, so direct, and so challenging. It is not just two different styles, it is two different ways of looking at how to deal with an issue' (Berrington 1985: 25).

The point that it is not just the Japanese language itself that creates international communication barriers is well made. Yet, the problem remains that few, if any, of Japan's overseas clients speak the language. Those whose native tongue is English should feel very lucky – and humble – that their language happens to be the language of international business. To the Japanese, this may seem to be unfair, but it is a fact of life that is not likely to go away. The many implications of this imbalance in language ability deserve further attention.

The language boom

Japanese managers who must communicate with foreign counterparts, whether in their own country or abroad, face a special communication hurdle. They must be fluent and comfortable in the true esperanto of international business – English. To achieve international understanding, managers need to be able to explain the major elements of their own management system to English-speaking contacts. In addition, they must know something about management practices, and the cultural context within which they take place, of the country with which they are dealing.

There are some optimistic individuals who assure us that Americans are busily learning Japanese and that soon the language scales will be in balance. It is true that Japanese is becoming increasingly popular in American schools and colleges. The Modern Language Association claims that college enrolments in Japanese language classes increased more than 40 per cent in the 1980s. At the high school level, California and Hawaii boast the largest enrolments. But even in far-distant New York state, twenty-five high schools offer Japanese courses.

All this, of course, is the good news. The bad news is that even today few business majors are studying Japanese. Most students of Japanese seem to be in the Humanities or the Arts. As a professor in the College of Business Administration at the University of Hawaii, the author has polled his classes on their language skills. In spite of the fact that more than half the class may be Americans of Japanese ancestry, few – very few – speak the language. Even at the MBA level, students are so engrossed in preparing to be high-level executives that they tend to push aside language instruction. It is, of course, a serious mistake.

The structural complexity alone of the Japanese language is a major barrier to its study. In addition, its subtlety and ambiguity seem to go beyond the average Westerner's comprehension. A well-known example is the many ways the Japanese avoid saying 'no'. To decline any request directly is very difficult. A simple 'no' might hurt the other person's feelings and make the speaker seem selfish and unfriendly. Some of the most common ploys to avoid this awkward situation are: (1) show your rejection by remaining silent; (2) ask a counter question as a distraction; (3) raise a totally different subject to derail the request; (4) simply exit without further comment; or (5) tell a lie – in this case a good trade-off for the unpleasant truth. One survey showed that the latter was the most-used path to avoid giving a negative answer.

Seasoned American business executives who frequently write to Japanese counterparts know that silence may also be used to avoid saying 'no' to a request from overseas. Business executives everywhere will, of course, have a natural tendency to put off answering any letter in a foreign language. But for the Japanese, reluctance soars when the reply must be negative. Therefore, simply not answering the letter is a very common way out of the dilemma. If more than two months pass without a reply, an anxious American would be well advised to recognize that the proposal has not been accepted.

The plain truth is that American business executives, present and future, simply will not make the tremendous personal sacrifice necessary to master spoken and written Japanese. This has been proved time and time again. Recently, a new institute was formed in Tokyo to cater exclusively to foreign managers, mostly Americans. Courses focused on the Japanese language, though some covered certain aspects of the Japanese management system. The writer warned that history offered ample proof that such a market was severely limited. Within two years the institute closed its doors because the few business executives who did enroll soon lost interest and dropped out.

This puts the ball squarely in the Japanese court. And, in predictable fashion, Japanese managers have been quick to accept the challenge. Once again, there is a veritable language boom in Japan – even greater than that in the post-Occupation period of the 1950s or during the time of the 1964 Tokyo Olympics. Wherever one goes in Japan, advertisements can be seen for English conversation classes. Roadside hoardings, underground walls, and bus cards as well as the newspapers, magazines, and TV carry the message. This is a big business and one that is growing larger every day.

There are at least two good reasons for this latest and greatest splurge on language instruction. First is the yen's rapid appreciation. Suddenly, and with very little warning, Japanese exporters have found it more profitable to produce overseas – and in some instances to then export back to Japan. These new foreign operations require that the whole Japanese staff, including management, engineers, and workers, learn to speak English.

Second, the rush of new 'business immigrants' to their shores has fuelled the need for the Japanese to learn English if they are to deal with these newcomers. Foreign lawyers, brokers, investment counsellors, management consultants, and a variety of entrepreneurs are setting up shop in Japan. As a result, the number of foreign residents – largely in Tokyo and Osaka – is sharply on the increase. This means that taxi drivers, waiters, kiosk attendants, as well as all the employees who work directly with the new wave of foreigners, must speak at least basic English.

The famed Berlitz Language Schools have enjoyed almost twenty-five years of successful experience in Japan's language-teaching market. With more than 30 schools throughout Japan, over 400 teachers, and more than 15,000 students, Berlitz clearly is a giant in the industry. Since Berlitz is a famous brand name and offers a quality service, the Japanese readily accept its leadership position and pay dearly for its instruction. For example, the tuition fee for a four-week total immersion course in which lessons are given from morning to night on a one-to-one basis is quoted at ¥1.4 million (about $10,000). Though all types of students are accepted, the businessman enrolled by his company remains Berlitz's prime market.

No one knows for sure just how large the total language training market really is. Some say it totals an incredible ¥10 trillion a year, comprising not only courses offered by schools such as Berlitz, but also correspondence courses, packaged manuals, tapes, and videos sold at bookstores, and even English telephone conversations offered by enterprising 'teachers' for perhaps ¥5,000 (about $38) per hour. Others are far more conservative, estimating total revenues at about ¥100 billion. Whatever the figure today, everyone agrees that the only direction in which the demand for English instruction can go is up! Already, it is estimated that 12 million persons, or one out of every ten in the population, are studying English in some way in Japan.

Not all English instruction, however, takes place in schools. For example, English 'tea salons' can be found in all of Japan's major cities. Japanese of all ages can attend for a small hourly fee or a modest maximum daily charge. Foreigners pay nothing in their role as informal instructors. Coffee, music, and magazines are free, and the opportunity to meet a variety of people with common interests is appealing. For those who already have some conversation ability, the tea salons can be excellent finishing schools – and even offer a chance to make new friends from a foreign country.

On an even less formal level are the frequent encounters with Japanese who approach foreigners appearing to be lost – a common dilemma. The businessman who went some distance out of his way to help the author meet a consulting appointment was indeed a friend in need. But it was also true that he received ten blocks of free English practice. Students, too, are not backward in using this approach on the underground and on trains to brush up their English conversation.

A persistent problem for Japanese managers studying English is the traditional separation of language training techniques from the content – that is, the principles, policies, and practices – of management. It is one thing to be able to direct a taxi driver or to order a meal in a restaurant. But it is quite another matter for a Japanese businessman to be able to give a thorough explanation in answer to the request, 'Please tell me all about the lifetime employment system we hear so much about.' Such unexpected requests all too often leave the Japanese manager speechless.

Furthermore, with the proliferation of Japanese subsidiaries and joint ventures in America from Maine to California, it has become essential that the Japanese management team be able to handle *managerial* English. The considerable friction between US and Japanese groups in such cooperative enterprises arises largely from the language barrier. The Japanese quite naturally discuss their problems in Japanese, and the Americans have no idea what they are 'plotting'. In one such case, the Americans commonly referred to their Japanese partners as 'the Japanese Mafia' – not a healthy state of affairs.

Some leading companies have recognized the need for English fluency on the part of their employees and are taking bold steps to deal with it. In 1987, C. Itoh Company, which has top sales among Japan's general trading companies, adopted a strict policy for its new recruits. After disappointment with the results of its regular English courses, the company enacted a 'no English, no promotion' policy for all new employees. Unless they pass a stiff exam, employees are disqualified for promotion from Class 3 to Class 2, which normally takes place in the fifth year of service. With sales shifting from exports to imports under pressure from the strong yen, not only those in export sales but every employee of the *sogo shosha* must be able to do business in English.

During the past ten years, the author has designed and promoted several highly successful programmes to meet the obvious need of Asian managers for English-language courses which combine the best of language-training techniques with the substance of international business. Known as 'Managers Speak English', and 'Let's Talk Business', these special courses have been offered by exclusive representatives to the employees of many leading companies in Japan, Korea, Taiwan, and Hong Kong. Toshiba, Sumitomo, Bridgestone Tire, Tokyo Electric, Hyundae, the International Bank of China, and many others have used these courses as a vehicle to develop the needed confidence and competence of their managers in dealing with business problems in English.

Much remains to be done in Japan if executives charged with international responsibilities are to be able to work in English. It is true that university graduates have already studied English for eight to ten years when they enter a company. But very few are able to use the language in their work assignments without additional training. In high school and university courses so much emphasis is placed on reading and writing that speaking and hearing skills are almost neglected. The pressing need now seems to be for specialized courses and well-trained instructors who can offer high-quality English education at a reasonable cost.

English in marketing

An interesting development in international communication is the mass marketing of consumer products incorporating English as a part of product design. In a very real sense, English in Japan has become an art form useful in attracting buyers to a variety of consumer goods.

This all started twenty years ago when the Sanrio Company introduced what it called 'shoppers' – shopping bags decorated with everything from Snoopy to 'Hello Kitty' characters. In addition, some of the most bizarre English yet produced accompanied the popular illustrations. Now equally mind-boggling phrases are found on T-shirts, stationery, pens, lunch boxes, clothes, and many other items. The fact is that for Japan's young people English, good or bad, is *kakko ii* – probably best translated as 'in' or 'now'. While foreigners attempt in vain to discover the meaning of the English phrases, very few Japanese even bother to read the words. The English has only an abstract visual effect and carries with it a sense of modernity and sophistication. A Sanrio executive admits that sometimes they take 'meaningless phrases' just to fit a particular design and space.

At any rate, the 'shoppers' and other items have found their way into Japan's export trade, and collecting them has become a fad in other Asian and Western countries throughout the world. The appealing characters, and the amazing English prose, combine to fascinate young consumers everywhere. Though such items hardly are an important medium for international communication, their use of English is a reflection of the widespread urge among Japanese to go beyond the traditional boundaries of their own language.

Thinking international

More than ever before, the Japanese are determined to become thoroughly international-minded and to communicate successfully with the rest of the world. And for them, communication with the outside world means knowledge of today's international language – English. We already have discussed a number of roadblocks standing in the way of achieving true internationalization: the language itself; reasoning patterns sharply different from those of Westerners; and the high cost and uncertain quality of training in English that is relevant for management purposes.

But perhaps the thorniest problem of all is the insular Japanese mentality. A leading expert on international competition and strategy, Kenichi Ohmae, offers this candid observation:

> Japan is at an awkward age between adolescence and adulthood. Its inability to form an accurate self-image is the greatest obstacle to its attaining maturity, for the key rite of passage in global society is acquiring the ability to view the world and oneself without bias. There is a real danger that unless we quickly succeed in weaning ourselves from our childhood illusions, we will repeat our past mistakes and be drawn into self-defeating isolation.
>
> (Ohmae 1987: 11)

Mr Ohmae and others are concerned that Japan will continue to overreact to foreign criticism and fail to act with the degree of independence, based upon understanding, appropriate for a leadership role in the global community. Thoughtful leaders in Japan worry that their country will succumb to an inner weakness often referred to as the 'British disease' or 'American malaise'. Neither Americans nor the British will happily accept this particular use of their countries as a reference point, but it is only natural that a *nouveau riche* and newly powerful country makes such questionable comparisons.

There are powerful forces at work to support Japan's drive to become a fully internationalized nation. The growing awareness worldwide of her position of strength shows progress has been made towards this goal. A *Washington Post*–ABC News poll recently found that 54 per cent of Americans interviewed named Japan as 'the strongest economic power in the world today'. Large majorities truly believe that Japanese workers and companies are superior to their American counterparts. But, quite realistically, most of the American interviewees still viewed the United States as the world's strongest military power.

In general, the *Post*–ABC poll concluded that Americans have a favourable view of Japan, though most were fearful of her growing presence in the US economy. The further fact that 60 per cent of those interviewed characterized Japan as a reliable ally indicates that some communication is getting through to the average US citizen. So, in spite of the reservations expressed concerning the international communication skills of the Japanese, they must be doing something right.

Careful studies indicate that recent tensions seem to be declining and that both Japanese and Americans now take a more positive view of the relationships between the two countries. There will of course be 'ups and downs' as specific trade issues, such as the 1989 targeting of Japan under the Omnibus Trade and Competitiveness Act, come under discussion. But it does seem that people in both countries are coming to understand that the Japan–America alliance was, and is, the most important bilateral partnership of modern times.

References

Barnlund, D. C. (1989) *Communicative Styles of Japanese and Americans*, Belmont, California: Wadsworth Publishing Company.

Berrington, R. A. (1985) 'Bridging the gap'. *Speaking of Japan*, February: 25.

Imai, M. (1981) *16 Ways to Avoid Saying 'No'*, Tokyo: Nihon Keizai Shimbun.

Nagata, K. (1984) 'Communicating with Japanese *zaikai-jin*'. *Speaking of Japan*, January: 27.

Ohmae, K. (1987) *Beyond National Borders*, Tokyo: Kodansha International.

Tasker, P. (1988) *The Japanese*, New York: E. P. Dutton.

Chapter twelve

Improving organizational effectiveness

In 1980, the Japan Productivity Center (JPC) celebrated the silver anniversary of its founding. During the preceding quarter century, JPC had sent 1,468 'study missions' abroad, involving 22,800 Japanese businessmen. Employing 600 people at regional offices throughout Japan, the Center also has overseas offices in Washington, Frankfurt, London, Paris, and Rome. The main purpose of early missions to the United States was clearly stated to be discovery of the secret of America's high productivity.

It should come as no surprise that today the JPC receives more study missions from the United States and Europe than it sends. As many as 60 groups of eager business executives arrive each year to learn the secret of Japan's phenomenal success. The roles of 'teacher' and 'student' at least temporarily have been reversed.

To illustrate the top priority given to productivity by the Japanese government, the First Order of the Sacred Treasure recently was awarded to Mr. Kohei Gohshi, founder and director of the Japan Productivity Center. It is significant that this highest of honours has not yet been bestowed on any of Japan's Prime Ministers. So ingrained in the thinking of all Japanese is the need for efficiency and productivity that Japan frequently is referred to as the 'productivity culture'.

Japanese corporations, or *kaisha*, have turned out to be the most aggressive and competitive players in the international management game. In one field after another, from automobiles to semiconductors, the Japanese have taken the lead in world markets. The *kaisha* seem incredibly efficient, and their success has become the source of both amazement and frustration for foreign executives.

There have been any number of explanations for the winning streak presently enjoyed by so many Japanese companies. Many are irrelevant or just plain wrong. Among the more popular myths are that labour costs are less in Japan, that the government really runs industry, that central banks will never let an important company fail, or that the Japanese protect all their important industries with a tight web of tariff and non-tariff barriers. Though there may be a modicum of truth in each of these claims, they are grossly overstated and do not reveal the real sources of Japan's leading competitive edge.

The purpose of this chapter is to evaluate carefully some of the more likely sources of the proven effectiveness of the Japanese *kaisha*. We already have emphasized the impressive overall concern for their employees. Rather arbitrarily, six additional sources will be discussed: (1) the emphasis placed upon technology and production; (2) forward-looking product diversification; (3) effective use of suggestion systems; (4) belief in the concept of total quality control (TQC); (5) commitment to robotization; and (6) a unique union-management relationship.

But first a word of solace should be offered to Japan's most formidable competitors – American corporations. When comparing productivity, the real bottom line is the output of a nation's labour force – the gross domestic product per employee. A decade ago, it was the rage to compare labour productivity *growth* rates, with little attention given to attained *levels* of output per worker. With the proper selection of years on which to base rates of growth, Japan was a winner every time. For example, it could be shown that between 1960 and 1980, Japan's labour productivity growth rate in manufacturing averaged a healthy 9.3 per cent a year while the US rate was only 2.7 per cent. But if we use the Japan Productivity Center's figures to compare the 1980 levels of output per worker in manufacturing, using Japan as a base of 100, the US results are more reassuring: overall productivity, 138; food processing, 225; apparel, 259; steel, 66 (a big disappointment); industrial machinery, 128; automobiles, 99 (a closer race than some suspect); commerce–services, 154; and agriculture a whopping 412. In other words, while Americans must improve their performance in selected industries, there is no need for them to be overly defensive. In many areas, US workers still stand tall in the international productivity ratings (JETRO 1982).

Productivity first

The first source of the organizational effectiveness of Japanese firms is the priority given to technology and production. It is true that Japan turns out a higher percentage of university graduates in engineering and the sciences than does the United States. It is also a fact that the recognized path to the top of a Japanese *kaisha* must include a good proportion of time in the production side of the business. Financial wizards, accountants, or lawyers seldom become presidents of Japanese companies.

Japanese business leaders like to – and do – recognize employees as their most important asset. However, the crux of the matter is that human resources are clearly seen as the means to effective development and use of state-of-the-art technology. Therefore, rather than being contradictory, the great importance attached to both technology and human beings results in a healthy synergism.

For his book, *Japanese Technology*, Masanori Moritani uses the subtitle 'Getting the best for the least'. This is the main thrust of the Japanese manufacturing philosophy. In the final analysis, personnel and financial policies must support the technical efforts of Japan's engineers. Technology or people – which is 'means' and which is 'end' – is a rather futile distinction that has been debated at great length over the years. There is no final answer, since both are essential in a strategy for improving organizational efficiency.

Two noted researchers, Richman and Reitsperger, add empirical support for this point of view in their in-depth study of successful Japanese companies, and comparable British and American companies, in Britain. In explaining the Japanese 'miracle' of high productivity, these experts conclude that 'their productive superiority is not rooted in quality circles or an emphasis on human relations. Rather it is the result of a strategic focus on manufacturing, the combination of industrial engineering and production techniques, and incentive systems which focus the efforts of the workforce' (Richman and Reitsperger 1986).

An extensive study of Japanese manufacturing philosophies in seven industries and 126 companies further explores this issue. A major conclusion drawn from the evidence is that 'unlike managers in the West, Japanese managers in manufacturing view production as an interactive system. Staff and specialists are an integral part of the manufacturing system, and even staff takeovers of operations are considered to be desirable when quality performance is at stake' (Reitsperger and Daniel 1988).

This is an important and revealing finding, and one that should be pondered carefully by Western managers. Perhaps a clue to Japanese success lies in their ability to bring all their managerial skills – production and human resource management – to bear on a single-minded commitment to production excellence. All members of the corporate family share the clear strategic focus upon increased productivity.

Even this brief discussion of Japanese production policies would not be complete without some reference to the famed Toyota Production System, now better known as the Just-in-Time (JIT) or *kanban* system. The term *kanban* refers simply to a special production control card. These cards are used to coordinate and control the production flow by indicating to each step the needs of the next step in the process. Therefore, each step produces, or supplies, only the items actually called for at the next higher level.

The most obvious result of the *kanban* system is the drastic reduction of investment in inventories all down the line. Suppliers deliver just in time to meet the current demand for materials and parts. This most-publicized advantage alone of the JIT process would make it a major contributor to cost reduction and to organizational effectiveness. But it does much more. By streamlining the production flow and injecting more flexibility in scheduling, changeover time and the costs associated with a varied product mix can be reduced dramatically.

It was the need to produce many models of Toyotas in small 'batches' that induced the company to pioneer the JIT system several decades ago. Today the concept is spreading throughout Japanese industry and is even spilling over to General Motors and other American companies feeling the hot breath of Japanese competition. As we shall see in a later section, rationalization of the production process, when combined with aggressive automation, can go far in explaining the successful Japanese invasion of markets formerly dominated by American and European manufacturers.

New products – new horizons

Japanese companies today are heavily involved in developing and implementing product diversification programmes which can lead to broad, new horizons. Unlike American firms which tend to diversify by takeovers and mergers, most Japanese *kaisha* thus far have followed an in-house approach for developing new products and services.

Admittedly, internal product diversification is more risky and time-consuming than restructuring through acquisitions. For example, all employees must be made aware of the reasons for the diversification programme and of changes in their responsibilities which may follow. Furthermore, the parent company is actively involved in, and is directly affected by, the fortunes – or misfortunes – of the new venture.

It is true that during the past few years some cases of merger, following the American model, have appeared on the Japanese scene. But such acquisitions still are not common in Japan's industrial society. To use financial power to take over a corporate body created through years of devoted work by all its employees somehow does not seem quite ethical. Furthermore, it must be remembered that an external acquisition in Japan means merging two closed, exclusive corporate families, each with its own well-established hierarchy and social system.

An additional difficulty is the legal requirement for unanimous consent of all directors of the two companies involved in a merger. Even when this is achieved, a problem remains in securing the support of the two distinct groups of employees. As one top executive points out, 'A Japanese corporate diversification program must be viewed in the context of the Japanese management environment – company-based unions, lifetime employment, seniority wages and promotions, and the employee's strong awareness of belonging to a corporate community' (Hattori 1985: 103).

Most Japanese diversification programmes have been successful, but there have been some disappointments. Earlier in this volume, reference was made to several efforts by Japanese companies which reached too far into unfamiliar fields and failed. However, the overall track record thus far has been good. By accepting the fact that not all management skills are readily transferable, and that industry-specific experience is essential in the management of new acquisitions, Japanese companies have taken a rather cautious approach to diversification. In most cases, they have concentrated on areas in which their present administrative skills and technical knowledge will be applicable.

An interesting story of diversification is that of the Seiko Group, which, until the time of the Tokyo Olympic Games, was concerned solely with the manufacture and worldwide distribution of high-quality timepieces (Hattori 1985: 103–21). In 1964 the company decided to diversify into new, but related, products. A controlling criterion for selecting products was that they must be consistent with the company's already existing management skills, markets, and technology.

By 1970, Seiko had made public its long-range plans for developing multidivisional business operations to enable it to move into many new fields. Early efforts concentrated on revitalizing watch production by introducing electronic and quartz timepieces. This was followed by setting up new divisions devoted to producing a variety of sophisticated electronic instruments and components, including digital printers, personal computers, and scientific equipment.

Such expansion took a long time – for some divisions longer than anticipated. First, a consensus had to be obtained from all members of the groups that would be involved in new operations. Then innovative production techniques and alternate market plans had to be developed. In some cases, it was estimated that eight to ten years might be required for new divisions to secure the proper balance of development, production, and marketing programmes.

A plan for the 1980s and 1990s has been promoted as the New Daini Project (ND), the purpose of which is to restructure and further expand Seiko Group operations. The ultimate target is to have revenues equally divided between watch sales and diversified product sales. At the time of writing, the project is said to be on target, and Seiko continues its steady, internal growth into a diversified, multidivisional conglomerate.

The unique strengths of Japanese management when operating in a 'closed' corporate setting often become formidable obstacles when shifted to a multidivisional environment. For example, the inner-directed dedication and loyalty of employees in Japanese companies can isolate them from contact with outside organizations.

As mentioned earlier, managers tend to specialize in a given company rather than in a particular function, since most have spent their entire careers in one organization.

There is a need, therefore, to bring into top management people with experience outside the company. However, the fact remains that almost 90 per cent of corporate board members in Japan are also operating executives in the company. It is a problem to divert the attention of these inside 'working directors' from their day-to-day operational duties to the broader problems of diversification. Basically, this is a communication problem, since all managers must be made aware of the critical factors, both internal and external, that have compelled their company to develop new products and to seek new horizons.

Suggestion systems – Japanese style

Encouraging ideas from employees through a suggestion system has a long history in the United States. As early as 1898, Eastman Kodak Company started a suggestion programme. The employee who submitted the first accepted idea was awarded a grand prize of two dollars – not too modest an amount in those days.

Japan's first suggestion programme, limited to management personnel, was started by Kanebo Company in 1905, after executives had visited the United States and observed a plan in action. But it was not until the 1950s that suggestion systems covering all employees became popular. To a reticent workforce accustomed to following orders with few comments of any kind, the idea of offering suggestions to superiors was not quickly accepted. However, in the 1960s companies began to integrate suggestion plans with a variety of small-group activities such as quality control circles and *jishu kanri* (autonomous control) teams. With this sort of appealing combination, the number of suggestions increased rapidly.

In 1976, Matsushita Electric reported an average of fifty suggestions for each of the 1,500 production workers in its Ibaragi television plant. In recent years, the company as a whole has been averaging over ten suggestions per worker (factory and office workers combined). At Matsushita, the acceptance rate averages about 10 per cent, a figure quoted by a number of other equally successful companies tapping this important source of creative ideas.

By 1982, a survey of 512 organizations conducted by the Japan Human Relations Association and the Japan Suggestion System Association showed an impressive 14.74 suggestions per employee. At Hitachi Ltd, 5.8 million suggestions (102.59 per person) were received. Other firms experienced levels as high as 400 suggestions per employee, and one person at Fuji Electric is said to have set a remarkable record of 13,173 suggestions in a single year. Without vouching for these figures, it seems safe to say that suggestion systems, when combined with other accepted group activities, have caught on in Japanese industry.

According to the 1982 survey mentioned above, the largest percentage of suggestions (35 per cent) deal with improvements in the work process. Other areas recommended for improvement and claiming more than 10 per cent of all suggestions included: machine tools; the work environment; and ways to save energy, resources, and materials.

In the adaptation of suggestion systems to the Japanese corporate culture and values, we have yet another clear example of taking a good foreign idea and making it better. A significant feature was their shifting from a passive mode, merely waiting for suggestions, to an active programme for educating personnel concerning all aspects of the plan. This shift fits comfortably with the typical commitment of Japanese management to developing the skills of all employees fully, and to recognizing that employees can make a real contribution to organizational effectiveness.

The fact is that studies continue to tell us that employees worldwide want their views to be heard. A consistent complaint of American workers is the failure of superiors to listen to their ideas, and the strong feeling that their bosses really don't believe they have anything of value to contribute beyond the performance of their jobs. A further complication is that the prevailing adversarial relationship between unions and management in the United States leads managers to feel that worker cooperation just is not possible to achieve.

The phenomenal success of Japanese suggestion systems and, as we shall see in the next section, of quality circle programmes, reflects a management philosophy which stresses the perfectibility of human beings. Truly believing that employees are their most valuable resource, Japanese managers naturally turn to subordinates for ideas that will yield economic returns to the company. Given encouragement and support, it is assumed employees will contribute substantially to the improvement of organizational effectiveness. The results seem to indicate that this is a most valid assumption to make within the Japanese management system.

Total Quality Control (TQC)

Total Quality Control is a philosophy – even a way of life – that permeates every phase of the process of management in Japan. The Japanese consider quality and productivity as one and the same. Quality by inspection is outmoded, while downgrading, re-work and scrap are not acceptable corrective actions. They stress that corrective action must be built into the entire productive process. To this all-encompassing concern for quality in every corporate activity has been given the name Total Quality Control (TQC).

Basic to an understanding of TQC in Japan is an appreciation of the fact that quality control has shifted from being a strictly engineering function, performed by specialists with little actual line experience, to being the responsibility of each and every employee. It is also important to keep in mind the egalitarian approach to management in Japan. Because every employee is a member of the same corporate family, different only in age and length of service, managers easily can accept the creative potential of subordinates in contributing their ideas for improvements in all phases of company operations.

A core building block in the Total Quality Control concept is the use of quality circles (QC). According to Robert E. Cole, Director of the Center for Japanese Studies at the University of Michigan, 'QC circles are small groups of people who do similar or related work who meet regularly to identify, analyze, and solve product-quality and production problems and to improve general operations' (Cole 1979). Objectives of circle activity include not only quality and productivity improvement, but also personal training, improved morale, leadership development, and job enrichment.

Experience indicates that circles should be kept small, perhaps ten to twelve members, to facilitate communication. Though participation is supposed to be voluntary, the author's questioning of circle members on this point indicates that the excellent participation rate may be more the result of pressure from superiors and peers. In answer to the query, 'Do you enjoy attending quality circle meetings?' a spokesman for one group answered: 'Not really. We simply have to attend.' A study of female employees in a leading Japanese bank further confirms this scepticism. While the majority felt that circle meetings were beneficial, almost half of these women said they would prefer not to participate, and only 5 per cent considered attendance to be voluntary.

There is no one best formula for QC scheduling or for payment of participants. If circle meetings are during normal work hours, no additional pay is expected. If employees must meet outside normal working time, the company may pay them the usual overtime rate or merely a small additional payment. In some cases, enthusiasm for participation is so high that even long meetings after work do not involve any extra pay. Decision on these matters will, of course, be made with the cooperation and approval of the company labour union.

A careful survey of twenty-four Japanese companies using quality circles reveals the major benefits realized from the programme (Ross and Ross 1982: 19). The top three benefits mentioned were improved communication, greater job satisfaction, and improved morale. Notice that all of these are human-relations centred. Next in priority were the benefits of productivity improvement, quality improvement, and cost savings. These results clearly show that the benefits realized from QC circles go far beyond the improvement in product engineering to equally important enhancement of 'human engineering'. This, after all, is the whole point of Total Quality Control.

Quality circles have spread rapidly in Japan since their establishment in the early 1960s. There are now well over 100,000 circles, with a total membership estimated as high as 10 million workers. Such 'total immersion' in QC activities is largely due to the efforts of the influential Japan Union of Scientists and Engineers. This coordinating organization conducts training sessions for circle leaders and 'facilitators', publishes relevant books and manuals, and sponsors a variety of conferences and visitor programmes. These activities encourage exchange of experiences among Japanese companies and, through foreign conferences and exchanges, foster the spread of the movement to other countries. Because exceptional quality is such a potent factor contributing to the competitiveness of Japanese products, it would be difficult to overstate the importance of Total Quality Control as a means of improving organizational effectiveness.

Robotization

To this writer, the worldwide explosion of advanced automation in factories, banks, offices, hospitals – everywhere – may well be the most significant development in organizational management during the remainder of this century. An important part of this scramble to automate is the substitution of robots, popularly referred to as 'steel-collar workers', for human beings. This substitution process has been dubbed the 'robotization' of industry, and its effects have only just begun to be felt throughout the world.

It will come as no great surprise to most readers that Japan today is leading in the use of industrial robots. In 1980, the American Robot Association reported that Japanese companies were operating 70 per cent of the robots in use at that time. Since then, the introduction of robots in Japan has progressed rapidly, not only in large companies but in the small and medium-size enterprises that account for the great majority of business organizations.

Most of these devices still are being used to relieve humans from performing the most tedious and hazardous jobs. Though used in all fields, demand for their services is greatest in the automotive and electronic fields. However, we can already see robots invading many other fields, such as social welfare, oceanography, forestry, construction, transportation, and services.

Not all robots are designed for strictly industrial use. According to a Japan Air Lines newsletter, the Tomy Company has developed a robot whose sole reason for being is to act as a stress reliever. It is programmed to hang its head apologetically when yelled at. Then it will cheer up and dance around until someone yells at it again. Named 'Rakuten', roughly translated as 'Mr Optimism', the robot sells for under $50 and is said to be targeted for 'households with no dog to kick'.

Returning to industrial robots, one might ask why Japan leads in their use. The answer basically lies in the considerable flexibility of the Japanese corporate structure. Job specifications are intentionally vague or non-existent; a worker displaced by a robot does not feel that he has been dispossessed of his personal property and can accept another job without complaint or anxiety. With promotions and pay raises still largely determined by length of service, fears of damage to one's career are minimized. Furthermore, job rotation is such an expected and regular feature of the Japanese management system that a change in work assignment, whatever the cause, is not a traumatic experience. Finally, the cooperative attitude of the company-based unions, described in detail in the section that follows, greatly eases the introduction of these efficient, obedient steel-collar workers.

A report in *Time* magazine describes the 'eerie science fiction' scene at the highly automated Yamazaki Machinery Works in Nagoya. Referred to as a flexible manufacturing lab, the operation is an impressive demonstration of the benefits of automation. Instead of employing 200 skilled workers at sixty-eight different machines to produce a monthly output of 1,400 parts, there are now only eighteen computer-controlled machining centres. Today, the plant is run by ten to twelve workmen on the day shifts and a single watchman on the night shift.

Castings that formerly took three months to complete now are turned out in three days. The robot-like machines select the correct tool to use for each job; if a drill bit breaks the machine will quickly replace it. The time required for drilling, milling, and grinding operations has been reduced to a minimum. Is Yamazaki management pleased with its $18 million investment? It would seem so from the president's conviction that 'the accuracy is better than humans can do, and the machines never have a blue Monday' (*Time* 1981).

New examples of the expanding role of 'intelligent robots' in Japanese industries can be seen almost daily. The Ministry of International Trade and Industry is backing a multi-million dollar plan to develop robots so versatile and smart that they may eventually be capable of producing an entire automobile. Quality can be controlled by robots far beyond the limits of human beings. Nippon Electric, for example, has developed an assembly robot that can position parts with a maximum error of four-hundred-thousandths of an inch. Fujitsu Fanuc Inc. has robots working that can recognize and sort parts before assembling them.

The truth is, robots with visual and tactile sensors are proving to be tremendously cost-effective, almost trouble-free, and capable of far greater output than human workers. Pay-back periods often are two years or less, since these willing 'employees' work twenty-four hours a day, seven days a week, and never indulge in extended tea breaks.

American companies are busily trying to catch up with Japan in both production and use of robots. General Motors, for example, set 1990 as the target date for installation of 14,000 robots. Though American unions are cautious, thus far they have been cooperative if the company gives a persuasive guarantee that no jobs will be lost due to automation. But with robots producing robots at an ever-increasing pace in Japan, most of these newcomers to the US labour force may be of foreign origin.

An international reputation for reliability and competitive costs already has led manufacturers around the world to prefer Japanese-made industrial robots for use in pursuing factory automation plans. In 1985, exports accounted for 25 per cent of the ¥295 billion of Japanese robot sales. Total sales each year have been increasing at a remarkable 30–40 per cent. According to some estimates, the combined domestic and international markets for the country's industrial robots could total a staggering ¥1 trillion by 1995. Robotics is, indeed, a growth industry, and Japan at present is leading the pack.

A promising approach to the US challenge of matching Japan in robotics is seen in the 1982 joint venture formed between General Motors and Fanuc, one of Japan's largest producers of robots. The resulting company, GMF Robotics, combines Japanese-made hardware with the sophisticated software developed in the United States. This move gave Fanuc an entry into the potentially huge US market for robots. GM, on the other hand, is now assured of a steady source of high-quality, low-cost robots. According to one analyst, it was a good marriage because 'GM, like other American manufacturers, had suffered badly in competition with the Japanese, and robotics was seen as a means of restoring competitiveness, both in quality and in price' (Schodt 1988).

With a decade of experience of robotization behind them, Japanese manufacturers are beginning to appreciate the broader impact the movement has had upon strategic decision-making. For example, the economics of plant location are changing rapidly.

Many industries that formerly were labour-intensive, with payrolls accounting for 25 per cent or more of total costs, have shrunk labour's share to 5–10 per cent. As a result, the former need to locate plant sites where low-cost, high-quality workers could be found no longer is a serious constraint. To low-wage countries enjoying the jobs and income provided by Japanese overseas plants, this comes as bad news. Many such foreign operations, not only from Japan but also from the United States, Germany, Korea, and other industrialized nations, will be moving home again.

A second impact of robotization upon management strategy is in lowering critical break-even points. With all the uncertainties of international business, profitable operations at 70 per cent of capacity seem to be a favoured goal. Toyota already has achieved this magic number. A few companies even claim that they can break even at 30 per cent by using robots for much of their operations.

Finally, robots ease the need of companies to meet the increasingly fickle demands of consumers for different models, styles, accessories, and colours of everything from automobiles to personal computers. For example, stamping machine changeover time has been drastically reduced at auto plants. Manufacturers no longer have to worry unduly about a trade-off between consumer desires for variety and the need for optimum lot size. Model life cycles have been shortened to the point that fashion, rather than costs, will dictate the variety of products pouring from Japanese assembly lines.

The amazing invasion of Japanese industry by robots can only serve to widen the competitive edge Japan holds over the West. The message is clear to business leaders throughout the world: robotize as quickly and as thoroughly as possible or be willing to accept a permanent spot on the second team of industrialized nations.

Working with unions

A final contributor to the effectiveness of Japan's *kaisha* is the unique relationship existing between labour unions and corporate management. To understand the present status of union–management relations, we must look briefly at the decade following the end of the Second World War. It was during this period that much of the philosophy underlying the present Japanese management system began to take shape. To forge an appropriate role for labour unions in the dire circumstances facing the country at that time was a particularly difficult problem for victors and vanquished alike.

For our purposes, we can consider the modern labour movement in Japan as starting in the immediate post-war years. Following the Manchurian Incident in 1931, Japan embarked on the development of a war economy in which there was little room for labour unions. Instead, workers were organized in each plant for the purpose of promoting cooperation with the nation's goals. This is an important fact to keep in mind later as we evaluate present-day, company-based unions.

The US Army was responsible for the Allied Occupation policy in Japan. Its first priority was to break, once and for all, the solidarity and power of the military–industrial complex which led the nation to war. Military leaders were purged, and the huge industrial cartels (*zaibatsu*) were disbanded.

A key part of the Occupation strategy was to establish a viable labour movement to discourage excessive managerial autonomy and to act as a counterforce to the latent socialist sympathies stirring in the devastated country. To establish a legal basis for the union movement, a Labour Union Law was enacted which was, of course, patterned closely after US labour legislation. It called for local unions to be affiliated with industrial unions which, in turn, would be coordinated by one or more national centres.

But, as with so many things, American seeds sown in Japanese soil bore uniquely Japanese fruit. The whole concept of what has been referred to as 'common-destiny management' clashed with the suggestion of any real control from external union sources. Japanese workers knew that they must share the uncertain fate of their companies, and managers realized their own dependence upon the cooperation of workers. A widely quoted expression, 'the union exists because the company exists' reflects the strong feeling of interdependence felt among all members of the struggling organizations. Therefore, only indirect ties developed between the individual unions and industrial federations or national centres.

The basic units in Japan's labour movement are the 'enterprise unions' (*kigyo-betsu kumiai*), so called because they organize the employees of only a single establishment. In their excellent analysis of the Japanese industrial relations system, Professors Okochi, Karsh, and Levine bluntly state; 'The most important feature of the Japanese labour unions is enterprise unionism' (Okochi, Karsh and Levine 1973: 235). In any event, it seems clear that the remarkable post-war growth of Japanese industry would have been impossible without the stable, cooperative union–management relations within companies made possible by enterprise unions.

Because of their importance, it may be useful to provide a summary of the major characteristics of enterprise unions. First, they enroll all regular employees in a single establishment regardless of occupation or job status. In other words, union members include all white-collar and blue-collar workers, college and high school graduates, who are fully fledged members of the corporation below a certain rank. In some companies, assistant section chiefs (*kakaricho*) and, in rare cases, even section chiefs (*kacho*) belong to the enterprise union.

The inclusion of even lower-level supervisors in the union comes as quite a surprise to Western managers. For example, with the clear dividing line between management and workers drawn in US firms, it is understandable that foremen, as the first level of management, are legally denied membership in the same union as their subordinates. From foreman up, every American supervisor is exhorted to think and act like a member of the management team. How, then, could they be union members and, in that sense, join the 'enemy camp'? When asked why lower-level managers were allowed to be members of the enterprise union in his company, one Japanese executive confided to the author 'How better can we find out what is on the union's mind?'

A leadership position in a Japanese union often leads to promising careers within management. Leaders in enterprise unions are elected from among the regular employees of the company. While American companies often label union activists 'trouble-makers' and deal with them accordingly, Japanese companies tend to view union experience as valuable training for responsibility in management. An impressive number of presidents of Japanese corporations previously demonstrated their managerial talents as labour union officers. One management association survey shows that one out of every six corporate board directors has served as a labour union chairman or secretary-general.

All regular employees automatically join the union, and their dues are collected by check-off. Since union membership is confined to regular employees, part-timers (including many women), temporary, and subcontract workers typically are excluded. The check-off feature in Japan, as in the United States, no doubt does lead to indifference on the part of members and to concentration of power in the hands of the leadership. However, the fact that enterprise-union offices are located on company property gives a degree of visibility that encourages an awareness of union membership on the part of employees. Though direct financial assistance by the company to the union is forbidden by law in both Japan and the United States, the Japanese have opted to exempt provision of company office space and administrative facilities from this restriction. This particular issue never would arise in the American context, since it would be unthinkable for any company to invite the union to set up shop on company property.

Membership figures released for 1988 show unionization rates in Japan and several other selected countries. Japanese unions claimed 12 million members, which was roughly 27 per cent of the labour force. Comparable US figures were 17 million and 17 per cent; West Germany 9 million and 41 per cent; and the UK 11 million and 49 per cent (Keizai Koko Centre 1990: 73). American union memberships have been declining in recent years, both in absolute numbers and as a percentage of the workforce. Membership in Japanese unions, at least to the present time, has remained fairly stable over a number of years.

At first glance, the overall structure of labour unions in Japan and the United States appears to be quite similar. In Japan, enterprise unions may be affiliated with industrial federations which, in turn, may join one of the national centres. Similar levels prevail in the United States, with local unions joining industrial/craft organizations, which may elect to join the single peak federation, AFL/CIO.

At the bottom level, the significant differences between Japanese enterprise unions and US locals, which organize similar workers from one or more companies in a given locality, already have been discussed. The second level, too, shows important differences.

Industrial unions in Japan provide fewer financial and educational benefits to the enterprise unions than do the large American nationals to local unions. Japanese industrial unions devote a major portion of their time and resources to political campaigns and to lobbying for their favourite candidates in the party with which each is aligned. American industrial federations play an active role in organizing efforts and contract negotiations at the local level, while almost all such activities are confined to the enterprise level in Japan.

Moving up to the top of the structure, a recent development has unified Japan's private sector unions under a single umbrella, the National Federation of Private Sector Unions, or Rengo. Until 1987, there were three major peak federations of unions in Japan – Sohyo, Domei, and Churitsuroren, each closely connected with a specific political party. With unification of private-sector unions in a single peak federation, not only will their economic power be increased but their political influence can be concentrated on a party of the leaders' choice.

A final important aspect of Japanese unionism which should be mentioned is the Shunto, or Spring Labour Offensive. These perennial labour demonstrations for higher wages and shorter hours take place every spring in March and April. After making public their demands for base-rate wage increases, the top union federations and the major employers' associations negotiate a guideline of a given percentage increase. Each company is then expected to come as close to the guideline figure as possible in determining their 'base-up' for the year.

The steam behind the Shunto seems to have lessened considerably in recent years. Average base-rate increases have been modest and probably no more than management would have offered without all the time and money spent on the annual spring ritual. Some labour experts predict the eventual abandonment of the Shunto. They feel that the impact is negligible due to the rapid growth of the service sector, professionalization of jobs, increasing use of merit-based wage increases, and the expanded employment of non-union part-time female and aged employees.

Looking to the future, Konosuke Matsushita, a leading Japanese industrialist, has said that he believes labour unions will, and should, survive, and that Japanese-style unionism will provide a viable model for Asia's newly industrializing countries. Matsushita sees unions and management as another example of the *yin* and *yang* dichotomy, being at once in conflict and harmony. Such symbiosis, so long as it is fully accepted by both parties, can make a significant contribution to the continued organizational effectiveness of Japanese corporations.

This chapter concludes Part III dealing with the major functions and strategies characterizing the process of management. Now we turn to the final two chapters in Part IV: Scenarios for the Future. The next chapter exposes some of the many challenges which Japanese management and, indeed, Japanese society is now facing. In the final chapter, an attempt will be made to sketch the role, as seen by this writer, that Japanese management is likely to play in the anticipated Century of the Pacific.

References

Cole, R. E. (1979) 'Made in Japan: a spur to US productivity', *Asia*, May/June: 6.

Hattori, I. (1985) 'Product diversification', in L. C. Thurow *The Management Challenge; Japanese Views*, Cambridge, Mass.: MIT Press.

JETRO (1982) 'Gauging and comparing economic productivity', *Focus Japan*, September: JS–A.

Keizai Koho Centre (1990) Japan 1990: An International Camparison, Tokyo.

Lillrank, P. and Kano, N. (1989) *Continuous Improvement*, Ann Arbor, Michigan: Centre for Japanese Studies, University of Michigan.

'Look no hands', *Time* (16 November 1981), p. 127.

Moritani, M. (1982) *Japanese Technology: Getting the Best for the Least*, Tokyo: The Simul Press Inc.

Okochi, K., Karsh, B., and Levine, S. (1973) *Workers and Employers in Japan*, Tokyo: University of Tokyo Press.

Reitsperger, W. D. and Daniel, S. J. (1988) 'Japanese manufacturing philosophies: empirical evidence', presented as a working paper at the annual meeting of the Academy of International Business, San Diego, California.

Richman, G. and Reitsperger, W. D. (1986) 'Japanese production excellence: lessons to be learnt', *Euro–Asia Business Review*, October, 5: 10.

Ross J. E. and Ross, W. C. (1982) *Japanese Quality Circles and Productivity*, Reston, Virginia: Reston Publishing Company.

Schodt, F. L. (1988) 'In the land of robots', *Business Month*, November: 72.

Part four

Scenarios for the future

Chapter thirteen

Current challenges to Japanese management

Today, Japan's vaunted management system, indeed Japanese society itself, is facing a number of critical challenges. Westerners who rub shoulders with free-spending Japanese tourists, or who read only the 'good news' of another Japanese conquest in foreign industry and real estate, are led to believe that the country is well on its way to becoming Number One among all nations of the world. However, for those who travel to Japan without the insulation provided by corporate expense accounts or carefully programmed tour groups, a different picture emerges. Well-worn clichés, such as 'all that glitters is not gold', come to mind. One of Japan's most candid observers summarizes his country's dilemma perfectly in these few words: 'We're rich in play money, but live as if we are poor' (Ohmae 1987: 128).

How – and why – can the Japanese be rich and poor at the same time? The truth is, Japan has experienced this seeming paradox throughout her history. Rich in culture, traditions and the arts – poor in the ability to communicate and to share these treasures with the rest of the world. Rich in the education and skills of her people; poor in their stifling insularity and ethnocentricity. And today, rich in deliberately over-valued yen; poor in the infrastucture of housing, roads, and space so essential to quality of life and self-fulfillment. As the subtitle of Frank Gibney's fascinating book tells us, Japan truly is *The Fragile Superpower* (Gibney 1975).

Some of the forces currently creating both problems and opportunities for Japanese managers originate within the country and some come from abroad. Whatever their source, the pressures they create demand change, and this writer has full confidence that the Japanese will once again successfully rise to the occasion. However, as mentioned earlier in this volume, it would be a serious mistake to assume the responses necessarily will emulate the West. More likely, new and uniquely Japanese ways will be developed to accommodate and adjust to new conditions. Only the most naive and unwary foreign analysts will fall in the trap of believing that Japan inevitably will begin to look 'more like us'.

Dealing with new challenges and taking advantage of new opportunities will have a significant impact upon the way the Japanese do business. Many winning management policies and procedures from an earlier era of rapid growth may have to be modified to fit a more mature, stable economic environment. If history serves as a guide Japanese managers will 'bend with the wind' and adapt skilfully to the dynamics of change.

In this chapter, an attempt will be made to evaluate the impact of major domestic and foreign pressures upon the Japanese management system. Perhaps this will give us some clues as to the future course we can expect the *kaisha* to follow in this most competitive of all Asian nations.

Domestic pressures

After several decades of obsession with exports and rapid growth, Japan now has reached the stage of maturity when her leaders must look inward. Unfortunately, the present scene is not as reassuring as that of the earlier 'miracle' years. A rapidly aging population, the drastic restructuring of the economy, a widely recognized need to acquire an international image based on trust and respect, and a spreading sense of anxiety concerning the future, are several such areas to be examined in this section. Each requires sensitive and constructive response from business and government power centres.

An aging population

A recent white paper from the Japanese Ministry of Health and Welfare lays plans for 'a bright, congenial environment for the elderly' in the twenty-first century. This concern is well-founded, since Japan's population is aging at a far more rapid rate than in other advanced nations. If three age-groups are identified (0–14,

Figure 4 Transition of age-groups in population

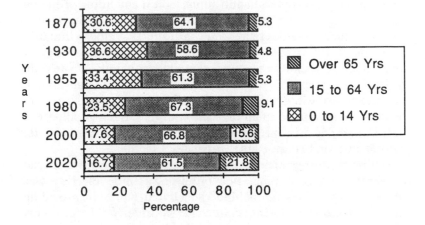

Source: JETRO, Focus Japan, August 1984: 2

15–64, and over 65) the trend towards concentration in the older segments is clear. Figure 4 projects this transition to older age-groups to the year 2020.

Another way of looking at this trend is to turn to the ratio of Japanese over 60 to total population. This senior group already represents 15 per cent and is expected to escalate to a huge 27 per cent by the turn of the century. In other words, one in every four citizens will be counted in the market for what is termed the country's 'silver business'.

Senior citizens with time and money present an opportunity that will not go unnoticed by business leaders in Japan. Little wonder, for estimates of the size of the 'silver' market by the turn of the century reach as high as $800 billion. If such estimates turn out to be true one effect upon management will be to stimulate the search for new products and services that will appeal to older people. Health products and home-care services immediately come to mind. Travel agencies, and a host of travel-related businesses, from rental cars to super-luxury ocean liners, can be expected to flourish. One travel agency that specializes in tours for seniors reports that its business has doubled over the past ten years. Such tours focus upon 'special events' that include singing competitions, 'do-sports' health tours, and many kinds of hobby tours.

Leisure-time activities increasingly are aimed at elderly citizens. All kinds of sports equipment and facilities already are in great demand. A new sports rage among Japanese seniors is 'gate ball' (a kind of croquet), which currently claims several million enthusiasts. Bowling alleys, golf driving ranges, and drive-in theatres are sprouting up all over the country. And a good part of their business is accounted for by older people with leisure time, good health, and comfortable incomes.

American entrepreneurs currently are investigating special segments of this distant, but promising senior market. For example, Japan lags far behind the United States in providing retirement and convalescent centres for the elderly. This is largely because tradition dictates that each family take care of its own. However, this is changing, and such American industry leaders as Beverly Enterprises and Manor Care are eyeing opportunities in this field. They will no doubt face stiff competition from aggressive Japanese firms such as Misawa Homes, which advertises its retirement centres as 'futuristic homes to increase the worthiness of life for the aged'.

Inevitably, the aging population has created some thorny problems as well as promising opportunities for management. Some of the areas in which adjustments have had to be made include corporate hiring, pay, and promotion policies. For example, one direct impact upon management may be seen in the gradual rise of the mandatory retirement age from 55 to 60 in most large companies. This shift is not very impressive when compared with American firms that have either totally abandoned the idea of forced retirement or have moved up to age 70. But it has had important repercussions throughout Japanese corporations.

In a relatively stable economy, workers remain longer in their jobs and fewer young recruits are hired. Reflecting this, unemployment figures in Japan, though not calculated on a comparable basis with other countries, have been creeping up. Furthermore, because salaries are closely linked with length of service, an older workforce means higher average rates of pay and a larger total wage bill. Response to this dilemma in many companies has been to flatten the wage curve by putting a cap on automatic increases at least at age 55 and, in many recent cases, as early as 40–45. Inevitable, too, is the fact that promotions will be fewer and less frequent as older employees are allowed to delay their exit from the firm.

A restructured economy

In Chapter 4, dealing with the modern environment, a description was given of the current programme for drastic restructuring of the Japanese economy. The plan, set forth in the Maekawa Report, is directed at expansion of domestic demand to reduce Japan's trade surplus. It proposes to do this by the promotion of housing construction and urban development; by the stimulation of private consumption through boosting wages and shortening hours of work; by tax reform; and by the promotion of investment in the social infrastructure by local government.

Such massive adjustments in the economy do, of course, create pressures which must be responded to by corporate management. The most significant response has been an intensified commitment to creative research and development (R&D) on a grand scale. As totally obsolete as the stereotype of shoddy products from Japan is the equally mistaken belief that the Japanese are not creative – that they are merely imitators. A much-quoted statement by Harvard's Professor Harvey Brooks may be worth repeating once more here: 'Successful imitation, far from being symptomatic of lack of originality as used to be thought, is the first step of learning to be creative' (Arima 1987).

Japanese artists, scientists, and engineers took that first step years ago and are now among the most creative people in the world. Superb Japanese design, style, form, and function characterize all fields of endeavour. R&D in industry has pushed Japan into a leadership position in cameras, small computers, semiconductors, robots, and office automation. Though still lagging behind the United States in such fields as computer software, aerospace, and biotechnology, Japan is determined that the gap should not be a permanent one.

There is a myth currently circulating that the reason for Japan's recent surge in innovative R&D is that 'the government pays the bill'. Nothing could be further from the truth. While about half of all research funds are raised by government in Europe and the United States, only one-quarter of such monies in Japan come from the government. Furthermore, of these limited funds, only half goes directly to private industry. The bottom line is that the Japanese *kaisha* finance almost all of the R&D they perform.

In addition to stimulating industrial R&D, restructuring of the economy has put a premium on experts in corporate planning. Japan's successful drive toward technological leadership has not been due to happenstance. Rather, it is the result of high-level, strategic planning in both corporate and government circles. Much has been made of the government's success in 'targeting' and supporting winning industries and products. But most of the 'winners' have been created through skilful planning in private industry.

It is true, as mentioned in Chapter 6, that corporate planners have become the heroes of the *kaisha*. During the boom years of the 1960s and 1970s, there was no time and little need for long-range planning. But today, the tremendous challenge of adapting to a drastically changed economic environment demands carefully planned strategies. The current scramble to diversify into often unfamiliar fields is further justification for careful corporate planning. Fortunately, Japanese planners are relatively free to design creative and ambitious scenarios for the company's future without undue constraints from its shareholders.

A final example of restructuring is the privatization of several long-standing public corporations in Japan. A series of reports from the government's Council for the Promotion of Administrative Reform presented convincing evidence that three such corporations – Japanese National Railways (JNR), the Nippon Telegraph and Telephone Company (NTT), and the Japan Tobacco and Salt Public Corporation (JTS) – could be more efficiently managed in private hands.

For many years, Japan had both public and private railroads, which together provided exceptional coverage the length and breadth of the land. However, JNR had suffered staggering deficits, amounting to roughly ¥2 trillion annually in recent years. Although NTT and JTS operated at a profit, this generally was conceded to be due to their monopoly control. In any event, these three powerful government monopolies have been deregulated and must now become more competitive as they face market pressures in the private sector.

Deregulation of public corporations typically leads to ambitious plans for diversification. An example is Japan Air Lines, now a privately owned carrier, which has targeted such fields as tourism, hotels, and real estate as promising areas for future development. In all these deregulated fields, new companies, both foreign and domestic, are bidding for potentially lucrative contracts. As the managements of former public monopolies have discovered, their role as private companies, particularly in an international setting, is tough and competitive, but offers many new challenges and opportunities.

An international image

One of the most urgent challenges to Japanese business leaders is to make their companies – and themselves – more truly international in outlook and behaviour. Though the centuries of isolation are now far behind, there is still a widespread feeling among Japanese that, once outside their island home, they really do not 'belong'. However, a desire to break the shell of provincialism and to gain acceptance as truly international citizens (*kokusai-jin*) is felt, and expressed, by people in all walks of life.

Recognition of the need to achieve a higher level of internationalization has induced Japanese government and business leaders to seek a broader role for themselves and their organizations in world affairs. In its excellent study, *Japan in the Year 2000*, the Long-Term Outlook Committee of the Economic Planning Agency's Economic Council, stressed progress in internationalization as one of three major trends to receive priority in government planning.

The Committee established the following prerequisites for internationalization:

(1) Japan must positively strive to reactivate the world economy.
(2) Japan must further open its economic society to be acceptable internationally.
(3) Japan must positively contribute to the settlement of various problems on a global scale, such as the North–South issue, and food, and environmental problems.

(Economic Planning Agency 1983: 179)

This is a big order, and requires that Japanese executives take steps to broaden their horizons and deepen their knowledge of world affairs. The so-called North–South problem refers to the gap between industrially advanced nations and developing countries. As the report points out, developing nations (including China) have three-quarters of the world's population, but only one-fifth of total world income. Furthermore, on a per capita basis their income is less than one-tenth that of advanced countries. Today, most Japanese people realize that they must continue to expand their private economic cooperation and official development assistance to less-developed parts of the world.

And, as the Committee recommends, the Japanese must think and behave in a way that will make them 'acceptable internationally'. For managers, gaining such acceptance will require a new determination to become international citizens, to cast aside persistent feelings of innate superiority, and to engage in dialogues with foreign counterparts in a context of equality and mutual respect. Only when this is accomplished will people throughout the world give Japan the international image she seeks and so desperately needs.

Communication remains a major problem in achieving acceptance internationally. Somehow the message Japan wants to impart to foreigners just does not come through. The results of a survey conducted by the Japan Institute for Social and Economic Affairs are especially disturbing as an example of this failure to communicate. The Institute sampled 200 foreign students in the greater Tokyo region, and 36.5 per cent said their impressions of Japan had become worse during their stay. Only 16 per cent reported that their impressions had improved. The remainder said they felt the same after face-to-face exposure over a substantial period of time.

Most disappointing was the fact that the same 36.5 per cent told of human relations problems with the Japanese, rating such discomfort equal to that due to high prices, crowded commuter trains, and poor housing. The 200 participants came from 29 countries, about two-thirds of them from the Asian region. These students will not be good ambassadors for Japan when they return to their home countries.

An anxiety syndrome

This source of pressure originates from within the heart of Japan and is psychological rather than demographic or economic in nature. In essence, Japan's managers share with their employees and the general citizenry a nagging sense of anxiety concerning the future. One source of this anxiety is the uncertain search for an international identity discussed in the preceding section. One of the country's most perceptive analysts writes of 'the soul-searching we in Japan are going through, because we are genuinely concerned and unsure about how to improve our relationship with the rest of the world' (Ohmae 1987: ix). When business leaders experience this lack of certainty as to how to think and act in their dealings with American and other foreign counterparts, the result is a good bit of tension and stress – a condition one member of the Japanese Diet has called 'enlightened despair'.

A second source of anxiety is the dread that Japanese workers are slowly but surely developing the 'American malaise' – an unwillingness to do the menial jobs in industry and a widespread feeling that everyone should be a white-coated professional. Smaller companies already have been plagued by a shortage of competent, reliable blue-collar workers. The answer to this problem for many companies has been a rush to automation. According to the Japan Institute of Labour, while the price of robots remained fairly constant for most of the 1970s, the wages paid to factory workers leaped 68 per cent. Coping with the inevitable trend toward automation, with all of its implications, has caused many sleepless nights for Japanese managers.

An additional source of executive worry is a concern that *gomu-shugi* is spreading among their employees. This is a term which means loss of five basic qualities – spirit, interest, emotion, sense of responsibility, and manners. In a 1981 New Year's editorial, the *Mainichi Shimbun* claimed that the reason for *gomu-shugi* was 'egoism that seeks indolence for oneself alone, caring little to what happens to others'. The writer then went to considerable lengths to separate egoism from 'the individualism upon which democracies are built'. The editorial was a plea to all Japanese to reverse this trend, and to return to the qualities that have brought the country to its present strength as a world power.

One final cause of the anxiety syndrome experienced by so many

Japanese these days is a frustrated yearning for what might be called 'spiritual affluence'. Although a recent public opinion poll conducted by the Prime Minister's Office showed almost two-thirds of the people were generally satisfied with their present life, one-third stressed their need for 'richness of the heart' rather than merely 'richness of things'.

Sated with every conceivable consumer good, and flush with inflated yen, the Japanese are enjoying more than their share of material affluence. This, however, is not enough! There is a search going on for riches of the soul as well as those of the body. With broad windows opened by international travel and communication, they have new benchmarks for comparing the pressures of Japanese life with the less-harried lifestyles in other countries. The national Economic Planning Agency describes this situation as being safe and rich, but lagging behind in leisure. A particularly sensitive problem arising from the still-limited leisure time is an apparent worsening of Japanese family life. The Agency's report attributes this deterioration to 'the increase of mother-and-child-only families and to a rise in the suicide rate of aged persons'.

Anxiety shows up clearly in surveys of Japanese expectations for the future. A recent Gallup Poll, for example, found 64 per cent of those questioned fearful of the future, with only 6 per cent saying that they were hopeful. Similarly, in a study conducted by the Prime Minister's Office, 43 per cent said they saw the future as being 'darker', while only 12 per cent saw it as 'brighter'.

The fact is, there is much evidence to suggest a rather widespread lack of confidence in spite of the exuberance and free spending seen among the hordes of Japanese tourists in every corner of the world. This ambivalence presents another challenge to the management of Japanese companies. The world-famous confidence and 'can do' psychology of Japanese employees is a precious asset that must be preserved in spite of the many pressures converging upon managers from both at home and abroad.

Foreign pressures

Western readers will be more familiar with the stresses and strains caused by pressures originating outside Japan – perhaps from their own country. The media in America and Europe have sounded the alarm and encouraged poorly informed 'Japan Bashers' to blame the 120 million Japanese for all the woes of the world. There is a favourite expression in US business folklore that 'nothing succeeds like success'. The past ten years of Japan–American relations might tempt us to revise the statement to 'nothing condemns and vilifies like success'. For her remarkable industrial achievements, Japan has been rewarded with jealousy and bitter accusations from competitors throughout the world.

Japan is quite accustomed to being something of a loner among nations. Cut off from the rest of the world for several centuries, a certain insider–outsider mental set persists. In spite of total dependence on foreign energy sources, and a terrifying susceptibility to economic or military blockade, the Japanese somehow manage to feel 'self-contained' and capable of becoming a model for developing – and even some highly developed – nations.

During her roaring 1960s and 1970s, Japan looked only at her own growth and profits with little regard for other people. But as a *Time* magazine article reported almost a decade ago, 'The Japanese post-war economic miracle is cresting. Japan is a fascinating success, as a business and as a society. Yet, paradoxically, Japan's very success has grown threatening, its future shadowed and complicated. The Japanese face new problems, inside, among their densely and close-woven tribe, and outside, with the rest of the world' (*Time* 1983: 20). Three such problems to be discussed here are the continued spread of protectionism, competition from newly industrializing countries, and foreign distrust of Japanese motives and goals.

Protectionism

The most obvious and persistent pressure from abroad has been the strident cries for protection of industries wounded by Japanese competition. Though protectionism has been shown to be shortsighted and self-defeating, it is like the proverbial 'bushel of eels'. Just when you think the slippery creatures are under control, they rise up to strike again. Few countries openly advocate protectionism as a national policy; fewer still do not practise it.

There will be no winners in the continuing battle of words over this issue. Claims and counterclaims are largely subjective, and what facts are used are too often distorted to support the user's argument. As one writer wisely points out, 'The blame for the present crisis of the liberal trading system lies both with the United States and Japan, and both countries have to take corrective measures if required stability is to be restored' (Maswood 1989: 3).

The 1985 Plaza Accord, which abruptly increased the value of the yen against the dollar and other major currencies, made it extremely easy and attractive for the Japanese to invest overseas. For example, the revaluation soon made it possible to acquire American real estate, securities, and manufacturing facilities for 50 cents on the dollar – that is, at half the price US investors would have to pay. To make foreign investment even easier, banks in Japan have been happy to loan funds at very favourable interest rates to eager borrowers. Having helped to set the stage with such irresistible incentives, it is ironic that Americans and Europeans alike now are expressing serious concern over the resulting Japanese economic 'invasion'.

Stimulation of domestic demand, as explained earlier, will help lessen Japan's excessive dependence on exports. But direct overseas investment probably will do more to correct the trade imbalance and thereby stem the tide of potentially dangerous protective legislation abroad. According to the Ministry of Finance, Japan's total overseas investments amounted to about $140 billion as of March, 1988. Of this sizeable amount, North America accounted for $53 billion, more than one-third of the total and double the amount in all Asian countries combined.

The rapid annual increase in Japanese overseas investment has continued in recent years and shows no signs of abating. Though most investments in developed nations by the Japanese formerly were largely in the commercial sector, since 1980 many have been for on-site production in such fields as colour TV sets, cars, office equipment, machine tools, semi-conductors, and communications equipment (JETRO 1981). Real estate investments have shown spectacular increases and more than tripled in one year from 1985–86.

Though not without its problems of cultural mismatch and resulting friction, moving production facilities offshore does dampen complaints of excessive exports and threats of protective legislation. Furthermore, there are many advantages for the receiving nations, not the least of which is the creation of thousands of new jobs. In addition, new management techniques are introduced, the local revenue base grows, and an element of healthy competition is injected. While some critics insist that the huge infusion of Japanese capital is an unhealthy development, the prevailing view seems to be that the net effect is positive and that more, rather than less, such infusion from Japan may be expected in the future.

In any case, there is every reason to believe that the need to reduce exports due to the ever-present threat of protective legislation, plus the obvious advantages of a greatly appreciated yen, will combine to continue the outflow of capital from Japan to many countries of the world. A decade from now, it is possible that today's debate over the US–Japan trade problem may seem curiously antiquated. Perhaps Americans will no longer be concerned with imposing tariffs on Japanese goods or with what is the proper yen–dollar exchange rate. Instead, many may be working for Japanese companies and even finding them the employers of choice. Still, cultural differences are vast and a great deal of accommodation will have to take place on both sides before such mutual acceptance is likely to become a reality. As author Clyde V. Prestonitz Jr warns us, the issue 'that will bedevil US–Japan relations far more than trade friction ever did in the past' is investment (Prestonitz 1989).

Competition from the NICs

To Americans, the script sounds all too familiar. It was not too many years ago that Japan was either totally ignored or looked upon as a country of penny-wages and shoddy merchandise. Now Japan is a leader among industrialized nations of the world, paying top wages and offering top-quality products on a global basis. Japanese competition is threatening foreign companies not only in markets around the world but also in their own backyards.

Similarly, countries which once provided cheap labour and parts for Japan to turn into high-value-added exports are now selling their own finished products in competition with the Japanese. Sometimes referred to as the four young Asian 'tigers,' but more widely known as newly industrializing countries (NICs), South Korea, Taiwan, Hong Kong, and Singapore are forcing Japanese business leaders to rethink their production priorities and market strategies. The hot breath of competition is being felt increasingly from these nearby Asian neighbours.

It may be interesting to take the outstanding 'fast tracker' among Asian NICs – South Korea – as an example of competition coming from these new sources. Described by an American Embassy official in Seoul as 'a major player on the industrial scene', Korea has made remarkable progress during the past twenty-five years (Whitehill 1987: 100). From the abject post-war poverty which persisted until the early 1960s, the country now boasts a GNP of over $120 billion which, on a per capita basis, amounts to an impressive $3,000. Growth rates have slowed down in the past few years, but even the 1988 rate of 8.5 per cent (compared with over 12 per cent in 1986 and 1987), reflects a robust economy which is the envy of many more-developed nations.

Japanese managers are watching Korean development from two points of view: first, as a strong competitor supplying world markets (including Japan's) with a broad range of sophisticated products; and second, as a shrinking market in the future for Japanese exports of materials and parts to be used in Korean manufactured products. Korea has made clear her intention to shift, as rapidly as possible, to domestic sourcing of materials and components. This will not happen quickly, but the Korean Traders' Association has expressed serious concern about the country's 'excessive imports of Japanese raw materials and parts' (Whitehill 1988:8). According to the Association, the problem is particularly serious because Japan continues to raise prices to offset the damage done by appreciation of the yen.

All the Asian NICs, including Korea, hold a decided cost advantage over Japanese industries. Wage rates in Korean manufacturing are only about a fifth of Japanese rates. Furthermore, the average Korean employee in manufacturing works about 2,800 hours per year while his Japanese counterpart toiled only 2,168 hours. With this sort of cost differential, and a greatly improved reputation for quality, Korean products are gaining market share throughout the world – often at Japan's expense. Today, Korean business executives are said to refer to the Japanese as 'the lazy Asians' (Halberstam 1986: 697–706).

The Japanese government is taking a surprisingly sanguine view regarding Korea's own 'economic miracle' of the 1980s. The prevailing view among top officials is that Korea is enjoying an export boom similar to that experienced by Japan twenty years ago. But, they caution, Korea is a relative newcomer with only about three decades of industrial experience. The resulting lack of depth in management is seen as a problem that will plague Korean business in the years ahead.

It is clear from this and other similar observations that the Japanese do not officially admit to a serious competitive threat from Korea. Yet there is increasing evidence that Korea is emerging as an economic power to be reckoned with. Her external debt has shown a decline for the first time in many years. Revision of the Foreign Capital Inducement Law has encouraged investors from all over the world who want a share of the action. Increasingly, Korean companies are shifting from labour-intensive industries to machinery, electronics, and a booming tourist industry. Furthermore, the country gained tremendous prestige in the eyes of the world through the impressive organization and hosting of the 1988 Olympic Games – an event many hold to be prophetic of even greater things to come.

Despite government optimism, many Japanese companies already are feeling the pinch of Korean competition in industries ranging from textiles to electronics. With this cold fact in mind, a recent article with the title 'The Koreans Are Coming' seems curiously outdated – they already have arrived.

Not all Asian countries, however, are 'tigers'. There is growing evidence that Japan is building a new power base in a number of East Asian countries where her leadership is not seriously challenged. Japan's investment in the area more than doubled from 1987–88. Such countries as Thailand, Indonesia, the Philippines, Malaysia, and China are prime targets for Japanese investors. Of course, every attempt is being made to avoid any similarity to Japan's economic and military exploitation throughout the region during the Second World War – the infamous and ill-fated Greater East Asia Co-Prosperity Sphere.

The extent to which these countries will be amenable to delegating economic power to Japan remains to be seen. Sometimes even presumed pussycats can become full-grown tigers who will want full control over their economic destiny. Thus far, no coordinated economic plan, with Japan at its centre, has been formulated for these countries. The possibility, however, is being watched with interest – and some anxiety – by all players in the international management game.

Foreign distrust

A less-tangible challenge from abroad, but perhaps one of even greater long-term significance for Japanese managers, is the discouraging lack of trust among foreigners concerning their behaviour, motives, and goals. William Ouchi, in his controversial book *Theory Z*, isolates trust as a quality of Japanese management worthy of emulation by Western companies (Ouchi 1981). But this trust is confined to within purely Japanese companies and somehow has not rubbed off on the increasing numbers of foreigners (*gaijin*) working with – or for – Japanese firms.

Expatriates living and working in Japan usually experience some apprehension when working in Japanese companies. Most with whom the author has spoken sooner or later express the feeling that they are being 'used'. Complaints range from being looked upon as an English-language machine to being treated as a 'token *gaijin*' whose primary role is to give the firm a multinational character. In Japan-based joint ventures, the few foreigners in executive positions often claim that they have no real authority and find themselves working as 'part-time consultants' tolerated only to appease their home office. These sorts of reactions reflect a distressing lack of trust and confidence concerning their Japanese colleagues and hosts.

The difficulty of establishing mutual trust becomes particularly apparent in Japan's overseas operations. An example is in the auto and electronics companies that have been forced by protectionism and the strong yen to transfer manufacturing to the United States. As the Japanese presence becomes increasingly apparent, fears of domination shake confidence and breed antagonism among American members of the management team.

A recent lecture in Hawaii by Sony Corporation's chairman, Akio Morita, shows clearly that the Japanese are fully aware of this problem. Mr Morita was speaking to a hand-picked audience of business leaders in a state in which the Japanese already own 40 per cent of Waikiki hotel rooms, 10 per cent of the private golf courses on Oahu, many multi-million dollar estates, and all the major shopping centres. He acknowledged that Americans still are wary of Japanese intentions, and asked the assembled Hawaiian executives to help convince US mainlanders that Japanese business activities are 'in good faith'.

Mr Morita has been a persuasive ambassador-of-good-will for his company and for his country for many years. Unfortunately, his credibility recently has been threatened by his self-styled 'accidental' co-authorship, with outspoken politician–novelist Shintaro Ishihara, of the highly controversial book, *The Japan That Can Say 'No'*. Ishihara argues that racial prejudice has been a crucial factor in shaping America's 'biased and incorrect views' of Japan, and suggests that Japan take a firmer stand when dealing with US demands. Though Morita does not explicitly support this blunt view, he does repeat his familiar, pessimistic assertion that 'the American economy appears to be deteriorating' (Morita and Ishihara 1989).

The challenge of building trust among the more than 25,000 American managers already working for Japanese 'bosses' is a difficult one. In many Japanese subsidiaries and joint ventures, Americans claim that they have been promised promotions, benefits, and salaries that never materialize. Perhaps the most-publicized case is that of Edward A. Newbauer, former senior vice president of sales and marketing at NEC Electronics in California. He has sued NEC on charges that the company owed him compensation and benefits, and that it had required him to break American laws. Newbauer is quoted as saying 'Professionally, I was used. I set up the sales and marketing organization, the contacts with major customers, and taught the company how to conduct business. Once I did that, my usefulness ended' (Nathans 1988).

Americans refer to their Japanese counterparts as their 'shadows' who allow them to hold important titles and to earn generous salaries. But the important decisions are made in consultation with Tokyo headquarters often, because of time differences, after US offices are closed. While American managers are hurrying home at 5 p.m., the Japanese are warming the fax machines or conferring with superiors – in Japanese – by telephone. Furthermore, the after-hours drinking sessions so important for building an intimate network usually is strictly 'for Japanese only'. Americans are, as one disgruntled executive complains, '*gaijin* in our own country'. This is not a good foundation for building the faith and understanding necessary for a solid, long-term relationship.

In closing this chapter, it may be well to emphasize that highlighting the pressures currently faced by Japanese managers has been only for the purpose of bringing a necessary sense of balance to our discussion. The real world of global competition presents a tough and dynamic environment for all participants. In such an environment, even a powerful contender such as Japan constantly must face new challenges and take advantage of new opportunities as they arise. Most experienced foreign analysts agree that whatever problems are encountered by the Japanese simply will give them an opportunity to demonstrate once again their characteristic determination and ingenuity.

Now our attention in the final chapter shifts to some predictions concerning this remarkable nation's role in the much-heralded 'Century of the Pacific'. The twentieth century clearly was the American century. Can we predict now that the twenty-first century will belong to Japan? This is not an easy question to answer, though most of the media in both countries would like us to believe it is a foregone conclusion. There are both driving and restraining forces which must be examined in our closing chapter before even a tentative answer can be ventured. Most important for our purposes will be an assessment of the impact of future trends upon Japan's management system.

References

'All the hazards and threats of success', *Time*, 1 August 1983: 20.

Arima, T. (1987) 'Habits of the Japanese heart', *Speaking of Japan* 8, 79: 26.

The Economic Planning Agency (1983) *Japan in the Year 2000* Tokyo: The Japan Times Ltd.

Focus Japan (August, 1984), p. 2.

Gibney, F. (1975) *Japan, the Fragile Superpower*, New York: W. W. Norton & Company Inc.

Halberstam, D. (1986) *The Reckoning*, New York: William Morrow Company.

JETRO (1981) *Zaibei Nikkei Shinshutsu Kigyo no Keiei no Zettai* (Japanese Manufacturing Operations in the United States), September.

Maswood, S. J. (1989) *Japan and Protection*, London: Routledge and Nissan Institute for Japanese Studies.

Morita, A. and Ishihara, S. (1989) *The Japan that can say 'No'*, New York: Knopf and Tokyo: Kobunsha.

Nathans, L. (1988) 'A matter of control', *Business Month*, September: 46.

Ohmae, K. (1987) *Beyond National Borders*, Tokyo: Kodansha International.

Ouchi, G. (1981) *Theory Z*, Reading, Mas.: Addison-Wesley Publishing Company.

Prestonitz Jr, C. V. (1989) 'Trading places: comment from a veteran negotiator', *Business Tokyo*, November.

Whitehill, A. M. (ed.) (1987) *Doing Business In Korea*, Beckenham, England: Croom Helm Ltd.

Whitehill, A. M. (1988) 'Korea at the crossroads', *The Journal of Applied Business Research*, Summer: 86.

Chapter fourteen

Japan in the 'Century of the Pacific'

If we focus upon the past three decades of exploding economic power in Japan and other Asian countries, and if we then project this spectacular growth on a straight line into the next century, the conclusion is inescapable: the twenty-first century truly will be the 'Century of the Pacific'. And should we be more specific and project only Japan's 'miraculous' growth rate along the same straight line, the result would be equally clear: the next century will largely belong to Japan.

To prepare for this presumably inevitable assumption of world leadership, former Japanese Prime Minister Nakasone has been named chairman of a new organization to meet the responsibilities inherent in what members refer to as 'the coming Asia–Pacific era'. Founded in the closing days of 1988, the Pacific Parliamentarian League for Educational, Cultural, and Economic Cooperation positions Japan in the vanguard of Asian nations as they become the centre of world economic power.

It is tempting to indulge in this sort of simple extrapolation of the past and present into the future. Such a scenario has spawned much flowery rhetoric on the part of futurists and journalists. But sober reflection and more realistic analysis paint a more 'iffy' scenario – a twenty-first century of many unknowns, many surprises and, we all hope, improved chances for peace and prosperity for people in every country of the world.

Rosy projections for the next hundred years or more are risky at best and, at times, cruelly misleading. What 1890 prophet, standing on the brink of the twentieth century could have possibly foretold the drama, the victories, the disasters, and the incredible technological advances that would materialize? While today's leaders in business and government cannot afford to 'take one day at a time', neither can they take a whole century in one gulp.

Without in any way demeaning the possibility that Japan truly may be entering a new 'Golden Age', this chapter first will attempt to present a brief picture of the sort of environmental constraints Japanese managers reasonably may expect during roughly the next twenty-five years. Then an attempt will be made to evaluate how the management system is likely to respond to these anticipated conditions. Finally, a concluding section will offer a prediction as to the extent to which the unique aspects of the Japanese management system may, or may not, be readily transplanted to foreign soils.

Environmental constraints

When viewed realistically, forecasts of the business climate in Japan during the next quarter century are encouraging and allow a fair degree of optimism. But they simply do not support the euphoric and carefree scenarios being churned out by the Economic Planning Agency, the Prime Minister's Office, the Ministry of International Trade and Industry, and other influential government agencies. Promises have been made that all Japanese soon will enjoy a rich and satisfying life in 'smart buildings' located in 'new media communities' – the great 'technopolises' that will be the wonder and envy of the world. For most Japanese, however, the brightest picture of the future would emphasize substantial improvements in such prosaic needs as housing, paved roads, and sewage systems.

The truth is, Japan must move towards her brighter future hampered by several persistent, hard-core constraints that cannot be ignored. Several of these limiting factors deserve brief discussion before moving on to our forecast of trends in the most important functions of management.

Space, people, and resources

Like it or not, Japan is – and will remain – an uncomfortably small island country, crowded to overflowing with 122 million people. With rugged mountains covering 80 per cent of the country, most of the population is crammed into the remaining 20 per cent of reasonably flat, habitable land. These are widely known facts and will not be laboured here.

However, experts seem to agree that any future attempts by Japan to acquire additional *lebensraum* will, as in the past, be doomed to failure. The growing colonies of expatriate Japanese in Hawaii, New York, or London provide only limited and temporary respite for a few from the enduring problem of population pressure at home. Crowded homes, crowded trains, crowded ski slopes – crowded everything – is an environmental condition not likely to change in this or the next century.

Inevitably, Japan's greatest resource is not her land but her people. With almost 100 per cent literacy, and an inborn love for learning and self-development, the Japanese people are a source of incredible strength and resiliency. Kenichi Ohmae starts his book *Beyond National Borders* with a statement of faith and hope: 'The key to a nation's future is its human resources.' However, he then goes on to say: 'Japan, with its 120 million well-educated and hardworking people, is better endowed with the resources vital to success than any other nation of the world' (Ohmae 1987: 1).

This writer is a great admirer of Mr Ohmae, and examples of his wisdom and insight have been quoted many times in earlier chapters of this book. But to claim that each and every Japanese citizen, including the very young and the very old, is well-educated and hardworking does stretch his credibility. Furthermore, if sheer numbers were the game, then nations such as the United States and the Soviet Union, with more than twice Japan's population, would be clear winners.

No one will deny that high levels of educational attainment are a tremendous asset to Japan. On the other hand, the educational system is not without flaws and is the subject of recurring programmes aimed at reform. Great pride is taken in the number of engineers produced by the system. Surely this is significant for the manufacture of high-quality, reliable autos, electronic products, and other goods upon which Japan has built her export boom. Technical knowledge is essential for such industries.

But a question frequently is raised concerning the ability of Japanese schools and universities to produce creative, inquiring individuals with outstanding communication and problem-solving skills. These are the sorts of people who may be in short supply in the years ahead. It is worth noting that America's education system, so loudly criticized abroad, continues to turn out graduates with the ability to visualize and to create sophisticated telephone switches, computer software, and semiconductor chips that set the pace for other producers throughout the world.

Turning to natural resources, the fact need not be stressed that, realistically, Japan has none. Her industries must continue, into the next century and beyond, to cope with dependency on foreign sources, limited control of price and quality, and the ever-present burden of shipping and handling costs in acquiring resources necessary for survival. It does not seem rational to claim, as some Japanese commentators have done, that an abundance of natural resources actually can be a handicap. The truth is, any nation is severely handicapped by dependence upon others for the basic energy and raw materials upon which industrial societies depend.

However, in spite of such intractable environmental constraints, most experts agree that Japan can look forward to the next quarter century with confidence. Her achievements since 1945 have been little short of miraculous, and the country now enjoys a secure position among the half dozen leading industrialized nations. If no serious blunders are made in economic or political strategy, and if the government can discard its rose-coloured glasses and come to grips with reality, Japan should command a well-deserved leadership role in the emerging global community of nations.

The 'new' Japanese management system

In bringing this work to a close, it seems appropriate to fit all the pieces together and assess their overall impact upon Japan's management system. Japanese business leaders in the past have been avid students and, in recent years, equally keen teachers and leaders in the management field. The resulting management system reflects an eclectic mix of European and American experience with a generous portion of homegrown adaptation and improvement. The nation was, after all, a latecomer on the industrial scene. Furthermore, the nation's business leaders literally had to 'start from scratch' in building from the rubble left by the Second World War.

When finally rid of the Occupation forces in the early 1950s, corporate leaders were quick to realize that this was no time to reinvent the wheel. Instead, the optimum strategy was to pick the best of existing technology and products, add characteristically Japanese top quality and stunning design, and then race to capture a major share of markets throughout the world. This was done with awesome success.

Now the global business environment has changed. Other countries are becoming more critical of Japan's industrial strategy. Perhaps a bit jealous of her success, and somewhat weary of merely responding to Japanese competition, Western nations are stirring with renewed vigour and determination to stay out in front. At the same time, Japan's business leaders are showing their uncanny ability to 'bend with the wind'.

As we move closer to the twenty-first century, and as even greater interdependence among nations grows, Japanese management will continue to adapt to changing circumstances. Already there are a number of clues as to what directions these adjustments will take. In the sections which follow, the seven major functions of management comprising Part III will be revisited briefly. For each of these areas, some predictions will be ventured regarding the shape of things to come. Though stated positively, such predictions must remain tentative in nature and their validity proved or disproved only by the passage of time.

Organization and planning

The organizational structure of Japanese firms is changing, and must continue to change in response to environmental pressures. Referring not only to Japan, one international business leader wisely suggests: 'While yesterday's executives were called organization men, today's might be called reorganization executives, transforming their companies to cut costs and to focus on customers and markets' (Ferry 1989).

Most large Japanese companies will grow 'leaner and meaner' in the tough years ahead. In their formal structure, position titles are likely to bear a closer relationship with responsibilities and duties performed. Characteristic overstaffing, and tolerance of non-productive 'window gazers' (*madogiwa-zoku*), will not be compatible with commitment to cost-containment policies in the future.

It is likely that corporate boards will remain large compared to those in US companies. Though titles for board members seem to be taking on a more Western flavour – for example, greater use of vice presidents – the multi-level hierarchy among directors is apt to remain. The reason for this prediction is the continuing Japanese desire to use lower-level directorships as a training ground for younger board members. Furthermore, the essentially closed nature of Japanese corporate boards is likely to continue. Though seating a few helpful retirees from influential government agencies will persist, there is little sentiment to follow US boards in welcoming professors, lawyers, or celebrities from the entertainment world to membership. Also, the legal requirements for 'representative directors' and 'statutory auditors' are under no immediate pressure to change.

Because of the 'one big family' image so carefully nurtured by Japanese *kaisha*, the clear US distinction between management and workers is not likely to develop. Instead, the present distinction between top management (directors) and all other employees seems sure to continue. With respect to annual stockholders' meetings, one likely change is the disappearance of the infamous *sokaiya*. Police crackdowns on these 'meeting mongers', and a broader public ownership of corporate stocks, are developing a more responsible use of annual meetings.

Staff positions, particularly in planning, are likely to continue to increase both in number and status in the years ahead. Corporate restructuring necessarily has demanded major changes in organizations as they diversify into new products and become more international in their operations. Overseas experience, and fluency in one or more foreign languages, can be expected to bring even greater rewards for upwardly mobile managers.

Turning to the informal side of Japanese organizations, few changes are anticipated. Old-school ties never have been stronger in getting things accomplished, and one's *jin miyaku*, or web of human contacts, can be expected to continue as a manager's major source of strength in the future. Cohesive cliques based on university attended, on one's home prefecture and community, or on other unchangeable criteria seem to be a permanent part of Japanese corporate life.

Staffing

In the next quarter century – indeed, in the next ten years – Japanese management will have to deal with some difficult

275

problems in human resources management. The employment system during decades of rapid growth was well-suited to the needs of production lines. Loyal, secure, well-disciplined employees, working in groups for organizational goals, were instrumental in churning out floods of products which were appealing to consumers worldwide. But is the same system equally suitable for creativity, product innovation, development of new materials, and entry to new industries? This question has particular relevance when discussing staffing policies and practices.

Some treasured practices of Japanese management are not likely to yield to the changes ahead. Lifetime employment is one such durable practice. A study by Keizai Doyukai of the type of management needed for the 1990s showed no sentiment among business leaders for discarding career-long job security for regular employees. It is likely, however, that lifetime employment will be extended to far more female employees as women begin to assume a more important role in Japanese industry. Though very slow, there is a trend toward promoting more women to management positions and to regard them as full-time, regular employees.

Lifetime employment, however, is only a psychological contract between the company and its regular employees. The uncertain years ahead will no doubt witness some situations where there will be no alternative to 'paring the rolls'. In such cases, Japanese managers can be expected to show characteristic ingenuity in avoiding outright terminations. For example, offering attractive incentives for early retirement will continue to be a favoured practice. Transferring redundant employees to subcontractors and subsidiaries will remain another viable alternative in the future. Most important, however, will be ambitious and, in some cases mandatory, retraining programmes so that regular employees can be shifted to new operations created by diversification programmes.

Turning to the recruitment of staff, several trends already are emerging. Greater initiative is being exercised by high school and university graduates in actively seeking jobs in the companies of their choice. And, as time goes by, the large companies may lose some of their glamour while smaller, flexible, and innovative firms with young leadership could gain in appeal. Though the numbers are not yet overwhelming, there is little doubt that a new generation of entrepreneurs is appearing on the Japanese management scene. This is a good thing, for the tradition-bound managers who have dominated manufacturing and marketing operations in the past may not be well-suited to the demands of the golden information era Japanese companies see as their future salvation.

It is likely that the present custom of hiring new recruits once each year will yield to year-round efforts to find scarce, talented candidates for employment. The prevailing gentlemen's agreement setting a limited 'open season' for recruiting each year's crop of graduates already is ignored by many companies and is likely to simply fade away in the future. A much more open labour market is bound to develop in the years ahead.

In the final screening of applicants for employment, most Japanese companies will further simplify and streamline their procedures. Written examinations as a part of the selection process are being quietly dropped by some firms. Interviews are becoming less stressful, more constructive, and definitely more work related. On the other hand, assuming the permanence of lifetime employment, attention must continue to be given to the whole person as a future member of the corporate family.

With a good deal of uncertainty likely to prevail in the years ahead, chances are good that part-time and temporary workers will continue to fill an important niche in Japanese industry. Companies that are facing drastic restructuring, and those moving to off-shore operations, are loath to make extensive long-term commitments to new staff. Furthermore, from the supply side, in a society actively seeking more time and opportunities for leisure, part-time work has obvious attractions.

Finally, increasing numbers of mid-career recruits and foreign employees seem certain to be needed. Their employment will create a far more heterogeneous workforce than Japan has experienced thus far. The specialized knowledge and experience required by high-tech, information-oriented organizations will stimulate competition for qualified individuals no matter what their previous employment status. A small trend already has started towards opening company doors to foreigners on an equal basis with Japanese nationals, provided the outsider has something unique to offer which is not available in the local labour market.

Leadership and career development

The days of a passive style of leadership in which a manager acts primarily as a facilitator of group action appear to be over. When this writer asked top executives of more than a dozen of Japan's largest firms what traits seemed most essential to successful leadership, not one mentioned the ability to act as a group catalyst. Instead, they stressed such things as 'ability to see the future', and 'willingness to make difficult decisions'.

Japanese managers were surprised by the oil shocks of the early 1970s, and again by the strength of the worldwide protectionist sentiments boiling up in the 1980s. The next quarter century has every likelihood of being a period of many surprises, and this time Japanese *kaisha* expect their leaders to minimize the shock waves. Contingency plans and 'what if' forecasts have assumed major importance in corporate planning. There is little doubt that companies will rely less on projections and guidelines from MITI and other government agencies and will put more credence in their own strategic planning. This would be wise, since at the time of writing the Japanese government seems overcome with general euphoria and obsessed with the fun of constructing unrealistically cheerful scenarios for the future. A recent controversial work by Van Wolferen is highly critical of what he calls 'the System', composed of politicians, bureaucrats and big businessmen, and singles out MITI as a prime culprit. He accuses the Ministry of collecting damaging information on corporate activities and then threatening 'exposure' if they fail to follow MITI directives (Van Wolferen 1989).

As for the uniquely Japanese *ringi* system of decision-making, it seems sure to continue in use, but increasingly as an after-the-fact confirmation–authorization process for decisions initiated at top levels. In more general terms, close personal relationships, senior–junior ties, and confidence in the intuitive abilities of subordinates will continue to colour leadership style. Furthermore, we can expect the present willingness of top executives to assume full accountability for all actions and events below them will persist. Resignations, emotional TV appearances, and even suicide will not disappear from the Japanese leadership scene.

A trend already in motion is the increasing desire of employees at all organizational levels to have more of their personal life quite separate from their work life. This does not imply a weakening of loyalty to the company. It does, however, reflect a societal as well as corporate trend toward providing more leisure time and more leisure activities planned solely by individual employees and their families. The general move toward two consecutive days off each week – what the Japanese refer to as 'twin holidays' – is spurring on this search for at least a degree of liberation from the traditional pattern of 'all work and no play'.

It is reassuring that Japanese executives no doubt will continue to amaze their Western counterparts by their courtesy, restraint, and avoidance of personal confrontation. Though sometimes suspected of being a mere facade, politeness and sensitivity to the feelings of others are very attractive cultural traits that will not readily change.

Finally, Japanese leaders are apt to continue putting their highest priority on employees rather than short-term profits. In an excellent commentary, a Japanese economist and an executive point out: 'Although Japanese firms are set up as stockholder-owned corporations, that's not how they're run. Management looks not to the people who put up the capital, but to the employees' (Moroi and Itami 1987).

Turning to career development, the most significant change anticipated is the increasing reliance that will be placed on individual merit in making personnel decisions. During the rapid-growth era there was room for everybody to move up as companies expanded to meet soaring demand. But in more stable conditions, and with many Japanese manufacturing companies reaching maturity, automatic promotions and pay increases based largely on length of service simply are not feasible.

Furthermore, successful diversification and entry into promising new fields, such as biotechnology and supercomputers, require recognition of individual employees who possess special knowledge and skills. Time constraints, and the universal problem of 'teaching an old dog new tricks', put a limit on companies developing their own such specialists. Young, creative people with state-of-the-art knowledge will be needed in greater numbers as Japanese companies shift from an export economy to one based on information and services. Seniority will continue to be given more recognition than in Western companies, but it is clear that merit will assume much greater importance in the years ahead.

The compensation system

As competition for scarce, highly-trained specialists increases in Japan's eagerly-awaited information era, the present relatively high degree of uniformity in wages and salaries will diminish. Furthermore, the gradual shift toward merit rather than seniority as the controlling factor in pay increases will work in the same direction. This means that wage spreads which today begin to appear after five to ten years of employment may occur earlier in career development. However, wage spread between top management and rank-and-file employees will likely remain modest compared with US standards.

Similarly, management will be keying wage rates more closely to job requirements. This will be true in spite of considerable difficulty in determining factors to be rewarded in evaluating jobs. However, it would appear that individual differences in need – compensated largely through special allowances – will continue to be an important feature of the Japanese compensation package. While the family allowance is declining in use, most companies intend to continue extra compensation for housing and commuting expenses aligned to individual circumstances.

Of one thing we can be sure. The twice-yearly bonus, presently equal to four to five months' base pay, will continue as a treasured part of employee compensation. The author found no sentiment among workers or managers to discontinue this practice. These substantial bonanzas at the beginning of the year and in midsummer, have become eagerly anticipated means for gift giving, vacations, and other special expenditures made by employees and their families.

Increasing numbers of Japanese companies are providing private pension plans to supplement Social Security benefits. More generous corporate pensions, with coverage for the retiree's lifetime, can be expected in the future. On the other hand, some lump-sum separation payment, so common today, seems to be a permanent part of leaving a *kaisha* after a lifetime of association.

As for hours of work, the movement has started toward narrowing the gap between the 1987 average of roughly 2,100 annual hours of work and the 1,800-hours target set in the government's 1988 'New Five-Year Economic Plan'. An example was set in 1989 when government and public offices were ordered to be closed on the second and fourth Saturdays of each month. Banks, postal savings and other financial services have followed suit.

To respond to consumer demand for a variety of activities to fill additional leisure time, new markets will expand rapidly in golf, resorts, sports facilities, and travel. Fitness clubs are sprouting in most urban areas, their numbers growing from 90 in 1980 to 837 in early 1989, with no end in sight. Also, an extensive range of culturally oriented workshops and classes already is available to those with more time and money to spend. For example, the Diner's Club of Japan operates a 'Diner's Culture Salon' with instruction in hobbies, health, beauty, sports, and even in how to organize successful parties. A number of theme parks, following the example of the fabulously successful Tokyo Disneyland, either are under construction or in the planning stage.

Only Japanese imagination – never known to be limited – will set the boundaries for enjoyment of newly found leisure time in the years ahead. Management associations, large and small business organizations, and even many employees do not welcome this shift from less work to more play at a time when Japan is facing many difficult challenges at home and abroad. But the trend is well under way and there seems little possibility of stopping it.

Motivation and evaluation

Turning to the 'million-dollar question' of motivation, much of the grief and apprehension expressed by the Japanese press – and the gloomy forecasts of the foreign press – should not be taken too seriously. The strong work ethic and impressive motivation to work of Japanese employees seem alive and well, and should not be subject to serious erosion as we move into the twenty-first century.

Cultural values do change, but only very slowly. Roots of the Confucian work ethic run deep, not only in Japan but in the 'four tigers' (Korea, Taiwan, Hong Kong, and Singapore) referred to earlier. In the original study of Japanese and American workers conducted with Professor Takezawa, and in the fifteen-years-after study, two very important conclusions were reached regarding the role of work in the lives of Japanese respondents:

(1) their loyalty and dedication to the company regarding *work-related matters* were, if anything, stronger and more binding in the later study; and

(2) their desire for greater freedom and initiative regarding *non-work activities* also had increased during the fifteen-year period.

(Whitehill and Takezawa 1968 and 1981)

There is another important matter which is relevant here. The fears expressed concerning the softening of the younger generation may also be given too much credence. In the tough world of global competition in which Japanese companies now find themselves, young people who are fortunate enough to find good jobs soon 'join the team' and become loyal members of a corporate family. True, they want to have more control over their increasing leisure time. But when immersed in the work of their group, and concerned about the fate of their company, their motivation remains very high.

This is reassuring news for managers, but does not relieve them of a continuing responsibility for creating a congruence between corporate goals and those of employees. With the drastic restructuring of Japanese companies now and in the future, this presents a difficult challenge. But in the author's opinion, the remarkable resilience of Japan's integrated management system demonstrated in past crises will prove equal to the tasks ahead.

Forecasting the future of the closely related function of performance evaluation does not present such a rosy picture. As more weight is given merit than seniority in promotion and salary decisions, Japanese managers have no choice but to develop valid, reliable systems for evaluating individual performance. Numerous surveys show this to be a real stumbling block for managers as they move into the new information era.

How to deal with this problem remains an unsolved puzzle as companies struggle with the underlying problem: selection and definition of meaningful criteria to be used in the evaluation of work. Traits and patterns of behaviour must be relevant, clear, and predictive of good job performance. New criteria must be found to supplement the traditional reliance upon length of service and educational attainment. This is an area of Japanese management which will bear close watching as companies grapple with the difficult issues involved.

Communication

To set the stage for looking ahead at the communication needs of Japanese managers, it seems essential to repeat the words of wisdom quoted in Chapter 11: 'It is time Japan learned to communicate in ways that will enable the world to understand it better' (Ohmae 1987: 43). The process of sharing information and understanding so that countries will accept and trust Japanese motives and goals is a matter that vitally concerns everyone, everywhere. Internal, corporate communication among Japanese managers and workers sets an enviable standard for others to follow. But greater efforts to improve Japan's scorecard in international communication are needed and cannot be left to chance.

The problem of different value systems, and vastly different perceptions of the world at large, no doubt will persist. Probably the best we can hope for is greater understanding of such differences. In order to build understanding, Japanese and foreign business people must speak, write, and interact through a common medium. The cold, hard fact is that the medium for international communication is now, and will be as far as we can see in the future, the English language.

The need for Japan's business executives is not just for workable, everyday conversational English. Their urgent need is to develop competence and confidence in discussing complex management issues in English. This writer feels some satisfaction from recognizing this need and doing something about it. Special seminars for executives, which combine the substance of international management with modern language-training techniques, are being made available in Japan and other Asian countries through certified representatives. Other schools and institutes increasingly are offering courses hopefully designed to accomplish this same goal.

There remain, however, a number of constraints preventing managers from taking advantage of these special programmes for developing working ability in the language of international business. Obviously, busy executives find it extremely difficult to allocate precious hours to such study. Experience will indicate increasingly, however, that this is an area of self-development for which time must be allocated. Furthermore, an equally serious constraint lies in the unwillingness of successful executives to admit to a need for further language training.

Not all Japanese employees will interact with foreign, English-speaking, counterparts or customers. But as opportunities continue to grow for all Japanese business executives to become truly internationalized, command of managerial English becomes ever more important. The present boom in English instruction throughout Japan reflects a widespread recognition of this need.

Improving organizational effectiveness

In Chapter 12, six reasons considered important in explaining the demonstrated effectiveness of the Japanese management system were discussed. It is appropriate now to appraise the sustaining force of these factors during the next several decades.

First, management's overriding concern for productivity and quality is not likely to weaken in the years ahead. Employees at all levels in Japanese companies are acutely aware that the company's continued success – and their own well-being – depend on this critical leading edge in global competition. The main thrust of Japanese manufacturing will continue to be 'getting the best for the least'.

Some uneasiness, however, must be felt by managers as they move from strictly manufacturing operations to more service-oriented businesses. The 'strategic focus on manufacturing', and 'the combination of industrial engineering and production techniques' emphasized as important sources of Japan's current productive superiority may not be as important in the coming era of diversification into such fields as housing, education, leisure goods, and other facets of the domestic market.

Turning to the use of takeovers and mergers as a path to diversification, this strategy shows every sign of at least modest increase in the years ahead. In spite of the special difficulties in merging two closed, exclusive corporate entities, the need for flexibility and speed in responding to new opportunities no doubt will mean more resort to external acquisitions in the future.

An important source of organizational effectiveness has been the sincere cultivation by Japanese managers of the brains, as well as the brawn, of all employees. Suggestion systems and quality-control circles will remain as key factors in human resources management. With continued encouragement and support, dedicated employees can be counted on to provide valuable input as Japanese companies face an uncertain and demanding future.

Japan's lead in robotization probably will persist at least into the next century – not in the total number of robots 'employed', but in the percentage of the workforce, and range of capabilities, accounted for by the steel-collar workers. With Japanese managers' longer-term perspective on investment, and the general acceptance of automation by employees and their unions, this could be one of the more important sources of Japan's industrial leadership in coming years.

Finally, cooperation from supportive rather than adversarial unions will serve Japanese management well in the future as it has in the past. Though union federations are attempting to gain greater power through consolidation and reorganization, the foundation for Japan's labour movement will remain firmly grounded at the enterprise level. With each union physically and psychologically a part of the company, collective bargaining, contract negotiation, and union participation in management decisions within each enterprise will continue to make a significant contribution to the on-going overall effectiveness of Japanese firms.

Is Japanese-style management exportable?

Because of its fascination and importance to managers throughout the world, the question of transferability of Japanese management practices to other countries should be addressed before bringing this volume to a close. Toshiro Nishiguchi, in a recent article published by the Japan Automobile Manufacturers' Association, refers to the 'Japanization' of the US auto industry and its extensive use of 'foreign' management techniques. Sober reflection, however, indicates that even in such successful joint ventures as the GM–Toyota plant in California use of the term 'Japanization' goes too far and is misleading (Nishiguchi 1989).

In dealing with the feasibility of transplanting Japanese management practices, several important points should be kept in mind.

Figure 5 Lifetime employment: systems interaction and support

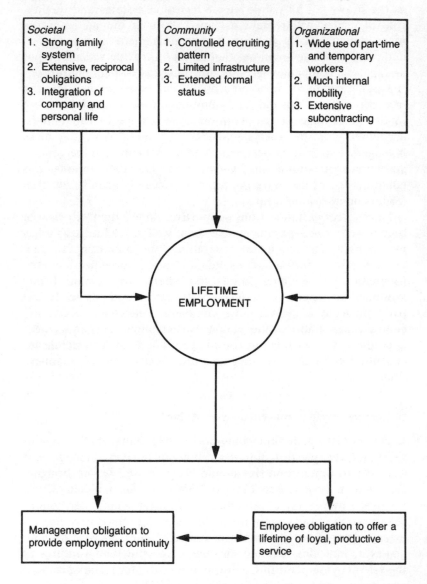

First, it seems hardly necessary to restate the fundamental fact that management is an integrated system, as discussed in detail in Chapter 5. The success or failure of a given management practice always is dependent upon many systemic 'conditioners', both internal and external to the firm. These conditioners originate at three levels: societal, community, and corporate (Whitehill 1976).

Figure 5 shows the impact of systems interaction and support, using the most-discussed and durable 'sacred treasure' of Japanese management – lifetime employment – as an illustration. The diagram shows that in Japan strong and lasting ties with groups are fostered at the societal level by a continued reliance upon family. In addition, the heavy burden of reciprocal obligations in society calls for long-term and intimate relationships. Finally, the willingness of the Japanese to merge their work and personal lives lends strong support to the close and lasting association of lifetime employment.

At the community level, a rather orderly, once-a-year recruiting pattern lends an air of stability and permanence to positions filled. Furthermore, many communities still lack an adequate infra-structure of housing and leisure-time facilities. Quite naturally, employees look to the company for much of their social activity. Additional fusing with the company arises from the practice of extending work-related status differences to all outside situations.

Many corporate-level practices also tend to support lifetime employment. Wide use of part-time and temporary workers provides an escape valve which helps protect the job security of regular employees. Loose job specifications, and acceptance of frequent job rotation, add a degree of flexibility which contribute to employment continuity. And finally, the very extensive use of sub-contractors tends to shift some of the risk from the parent company and allows it to offer stable employment to its own employees.

Experiments in the United States with employment guarantees, even for the 'lifetime' of the union contract, have had limited success. Reviewing the factors in Figure 5 which support lifetime employment in Japan, we find none which are applicable in America – in fact, just the opposite prevails in each case. This lack of fit between 'conditioners' and practice is fatal. In short, there really is no reason to expect this pillar of Japanese management to survive in American soil.

A similar analysis imposes a similar fate upon most other Japanese management techniques, including such star performers as seniority-based promotions, housing allowances, consensus decision-making, and enterprise unionism. They simply do not fit the values and lifestyles of American workers or managers.

Furthermore, the so-called 'foreign' management techniques claimed by Mr Nishiguchi to have permeated the US auto industry actually are those known and emphasized long ago by well-managed, competitive US companies. Cost reduction, inventory control, supply strategies, quality-control circles, and effective communication with customers and suppliers are not alien terms to American executives.

To summarize, those techniques which are unique to the Japanese management system, and are strongly conditioned by systemic forces, are not likely to succeed when exported to foreign – particularly Western – cultures. However, there will always be certain policies and practices which are of universal concern and applicability. It is in connection with these that the phrase 'Good management is good management' takes on significant meaning. These aspects of management in most cases originated in Western industrial societies, though they certainly were honed and sharpened by the hardworking Japanese as they sought and won economic victory following military defeat.

This common brew of good management did not – and does not – come solely from Japan. But to their great glory, Japanese managers have stirred in some special ingredients which have contributed to yet another 'economic miracle'. Though US managers may not be able to stomach these special ingredients, they surely can gain inspiration from the highly successful example set, in their own way, by Japanese counterparts.

Conclusions

In this final chapter, several basic premises have been ventured concerning the future of Japanese management. First, to describe the coming century as the 'Century of the Pacific' may be exciting but ignores the realities of forecasting. Few, if any, sane predictions can be made for the next one hundred and ten years. The best we can do is peer ahead for the next twenty to twenty-five years. When this time frame is used, there seems to be much 'good news', and some 'bad news', for Japanese corporations.

Taking the latter first, the 'bad news' lies in a number of stubborn constraints which simply will not go away. Limited *lebensraum* for 122 million people will continue to plague Japan with population pressure and stress. Then, too, the praiseworthy educational system in Japan none the less begs for reform to meet changing conditions and needs. And a final intractable handicap is the simple fact that Japan lacks any significant natural resource except her people. Total dependency on others for survival is not an enviable condition, particularly for an island nation.

But, fortunately, there is much 'good news' with which to battle these stubborn constraints. In the 1980s, the leaders of Japanese *kaisha* demonstrated remarkable resilience and flexibility in an uncertain environment. An incredible willingness to accept the risks of internal diversification, continued ability to take a long-term view and to 'hang in there' when the going gets tough, are only a few of the impressive strengths of Japanese management which bode well for the future.

In every one of the seven major functions of management discussed earlier in this chapter constructive changes already have occurred with encouragement, rather than resistance, from all parties – top management, employees, and enterprise unions. Notable is the slow but steady move towards utilizing the previously untapped skills of women in the workforce. Some bending of traditional staffing practices, and considerable adaptation of leadership style, are going forward to find a better fit with expected changes in the next quarter century. And, finally, the course has been set for achieving a more richly satisfying and rewarding quality of life for all Japanese people.

A leading Japanese critic and editor perhaps says it best in these few, well-chosen words:

> It is never easy to know what the future holds. Globalization and technological advancement are to be expected, but these trends alone do not provide a clear blueprint of what will transpire. Much will depend on how well we learn the lessons of our past successes and failures. To ensure that the success of the past 40 years is not squandered away in the next 40, we must reinvigorate the country's institutions to promote and maintain a dynamic society.
>
> (Kasuya 1989)

Such reinvigoration is proceeding at full speed in at least one vital Japanese institution – corporate management. If international understanding and trust concerning the goals and practices of the *kaisha* are carefully nurtured in the years ahead, there seems no reason to doubt that Japan and her industrial leaders can move forward with confidence and high expectations into the twenty-first century.

References

Ferry, R. M. (1989) 'The key to survival', *Business Strategy International*: 122.

Kasuya, K. (1989) 'The showa era', *Nihon Keizai Shimbun*, 11 January; reprinted in *Economic Eye* 10, 1 (Spring): 31.

Moroi, K. and Itami, H. (1987) 'Changing Japan's corporate behavior', *Economic Eye*, September: 20.

Nishiguchi, T. (1989) 'Good management is good management: the Japanization of the US auto industry', *The JAMA Forum* 7, 4 (April): 3–7.

Ohmae, K. (1987) *Beyond National Borders*, Tokyo: Kodansha International.

Van Wolferen, K. (1989) *The Enigma of Japanese Power*, New York: Knopf.

Whitehill, A. M. and Takezawa, S. (1968) *The Other Worker*, Honolulu: East-West Center Press.

Whitehill, A. M. (1976) 'Management transplants: practice or system?' College of Business Administration, University of Hawaii, *Working Paper Series* 14.

Whitehill, A. M. and Takezawa, S. (1981) *Work Ways: Japan and America*, Tokyo: The Japan Institute of Labour.

Index

age: of population 91–2, 185–6,
252–5; respect for 44, 76; (*see
also* loyalty to superiors;
seniority); at retirement 76, 116,
142, 180, 181, 254; (pensions
184, 185–6)
agreements *see* contracts; written
communication
agriculture *see* farmers
Akihito, Emperor 31
allowances 171–2, 173, 176–9, 187,
280, 288
amakudari 93, 117
Amaya, Naohiro 32
ancestors, veneration of 16–17
annual meetings 112–13, 275
anxiety: concerning the future 259–
60
appraisal *see* evaluation
armed forces 26–8, 29
arsenals, military 19
art and artists 4, 7, 14
artisans: in Tokogawa era 4, 13
Asahi Glass 96
Asahi Shimbun 219–20
atomic bomb(s) 28
auditors, statutory 111, 116, 275
Australia, emigration to 26
authoritarianism 7, 20, 24, 25
automation *see* robotization
automobile industry 98, 144, 230,
240, 266; *see also* Honda; Toyota

banks 14, 93, 95–6, 117, 231, 262
Benedict, R. 12
benefits, employee 7, 182–7, 280

Berlitz Language Schools 224–5
Berrington, Robin A. 222
blackmailers, corporate 113, 275
blame, acceptance of 156–7, 278
bonus, semi-annual 171–2, 176,
179–80, 280
Brooks, Professor Harvey 255
burakumin 76
bureaucracy 3, 8, 14, 21, 22, 29; as
a social force 49–50; *see also*
government
Bushido code 7
business cards 43, 114, 187
Business Council for International
Understanding 43

Canon 95
capital 90–2, 96, 97; *see also*
investment
cards, business 43, 114, 187
career development 115–16, 128,
162–7, 172, 279; evaluation
during 167, 174, 193, 201–10,
282–3
cartels 92, 95–6, 99–101; *see also*
zaibatsu
Chiba Prefecture 11, 67–8
China 5, 7; immigrants from 69, 70;
Occupation of 26–7, 244;
stereotype of 60; trade with 94,
102, 258, 265
chuto saiyo 144–5, 277
class: and organizational structure
111–12; and quality of life 70–1
cliques *see* *gakubatsu; habatsu*
clothing *see* dress